Praise for Nada Bakos's

THE TARGETER

My Life in the CIA, Hunting Terrorists and Challenging the White House

"Nada Bakos takes you deep inside the tense, stressful, and driven world of the CIA's analysts as few others have. Life-and-death issues are on the line more than most know — but Ms. Bakos is one who does, and she shows you that in *The Targeter* with candor, drama, integrity, and grit."　　—John McLaughlin, former acting director and deputy director of the CIA

"An exciting tale of cutting-edge espionage and a rueful account of how political exigencies can blunt tradecraft's effectiveness."
　　—*Kirkus Reviews*

"Part *Zero Dark Thirty*, part memoir, *The Targeter* provides a rare inside look at the CIA's analysis shop at a particularly difficult time: the run-up to the American invasion of Iraq and the early years of the war...The narrative will appeal to those who want to learn about the events that presaged the rise of the Islamic State and are curious about the CIA's inner workings."
　　—Dina Temple-Raston, *Washington Post*

"A remarkable book."　　—David Priess, *The Lawfare Podcast*

"Nada Bakos had a frontline assignment during some of the most important chapters of America's post-9/11 wars. Her well-written account of her work at the CIA is fascinating and underlines the many sacrifices she and her colleagues made in the fight against al Qaida. Bakos has also written one of the most clear-eyed and interesting accounts of what it is really like working at the CIA."

—Peter Bergen, author of *Manhunt: The Ten-Year Search for Bin Laden from 9/11 to Abbottabad*

"Bakos writes with authority and searing honesty about the demands of her work as a targeter and the dangers and dysfunction of post-invasion Iraq. The result is a gripping behind-the-scenes account of the hunt for one of the world's most brutal terrorists. The combination of a sharp, analytical mind and a genuine humility and humanity underscores why women make some of the best CIA analysts."

—Clarissa Ward, chief international correspondent for CNN

"A revealing and utterly engrossing account of the campaign to stop the terrorist mastermind behind the rise of ISIS. Former intelligence officer Nada Bakos takes the reader deep inside the CIA's secret war in Iraq with a fast-paced narrative that is by turns thrilling, funny, maddening, and remarkably candid."

—Joby Warrick, author of *Black Flags: The Rise of ISIS*, winner of the Pulitzer Prize

"*The Targeter* reads like a suspense novel written in Hollywood. But it's the true story of an unsung hero working to keep America safe and speaking hard truths to those in power. I relied on public servants like Nada to fight the Islamic State. Our country is indebted to their rigor, tradecraft, and dedicated war zone service, which carries a personal toll. This is the first inside account of what it's really like."

—Brett McGurk, former special presidential envoy for the campaign to defeat ISIS

"*The Targeter* is a raw, honest, and gripping account of the thrilling but daunting task of a CIA analyst answering her inner call to keep America and her people safe. Nada Bakos is the real deal... Nada shares the lessons she learned when serving the United States and does not shy away from acknowledging that in counterterrorism, tactical wins do not always translate into strategic successes. This book is an important asset for any analyst, policy maker, or thought leader looking to make a difference in counterterrorism in the twenty-first century."

— Ali Soufan, chief executive officer of the Soufan Group and former FBI supervisory special agent

"For the last decade, Nada Bakos has been a go-to source for understanding terrorist networks. Her memoir offers a gripping tale on how terrorists, and the counterterrorists who hunt them, actually operate in the real world."

— Clint Watts, senior fellow at the Foreign Policy Research Institute and author of *Messing with the Enemy: Surviving in a Social Media World of Hackers, Terrorists, Russians, and Fake News*

"Bakos takes us deep inside the work of the CIA targeters who were tracking al Qaida and the Zarqawists during the height of the Iraq War, showing us both the professional dedication and personal costs of these most quiet professionals."

— Doug Ollivant, senior fellow, New America Foundation

"An important contribution to our understanding of the intelligence wars that erupted in 2001 over Iraq's alleged connections to the 9/11 attacks and the George W. Bush administration's bungled efforts to stabilize Iraq after the 2003 invasion... One of the most important insights this book offers is that women have been at the heart of the CIA's war with al Qaida from well before 9/11."

— Bruce Riedel, the Brookings Institution

THE
TARGETER

MY LIFE IN THE CIA,
HUNTING TERRORISTS AND
CHALLENGING THE WHITE HOUSE

NADA
BAKOS

with Davin Coburn

BACK BAY BOOKS
LITTLE, BROWN AND COMPANY
NEW YORK BOSTON LONDON

Back Bay Books / Little, Brown and Company
Hachette Book Group
1290 Avenue of the Americas, New York, NY 10104
littlebrown.com

Originally published in hardcover by Little, Brown and Company, June 2019
First Back Bay trade paperback edition, May 2020

Back Bay Books is an imprint of Little, Brown and Company, a division of Hachette Book Group, Inc. The Back Bay Books name and logo are trademarks of Hachette Book Group, Inc.

This does not constitute an official release of CIA information. All statements of fact, opinion, or analysis expressed are those of the author and do not reflect the official positions or views of the Central Intelligence Agency (CIA) or any other U.S. Government agency. Nothing in the contents should be construed as asserting or implying U.S. Government authentication of information or CIA endorsement of the author's views. This material has been reviewed solely for classification.

The publisher is not responsible for websites (or their content) that are not owned by the publisher.

The Hachette Speakers Bureau provides a wide range of authors for speaking events. To find out more, go to hachettespeakersbureau.com or call (866) 376-6591.

ISBN 978-0-316-26047-3 (hc) / 978-0-316-26046-6 (pb)
LCCN 2016944050

10 9 8 7 6 5 4 3 2 1

LSC-C

Printed in the United States of America

To E, H, and R
My love and gratitude for your support

Contents

THE
TARGETER

Introduction

On a moonless night in May of 2011, an elite team of Navy SEALs blew the doors off their hinges at a compound in Abbottabad, Pakistan. They stormed up the darkened stairway to the third floor, and there, in a spartan bedroom, they shot Usama bin Ladin multiple times in his head and chest.

The 2011 strike should seem like a bookend to a winding tale of tragedy that began on September 11, 2001, when nineteen al Qaida terrorists hijacked four airliners over the United States. It was an event that would not have been possible without CIA officers mapping out the elaborate, evolving terror network that was unlike any foe the United States had faced before. Ultimately, by identifying and locating key players — a form of analysis known as targeting — Agency personnel tracked bin Ladin's trusted courier to a guesthouse near the Afghan border, and US forces were able to launch operations to capture or kill the emir of al Qaida.

Counterterrorism timelines, however, do not have fixed start or end points; ideology exists outside of one individual. The death of bin Ladin was dramatic, but it was not the final act in a series of events that began well before 2001 — and similar Agency work continues today against al Qaida and organizations like the Islamic State. It is almost impossible to quantify the exact number of people at the CIA who were involved in this fight over the years — an array of employees who brought vast regional and intelligence expertise to the battle against al Qaida.

My contribution to the United States' effort to combat terrorism came not in Afghanistan, the ancestral home of al Qaida, but farther west, in Iraq. I started working at the CIA before the attacks in New York, Pennsylvania, and Washington, DC, on September 11, 2001 — though this book focuses largely on 2003, the year the US-led coalition invaded Iraq and toppled Iraqi president Saddam Hussein, and on the fiery chaos that unfolded in the years following. My role throughout those years began as that of an analyst focused on whether there was a connection between Iraq and al Qaida and later as a targeting officer in the Directorate of Operations. My focus, and the focus of my team, was the movement sparked by Abu Musab al-Zarqawi — a Jordanian who quickly became a leader of terrorism in Iraq and differentiated himself from al Qaida by focusing on not only US targets but also Iraqis.

In the three years following the invasion of Iraq, as the United States struggled to institute democracy and implement basic security, no insurgent group caused more bloodshed — with more recklessness and indiscriminate focus — than Zarqawi's. A high school dropout turned religious fanatic, Zarqawi found in the power vacuum and lawlessness that was post-Saddam Iraq the chance to be recognized as a leader, and he became responsible for literally thousands of deaths. His legacy carries on in the actions of the Islamic State, or ISIS; the climax of his bloody reign was the 2006 civil war between Iraq's rival Sunni and Shia factions, which many believe continues to this day. Removing Zarqawi's network among the insurgency was crucial if Iraq was to have any shot at a stable future.

At the height of his power, Zarqawi commanded a regional terror network known as Al Qaida in Iraq (AQI). It was the most prominent regional franchise of al Qaida central. Zarqawi corresponded with bin Ladin personally; toward the end of his short life the man who would be nicknamed by his supporters the "slaughtering sheik" was in regular contact with al Qaida central command. The intelligence we gathered in dismantling Zarqawi's network was crucial in building a response to al Qaida.

By the time of bin Ladin's death, I'd retired from the CIA. Today, the "targeting" of terrorists forms the backbone of *Zero Dark Thirty* and *Homeland*—a topic that invariably comes up whenever people learn about my former life. People initially asked if I'm the real-life Maya, the main character from *Zero Dark Thirty*. I am not and was not working for the CIA at the time; Maya's character was based on someone else. In my experience, it took a team of people more than twenty years to find bin Ladin.

Many tenacious women and men led targeting operations for significant al Qaida figures, including bin Ladin. My team's efforts directly preceded the climactic action in that movie, just as our work built upon the groundbreaking analysis of the women and men who came before me. Additionally, while it's rarely the crux of the initial question, those shows and their heroines—Maya and Carrie Mathison—hint at a larger truth that reflects my own experiences: women initially made up the majority of the CIA targeters charged with hunting the most dangerous figures in the most dangerous terrorist organization the United States has ever known. Women were critical to defining al Qaida and managing the ramp-up at the CIA's Counterterrorism Center (CTC) after 9/11.

When I worked at the CIA, I—like all of my peers and counterparts—worked in quiet obscurity; the long hours we put in to keep our families, friends, and fellow citizens safe were simply part of the job. Today, I am a far more public figure. As a former analyst and targeting officer, I can now speak more freely about the challenges I faced inside the Agency, the successes my team helped deliver, and the failures we suffered. The lessons I learned may never be *more timely* because of how much has not changed with regard to ideologically driven individuals and groups who inexplicably see violence as the best way to accomplish their desired goals.

At the funeral of Julius Caesar, William Shakespeare's Antony said, "The evil that men do lives after them," a line I've thought of often regarding extremism. The shock waves from Zarqawi's short time on earth seem to only have intensified in the years following his death, in 2006.

The Islamic State of Iraq and Syria, or ISIS, has risen from the ashes of Zarqawi's organization in Iraq to temporarily claim the mantle of deadliest jihadist group. ISIS's brutal approach to establishing a twenty-first-century Islamic caliphate is taken almost entirely from Zarqawi's strategy. If we are to have any hope of countering violent extremist groups in the future, it is crucial to understand not only Zarqawi's rise to prominence but also the complicated social, political, and military factors that enabled him to unleash a wave of destruction that few people would have believed possible. Only then can we effectively map out a strategy for defeating the latest extremist movements. Simply put, we cannot kill our way out of a conflict rooted in ideology; to defeat ideological extremism, we need to address the political, economic, and societal issues that give rise to and sustain extremism. As a person who came to know that terrorist, I can say that the brutality he unleashed plagues me to this day.

CHAPTER 1

Murder Boards

"C'mon, c'mon..."

I jabbed at the Door Close button and caught my reflection in the elevator's brushed aluminum interior. My pulse raced.

With a final jab, the doors clamped shut on the third floor of the Central Intelligence Agency's New Headquarters Building, in Langley, Virginia. It was early June of 2004, nearly four years after my first day at the Agency.

"Fuck this," I muttered.

It had been ten months since I'd returned from Iraq to the cubicle farms of Agency headquarters. I spent the prior summer as the CIA's point person for our Iraq terrorism analysis group in Baghdad. At that time, I was working in the Iraq unit, within the CIA's Counterterrorism Center, or CTC. In May 2003, I volunteered for a temporary-duty assignment to Iraq for multiple reasons: first to support my team at headquarters, which was continuing to answer questions from the administration about Iraq or al Qaida and report anything new, and, second, getting out of headquarters would give me a chance to find signs that Abu Musab al-Zarqawi was still in Iraq. Until early 2004, a year after the war started, Zarqawi's group was not part of al Qaida.

My job with that team had initially been focused on analyzing the Iraqi Intelligence Service, or IIS. Our question was: To what degree did the IIS facilitate regional and global extremist organizations and terrorist movements? But we knew the IIS had a greater reach under Saddam: it could have acted as the facilitator through which Iraqi forces had trained and harbored Palestinian terrorists, plotted assassinations, and carried out other international crimes. By mid-2003, in the wake of the US-led coalition's invasion of Iraq, we were fielding endless backward-looking questions about what connection Saddam might have had to Islamist extremists.

Almost immediately in the aftermath of the September 11, 2001, attacks — when nineteen al Qaida extremists under orders from Usama bin Ladin hijacked four passenger planes and, along with them, a generation of American foreign policy — the White House had begun delivering the singular question to CIA analysts, day after day: *What's the connection between bin Ladin and Iraq?*

Everyone within the Iraq unit sweated under the demands from George W. Bush and his administration for more answers about a possible Iraq–al Qaida collaboration than we could plausibly provide. The administration didn't seem to like the answers we offered, through a steady flow of President's Daily Briefs, or PDBs. As a result, we found ourselves locked in a contentious relationship with the White House.

The foundation for the divide was laid not long after the 9/11 attacks, when, in a little-remembered bureaucratic line item, Secretary of Defense Donald H. Rumsfeld and his head deputy, Paul Wolfowitz, created a brand-new department to provide answers they'd like to hear that were consistent with how they and other neoconservatives saw the world and America's role in that world. The Office of Special Plans consisted of roughly a dozen personnel working on the fifth floor of the Pentagon. The people assigned to that office data-mined information gathered by the CIA and another intelligence agency, the Defense Intelligence Agency, then formulated intelligence reviews for an administration growing increasingly skeptical of CIA analysis.

You need to understand something about intelligence analysis; it is not an academic exercise. The CIA's analytic cadre are professionals who spend the majority of their time developing expertise on the issues they follow. That there are disagreements over the analytic findings based on the source material to build an argument is not surprising. Analysts often experience heated coordination meetings with their colleagues, and that is before a draft is submitted for a thorough editing and review process.

The Office of Special Plans seemed to utterly disregard the analytic tradecraft the Agency holds dear. Overseen by the undersecretary of defense for policy, Douglas Feith, the number three position within the Pentagon, the OSP often passed along raw intelligence without context and without explaining the reliability of the source to the White House. Feith's team latched on to any single thread of information while ignoring a half century of established intelligence protocols. In other words, it was "Feith-based intelligence."

OSP's clear satisfaction in the administration's end run around the CIA was particularly galling. In one press conference I watched, Rumsfeld practically gloated about its effectiveness: "In comes [my daily CIA] briefer and she walks through the daily brief, and I ask questions," he said. "Gee, what about this? Or what about that? Has somebody thought of this?"

Skepticism about the CIA's analysis was born early in the run-up to the war. In mid-2002, the predecessor to my team at the CIA prepared a product titled *Iraq and al-Qa'ida: Interpreting a Murky Relationship.* The report acknowledged, "This Intelligence Assessment responds to senior policymaker interest in a comprehensive assessment of Iraqi regime links to al-Qa'ida. Our approach is purposefully aggressive in seeking to draw connections." On June 25, 2002, four days after the paper was published, the CIA ombudsman for politicization received a confidential complaint claiming that the CTC paper was misleading in that it did not make clear that it was an uncoordinated product that did not reflect the views of other analysts outside the CTC unit.

Still, the uneven give-and-take with the White House put us all on edge — only more so throughout 2002 and early 2003, as the unmistakable drumbeat of war grew louder. In fact, I saw Vice President Richard Cheney and I. Lewis "Scooter" Libby, his chief of staff, visiting Agency headquarters themselves — an unnerving shift in protocol from the long-standing CIA briefings at the White House.

I was thankful that in our briefings with the vice president, crucial top cover for our unit's work came from our brazen, brilliant branch chief, "Katherine," who had a remarkable ability to deliver workplace-appropriate words in ways that left little doubt about the profanity they stood in for. (Unfortunately, I don't have the same skill.) As Libby's personal daily briefer, she had enough credibility among White House personnel to act as a barrier between the vice president and analysts like me, who had less experience with the administration.

———————

By late 2002, we had a much higher degree of confidence in our understanding of Saddam's connections to terrorist groups, though we did not see evidence of a connection to al Qaida. In the parlance of the Agency, Cheney was a "tough customer" — he knew enough about the substance of terrorism to ask pointed questions of the men and women who briefed him. In the years since those Langley meetings with top administration officials, various Agency personnel have described them as "unprecedented," "highly unusual," and "brutal." Inside our unit, Katherine made the decision to put analysts in front of Vice President Cheney. To prepare us, she skewered our analysis during practice briefings, which we called murder boards, in which she acted patronizing challenging, unfair, and insulting to prepare us for the real sessions.

At the time, there was a widespread belief that an attack of similar magnitude could happen again and the CIA needed to act as a bulwark against such attacks. The consequence, in the near term, is that analysts were given the opportunity to work in CTC. Even longtime counterterrorism analysts were new to the Iraq unit. After all, it hadn't existed on September 10, 2001. In my case, a coworker on my first day there dumped a dozen giant three-ring binders on my desk and said, "Here's what we've written so far about al Qaida and Iraq. That's for Congress, this is the White House, this is all our sourcing and research, and there is more in that filing cabinet outside the bullpen." This process is called reading in to a new account, which usually takes weeks or months. I had about three days to get up to speed.

"Murky," I muttered to myself in the elevator. I checked my watch: just after 2:00 p.m. I scowled; by then, I'd heard that word — *murky* — around the office so much it had come to make me cringe. The questions from the administration were about Iraq's connections to any and all terrorism, not just al Qaida.

Even the most aggressive attempts at drawing a connection between Iraq and AQ, however, had failed to produce the kind of smoking gun the White House wanted. So, in late 2002, the administration pinpointed a new bogeyman to bolster the justification for its hegemonic intent: a thirty-six-year-old former drug-dealing street thug from Jordan named Ahmad Fadil al-Nazal al-Khalayleh. Khalayleh had recently adopted a new name, Abu Musab al-Zarqawi. He would eventually join al Qaida after the invasion, and his group would be embraced as the prototype for the Islamic State of Iraq and Syria, also known as ISIS.

On October 7, 2002, I listened as President Bush, in a prime-time speech delivered in the massive rotunda of the Cincinnati Museum Center, in Ohio, laid out the broad strokes of what he said was the "link between Iraq developing weapons of terror, and the wider war on terror." Much of the speech focused on Saddam Hussein's long-standing efforts to develop chemical and biological weapons of mass destruction—and Bush's assertions that Hussein continued to do so. That particular assessment had come from another CIA branch down the hall, the Weapons, Intelligence, Nonproliferation, and Arms Control Center (WINPAC)—which, we in the Iraq unit knew, was feeling similar heat from above to justify the war effort. Thanks to WINPAC's findings, the president announced that Iraq possessed ballistic missiles theoretically capable of delivering those weapons to nearby countries, "in a region where more than 135,000 American civilians and service members live and work."

If Bush's assertion was true, I thought, it would be a serious issue. From my perspective, the president's remarks had the sheen of grasping at straws, particularly when he turned to his second rationalization, threats against the American homeland. "Of course, sophisticated delivery systems aren't required for a chemical or biological attack," Bush said. "All that might be required are a small container and one terrorist or Iraqi intelligence operative to deliver it."

I immediately recognized that for the president's assertion to have any real credibility, the administration needed to pinpoint *someone* who could somehow connect Hussein's regime to the single international terrorist organization to have struck within the United States.

"We know that Iraq and the al Qaida terrorist network share a common enemy, the United States of America," the president continued. "Some al Qaida leaders who fled Afghanistan went to Iraq. These include one very senior al Qaida leader who received medical treatment in Baghdad this year, and who has been associated with planning for chemical and biological attacks."

A "very senior al Qaida leader?" I said to myself. Everyone in the growing Iraq unit recognized that this phrase referred to Zarqawi, even though he was not mentioned by name. We knew he wasn't part of al Qaida and didn't seem to coordinate operations with them. We also knew that the CIA had determined that Zarqawi's organization didn't know about the 9/11 attacks, much less participate in them. Nor was Zarqawi's organization capable of developing sophisticated chemical and biological weapons; they were, however, working on the development of crude toxins and poisons—our terminology for Zarqawi's loose affiliates at the time was the "poisons network."

Everyone in the Agency realized that the United States was about to invade Iraq, and the role Bush's administration had chosen for Zarqawi had become clear.

Before the invasion, my standard Agency workday began at 3:00 a.m. Baghdad was eight hours ahead. A typical day started with the drive to the Agency's sprawling Langley campus in the middle of the night and presenting my ID badge to the heavily armed security guards. As I was one of the first ones to arrive for the day, my ground-floor office in the New Headquarters Building was typically quiet at that hour.

Upon arrival, a colleague and I quickly got to work examining incoming cables from the field, other intelligence reports, cyber collection, signals collection, news material, and written products—memos and briefings for lawmakers—our branch had written the night before to gather the latest insights on terrorism connected to Iraq or the IIS. By 4:00 a.m., we were scouring any last-minute intelligence that had bubbled up before sprinting to the Original Headquarters Building, on the other side of the campus, to update senior Agency briefers who were preparing to brief the president, vice president, and a small number of cabinet-level officials. We had to make sure those senior briefers were up to speed on any late-breaking intelligence and answer any questions they might have about the products our unit had written the day before.

Once the briefers headed off to the White House and other buildings across Washington, DC, to meet with their principals, my colleague and I headed off to the cafeteria for our first shot of Starbucks. Then we dragged ourselves back across campus, punched in the code to the cipher lock on our team's "vault," or room, and dug in for a few more hours of reading through traffic before the rest of our branch trickled in for our morning meeting.

For some reason, our vault was always roasting at that hour, so my colleague and I would "sing" Nelly's "Hot in Herre" because we couldn't play actual music due to the security policy. Our off-key version of the song was enough to wake us up and counterbalance the increasingly dark reports we were receiving from case officers in the field.

Lunch came around 9:00 a.m., as I wolfed down whatever was within arm's reach. Then, if all was calm, at around 12:15 p.m. I met with my counterparts on the next shift for the handoff. From there, I was off to the burn chute.

At the Agency, each analyst finds at his or her desk every morning a brown paper bag decorated with red-and-white candy-cane stripes. Known internally as burn bags, they're used to hold classified documents until they can be irretrievably destroyed. I set mine up under my desk; every incoming cable I would print throughout the day, as soon as I was finished with it, got dropped into the burn bag. Once the bag was full, I folded it over at the top a few times, stapled it as many times as was necessary to keep it shut, then carted it down the hall to the equivalent of a laundry chute, where the bag plummeted to the sub-subbasement of the New Headquarters Building. Eventually, the collected bags were tossed into an incinerator.

The great thing about the burn chute is that it's part of a long-standing tradition to welcome rookie team members by hazing them by playing on their paranoia of violating a security policy. We insisted that one rookie needed to yell his badge number into the abyss of the chute before he dropped the bags down to ensure that the worker at the bottom knew where they came from. Then, we told the same rookie, he should stand and wait for confirmation from below. "Just keep standing there," we said. "Sometimes it takes a minute or two." After around three minutes of standing by the chute, thinking someone in the basement might actually yell back at him, he caught on to the game.

In the run-up to the invasion, it really was the little things that kept us going.

As the administration had begun preparing its case for war, of course, there was less time for fun. If I could climb into bed some-time around sunset, then be back up at 2:00 a.m., it had been a "standard" day. Very quickly, the environment in the Iraq unit became anything but standard.

Hours at the office piled up. I was scouring practically a novel's worth of written reports, records, and cables every morning — what the other analysts and I called "drinking from the fire hose." Out of that mass of information, I set aside perhaps a dozen of those reports daily because they contained information that didn't seem to fit an established pattern or because I simply thought they might come in handy someday. Analysts, like most people, tend to look for patterns; anything that fell outside of (or was inconsistent with) established patterns often warranted closer scrutiny if we deemed the information reliable. I was keeping an eye out for literally one or two sentences that would trigger my next written product, information that would somehow further our understanding of the Iraqi Intelligence Service's plans or associations, so I could deliver it to a policy maker.

Some of the most intense days came when the information flowed the other way. If a policy maker had a question, it was our mission — and, frankly, our job — to provide that person with a thorough answer ASAP. Even though I learned quickly that that's not necessarily the same thing as an exhaustive answer.

Analysis is an ambiguous word; new analysts soon learn that analyzing is as much an art as a science. Once I moved beyond the simple recitation of facts, because no single fact explains the larger trend or picture, I then focused on the motivations of the actors, contextual dynamics, likely outcomes, signposts, and their possible implications. In intelligence analysis, there may be no complete answer to any given question. Painting a detailed picture of the trends is difficult, particularly when there is too little information and even when there's too much.

Having an incomplete picture of a given topic presents obvious limitations. Today, however, in the era of "big data," the opposite is often the case. Collecting massive volumes of information these days isn't the problem; even if you have volumes of documentation at the ready, an analyst has to learn how to make sense of it. How do you teach a gut instinct for accurately and objectively characterizing information?

Experience and expertise with a given topic make it easier to assign a degree of confidence to data. For me, particularly during those months prior to the invasion of Iraq, analysis was about creating a reasonable assessment of events within the context of a specific question — did Iraq have anything to do with 9/11 or al Qaida? Typically, we would approach a topic based on available information and then use our individual expertise, and the expertise of our colleagues, to tell a larger story. This point was made by Michael Hayden during his confirmation hearing to become director of the

CIA in 2006: he told Senator Pat Roberts that intelligence gathering "is shrouded in ambiguity...if these were *known* facts, you wouldn't be coming to us for them."

In March of 2003, the Bush administration green-lit Operation Iraqi Freedom, the invasion of Iraq, despite CIA analysis finding no connection between the country's regime and al Qaida. Three weeks later, US tanks triumphantly rolled into Firdos Square, in central Baghdad.

Soon my teammates and I were provided with an array of new streams of reporting we felt warranted further study. The new reporting did not validate the administration's original case for war. In the face of a growing number of questions from Congress, the Agency was pressed even harder to search for historical ties. For months, we answered questions about connections Hussein had or might have had with extremist groups in the past that would have helped justify the administration's case for war.

One frustrating moment that came in 2004 was when a member of Wolfowitz's team inexplicably asked me what type of underwear Zarqawi wore—a line of inquiry that begged more questions about the person asking. What did they expect to hear? He wears a thong and that might contribute to his inner rage? Indeed, I'd never thought to look into it. Our team was focusing on the growing potential for extremism following the invasion.

By early 2004, the insurgency was beginning to expand across Iraq. Zarqawi was well on his way to solidifying his control over the insurgency, while Iraqi civilians and coalition troops were dying. In Langley, I'd watched many of my exasperated coworkers leave the team for different jobs at the Agency—or simply burn out and leave the CIA for good. Katherine was part of that second group: she quit the Agency to become a successful entrepreneur.

The real intelligence story was the growing connection between Zarqawi and Usama bin Ladin. Zarqawi was not only becoming a subject of interest for the United States; he also was inspiring disparate terrorist networks that had not necessarily trained directly with al Qaida. My colleagues and I kept wondering why the administration wasn't paying more attention to the growing threat and instead remained focused on trying to piece together a case for the invasion. I was starting to become a very angry person watching people die inside Iraq as the United States struggled to find an effective way to stop the violence.

At work, I could feel the gradually rising tide of frustration as an endless stream of grim cables filtered through my computer system, followed by a never-ending stream of backward-looking questions from the administration. It took a few months, but in June of 2004, I reached the end of my patience and decided to quit.

I was lost in thought about all that when a soft *ding* snapped me back to the present. The elevator doors opened on the ground floor of the New Headquarters Building, and I walked through the sun-filled lobby. Even through the cloudiness of that early summer afternoon, it felt warm outside. I began to think of a job offer I had waiting for me at home.

I climbed into my car and picked up my cell phone—mobile devices aren't allowed inside Agency buildings. I cranked the ignition, dialed my boyfriend, Roger, and headed for the George Washington Parkway. He picked up as I merged onto the parkway.

"I did it," I said into the phone. "I'm *done*."

By the time I pulled up outside our house and made my way up the sidewalk, my frustration had lost its edge.

I pushed open our heavy wooden front door and stepped into the entryway. Gus, the three-year-old Saint Bernard we'd recently adopted, poked his head out from around a corner at the top of the staircase. I paused to see what came next: in Gus's previous life, spent chained in a yard in southern Virginia, he'd never seen stairs. When we first brought him home he spent an hour on the stair landing trying to muster up the courage to make his way down while I tried to convince him with hot dogs. But on that early June afternoon, he trotted right down to see me. He groaned once and flopped onto his side for a belly rub. I might not be able to fix US foreign policy or stop the endless stream of violence in Iraq, but I could do this for my dog.

The light streaming into the living room looked different at that time of day. I was so used to the long and unusual hours in counterterrorism, I didn't know what the afternoon light looked like in my own home. The shine from the hardwood floor gave the whole room an eerie glow; I felt like I'd stepped into an alternate universe. For as frustrated as I was, I felt like I was playing hooky, and I didn't like it.

I needed something productive to do—so I headed upstairs to put some laundry away. Then, when I didn't find any, I did a load just to have some clothes to put away. I noticed how quiet our Barnaby Woods neighborhood was. Lately I'd found that quiet was good.

I'd recently turned thirty-four and was struggling with an all-consuming, incredibly stressful job and new home ownership. My readjustment to life back in DC had been harder than I'd anticipated after a few months in Iraq. Unexpected sounds—even the doorbell—made me jump. I'd been snapping at Roger over little things; I didn't realize at the time how overblown my reactions had become.

At work, I focused all of my energy on Zarqawi and his network. But at night, distractions were harder to come by. I spent all my time trying to avoid thinking about Iraq, not just my time in country, but also everything I was reading on a daily basis.

Quiet was good, except when it was filled with guilt.

Laundry done, I sat down at the library table I inherited from my great-grandmother. The table had remained in her tiny one-bedroom cabin on Plum Creek Ranch in central Montana for years after her death. That farm and ranch is where her daughter—my grandmother Henrietta Ellis—grew up; sitting at the table in my living room, I thought back to the beautiful wood-burning range in that cabin, which was filled with knickknacks and western art. The whole thing felt like a Norman Rockwell painting. Whenever I stayed at Plum Creek during harvest, or during a few weeks of a lazy childhood summer, I felt a renewed sense of calm. I thought that cabin was paradise. Years later, when the building had fallen into disrepair, I claimed that table and had brought it along to every home I'd lived in since.

At the other end of the table was an offer letter from the Science Applications International Corporation. Better known as SAIC, the contracting giant, based in Virginia, had recently offered me a position managing one of their Middle Eastern counterterrorism research programs. I could have done the work well, I thought, and the federal government pay scale certainly left something to be desired, but no one enters into service at the CIA for the money. Taking a contracting job was a well-worn escape route from the CIA, even more so now that former Agency personnel didn't necessarily have to change their commutes. After 9/11, the CIA had begun to fill its expanding need for staff by bringing in private contractors with security clearances—who were described as "green badgers" because of the green ID badges they carry (CIA employees carry blue badges). We'd all seen coworkers leave on a Friday, then show right back up on Monday doing the same job—but with a different boss, a different color badge, and twice the pay.

Yet even though I'd thought about leaving the Agency at some point and had wondered how I'd do it, that offer letter had just sat there on the table for days. There, in the middle of the afternoon, it occurred to me that I should probably read it.

As I reached for the letter, I realized I was still wearing my clothes from the office — a purple button-down shirt over black pants. It had the comfortable feel of a uniform I wore often. Fit and function were always the most important things to me in my wardrobe; form, not so much. Government work doesn't exactly lend itself to high fashion, and that was fine with me. On the table next to my keys, I noticed my blue ID badge, and I drew in a long breath. I thought back to the day they'd first handed it to me.

That morning, in 2000, I and a few dozen other new hires had been led across the gray granite Central Intelligence Agency seal, which dominates the minimalist lobby of the Original Headquarters Building, in Langley. The lobby is surprisingly quiet given that it's all marble and massive. The eagle's head sits resolutely above a shield emblazoned with a sixteen-point compass star, representing intelligence gathered from around the world and filtered back to a single point. The symbol is unmistakable in its strength and unwavering in its focus. The seal is the first thing most outsiders envision when they think of the CIA. It's the first thing I saw on the day I became an insider. Simply walking across it on the way to my new-hire orientation, I felt a rush of pride and a sense of how much my life was about to change.

A few steps past the seal, the Agency's Memorial Wall comes into view to my right. In 2000, seventy-nine stars had been chiseled into the gleaming white marble, each star representing a man or woman who had given their life in service to the Agency and our country. More than thirty more have been added in the years that followed, some for men and women who were colleagues — friends — of mine doing the same kinds of counterterrorism work I did. Above those stars are etched the words IN HONOR OF THOSE MEMBERS OF THE CENTRAL INTELLIGENCE AGENCY WHO GAVE THEIR LIVES IN THE SERVICE OF THEIR COUNTRY.

Below the stars, the Book of Honor spreads out forty inches across a blue-gray marble ledge, encased in glass. The first time I saw the gold stars in that book—and so many of the blank lines that followed, indicating employees whose identities can't be revealed, even in death—it nearly took my breath away.

The other new hires and I had flowed forward to the ID scanners up ahead and soon through the underground tunnel that winds from the Original Headquarters Building to the Agency's igloo-shaped auditorium, a seven-thousand-square-foot relic of the 1950s everyone just called the Bubble. We took our seats; making small talk with those closest to me, I was impressed with the range of talent among those new employees: aerospace engineers; analysts; economists; translators; experts on everything from bridge building to bomb wiring.

From that moment on, I understood the Agency's mission on a whole other level, even with its infuriating bureaucratic potholes.

I hadn't been prepared for the way it would actually feel to leave.

I tossed SAIC's offer letter back on the table. Which is when my phone rang. It was Jim, an analyst from another counterterrorism unit's chemical and biological weapons group. I held Jim in high regard because he was one of the first analysts to begin mapping Zarqawi's poisons network in the '90s. He said his group chief, Scott, was familiar with my work and wanted me to come in and talk. I agreed to meet with them the following day.

In broad strokes, Scott told me about the ways in which the Agency was expanding to become a bigger part of the Global War on Terror and the new roles that were being created in the process. There were roles, he said, that needed to be filled by people with substantive experience. "Would you come lead a targeting team to go after Zarqawi?" he said. Scott effectively told me during our meeting that they wanted to retain my expertise and I would not have to continue answering the same backward-looking policy-maker questions on al Qaida's connection to Iraq.

"You mean I can actually *do* something about him?" I said. "I don't have to just answer questions about his past or his underwear anymore?"

I was sold.

CHAPTER 2

The Farm

Denton, Montana, is an approximately fifteen-square-block town in the center of the state, near the Upper Missouri River Breaks and two hours by car to the closest town most people have heard of, Great Falls. In many ways, not much has changed there since Lewis and Clark first explored those grasslands in 1805, and it is still one of my favorite places to roam.

Denton is a farming community where sixty-something families mostly live off the land, and mine was no different. My parents had a house in town, a stone-and-redwood home with big bay windows and a little yard where my older brother, Keith, and I made up SWAT team imagination games while wearing jean jackets my mom had embroidered with the words SWAT TEAM. But many of my childhood memories come from the summers at my grandparents' ranch in nearby Everson, a collection of family farms that lined the Judith River breaks, with a view so vast the world seemed full of endless possibility.

I learned to ride horses at the age of two—first on a Shetland pony, then on a succession of larger horses with names like Socks, Britches, and Jet. Then, when I was twelve years old and a member of 4-H, my mom bought me the first horse that belonged entirely to me, a chestnut mare with white feet and an elegant stripe down her nose named Coy Lady. I loved riding her into the nearby pastures, disappearing for hours at a time, pretending I was on my very own Victorian foxhunt. My friend Valerie and I even purchased inexpensive English saddles and set up straw bales so we could practice jumping. I used to imagine that I was a character from an old British novel riding through the English countryside. My rides with Valerie also taught me to conquer my fears while riding across the knife ridges of the Judith River breaks, where one misstep on your horse's part would have meant tumbling together three hundred feet down a sheer shale cliff. When I was twelve years old, it didn't seem dangerous; it was the most fun I had ever had.

Self-reliance was less an ethos than an expectation in Denton. My appreciation for the law of the land was first branded into me at age nine, when I stood along the fence and watched my dad and a hired hand put a bullet into a steer's head, then slit its throat to bleed it out before butchering the animal. I was hardly stoic about the slaughter, but the sight of blood didn't shock me by then. Mostly it was a matter-of-fact lesson in the cycle of life and in respecting the stewardship of farming and ranching. At least, I decided, the steer had simply been going about his day in his pen, with no fear, stress, or sense of impending demise. A lot less stressful than commercial slaughterhouses.

The animals I grew attached to were the orphaned calves—the ones I'd wrap in an old quilt, the ones whose necks I would adorn with scarves or ribbons. I used to sit on the straw next to the calves, feeding them from a two-quart calf bottle, feeling sorry that their moms weren't there to help them. When those calves grew large enough to be sold to the local market—when they were crammed into the back of a truck, which I knew delivered them to a stock lot where they'd be funneled into a factory chute, mooing in terror until the moment some guy ended their brief lives by slamming a bolt into their skulls — that's when I'd bawl.

As the youngest child, I was tasked with my least favorite job on the farm: replacing the duckfoot shovels on my grandparents' plow after they fell off or wore down after churning through more than two thousand acres of wheat fields. During seeding season, a broken plow was one step shy of a crisis that could set the entire operation back days. That and unexpected weather delays could affect my grandparents' livelihood.

So as soon as my grandpa called me from the barn, I'd drop what I was doing and reluctantly make my way over to the shop. My grandfather would hand me an air wrench, and I'd shimmy under the duckfoot, between the rear wheels. There was less than two feet of ground clearance under the plow, and I invariably whacked my head on the hard steel. Then I'd fumble for the bolts that secured the shovel, zap them loose with the wrench, and switch out the shovel for a new one. Then I'd tighten the bolts down again as the chattering of the wrench vibrated my whole body.

The dedication paid off, in a way. At ten years old, I got promoted to the role of temporary combine driver during harvest while my grandpa or brother took a break, which meant an air-conditioned cab and longer days. I loved being in the center of the action, and it meant I didn't have the labor-intensive job of driving the truck to load and unload the grain. To sidestep my allergies, Grandpa found me a mask that made me sound like Darth Vader, which I thought was an added benefit. Before long, I was spending those late summer mornings piloting Grandpa's half-million-dollar combine back and forth, in seemingly endless straight lines, at five miles per hour. I loved the responsibility, and it was a meditative activity — right up until the moment I accidentally harvested a skunk.

The TV picked up CBS and ABC; NBC didn't arrive until I was

close to junior high. On Sunday evenings, I watched whatever Disney show ran for half an hour, then stuck around as the family all gathered in the living room for *60 Minutes*.

When I wasn't working on the farm, my natural curiosity kept me occupied. Once, at the age of ten, I decided I wanted to learn a foreign language—which one didn't matter at all. So I began flipping through the *Encyclopaedia Britannica* set my grandparents kept on the bookshelf in the hallway. This was before the age of the Internet; there was no Google or Rosetta Stone online. The entry entitled "French" included a handful of mundane words—such as *oui* and *monsieur*—and the entry entitled "Spanish" did the same. But under "Sign language," I found the entire alphabet. I spent the next three nights sitting in the hall, memorizing all twenty-six letters.

I especially loved when my maternal aunt Harriette came to visit the farm, bringing my cousins Brian and Lori. I was completely fascinated by their stories of life outside Montana, brushing my aunt's long, dark hair until late in the evening, asking endless questions about their adventures in far-off Illinois.

My fascination with the wider world took root in 1976, when I had taken my first trip out of state to attend the wedding of my other maternal aunt, Henrietta, in New York City's borough of Brooklyn. The energy of New York was new and exciting and I'd found friendly faces everywhere I turned—most notably in the person of one of Henrietta's new in-laws. Days before the wedding, we went to a horse race at Belmont Park, on Long Island, feeding my love of horses. One of my prized possessions from the trip was a 1970s-era polyester shirt with variously colored racehorses that I instantly loved and held on to until college.

For the rest of our time in New York, we bounced from the Empire State Building to the Statue of Liberty, then to the newest tourist attraction at the time: the Top of the World observation deck atop the World Trade Center's South Tower. For years after that trip, my grandparents kept a photo on their refrigerator of a six-year-old me in a blue dress, with big white socks and sandals, sporting awesome '70s bangs. In the photo, I'm standing next to Keith, my grandpa, and our mom. The clouds had parted moments before my grandmother took the picture; the moment after the shutter clicked, I'd turned back to rest my chin again on the white guardrail, gazing out at the vastness of upper Manhattan and New Jersey beyond it.

My mom eventually had to pull me away from that railing to get dressed for the wedding. The city offered a view as enormous as those back on the farm. A few hours later, my aunt Henrietta introduced Keith and me in front of three hundred people at the start of her wedding reception to perform our practiced routine, the hustle.

From my perspective as a child, my parents were largely estranged during most of their marriage. After their divorce, when I was eleven, my father wasn't around much of the time; the anger between my parents was evidently too much for him to be interested in attending any of my school activities, my graduation, my wedding, or any other milestone event in my life. Particularly when I was a child, that sense of abandonment was a hard one to shake. Especially in a town like Denton, where he lived literally a block and a half away. To his credit, he reconnected with me many years later of his own accord. I know now that divorce makes people do strange things and that the marriage wasn't easy for either of them.

Without admitting it, or perhaps fully understanding it, my mother, Eloise, spent the majority of my early years feeling shackled to Denton, caught in the grips of a depression that only let up once she finally escaped that small town years later. In fact, she raced out of town to finish her bachelor's degree at the same time I did, then went on to earn a master's degree in social work and built a career at a point in her life when many people are thinking of slowing down. My mom was born with cerebral palsy, which manifested as tremors in her arms. She was frustrated at not being able to do everything for herself, and at the same time accepted it as just another challenge that added to her determination to succeed.

When I was growing up, my maternal grandmother, also named Henrietta, had a big impact on my love of learning. She turned everything into a lesson — and usually a fun one. She not only worked on the farm; she was also the business manager of the place, and she taught me about grain and livestock markets and keeping a ledger. She used to encourage my knack for memorizing numbers, quizzing me on details she'd just shown me.

I loved afternoons in her kitchen, leaning over the flour-covered table, assembling her infamous raspberry-rhubarb pie or Czech *kolaches*. In the 1930s, my grandmother had played violin in a band, so sometimes she'd belt out "I Double Dare You" or other standards from that era as I measured the next ingredient or watched the horses move around the pasture while grazing.

Other things my grandmother taught me shaped my entire world-view. She had grown up on her parents' homestead farm, an hour from Lewistown, Montana, back when her last name was still Van Haur and her family had nicknamed her Hanke. She'd become one of the first women, along with her sisters, in the area to attend college, in nearby Billings; then she raised my mother and her two sisters on the farm in Everson with her husband, Floyd Ellis. My grandmother's tenacity and grit demonstrated to me the extraordinary things of which women were capable. The life she lived was a driving force that compelled my own passion for women's rights — in part because of my grandmother's accomplishments.

My grandparents were hard workers, and life on the farm left little time for fun. My grandpa Floyd was nicknamed Bus because he'd won the local Buster Brown baby contest.

Harvest was stressful for everyone, the endless days and late nights racing to cut the grain before rain, hail, or wind knocked it down. In my younger years, to avoid the stress I'd run outside to hide in the barn with my dog and Coy Lady when I wasn't needed.

As a child, I was an eager student at Denton public school—and disciplined, too. I used to rush home to finish my homework right after school before a playdate, or, at the farm, a ride on Coy Lady. I loved puzzles and the fundamental logic of a good equation.

However, by the time I entered my freshman year in high school—in the same building as the elementary school and middle school, because Denton's population didn't exactly support multiple schoolhouses—I had lost the confidence I had in my younger years. Some of that may have been a result of my rocky home life. Partly it was apathy, and maybe it was a little boredom, because I never particularly struggled. Mostly, I think, a fear of failure cast a pall of mediocrity over my scholastic career. I couldn't underperform at what I never tried to achieve.

At one point during my freshman year, my mom asked the principal to arrange an IQ test for me so we could pinpoint where I fit in academically. Mom hoped it would boost my confidence—and to my surprise, I was told that I'd tested roughly two to three years ahead of my grade level. I don't know if it was a perception-changing moment in my life, but it did give my fourteen-year-old self more confidence, which I harnessed in various ways.

Small-town high schools can collect an odd array of teachers, and one dictatorial algebra teacher used to become so enraged over tiny things—such as students talking while he scribbled equations on the chalkboard—that he regularly berated my classmates and even threw desks. I couldn't believe his outbursts, and one day, after a galactic tantrum left one of my classmates in tears, and after he made inappropriate comments to one of my girlfriends, I finally went up to him after class and looked him in the eye—because by then, I was as tall as many of the adult men at the school. "Knock it off," I said. I think the teacher was so shocked that he never did figure out the right way to punish me. Soon the mutual resentment between us became its own sort of drama, and he subsequently asked my mom to stop me from enrolling in his math class the following year. It wasn't a huge loss.

I had some great teachers, too. My favorite English teacher, Mrs. Hassinger, wouldn't let me off the hook if I showed low self-esteem. She insisted we could all achieve great things if we applied ourselves—which included reading Shakespeare every year and performing on the school's tiny stage every spring, whether we wanted to or not.

I was a typical teenager. I once shaved the right side of my head, because it was the 1980s. And my high school friend Lynn Donaldson and I would spend our weekends walking around Lewistown, the nearest "city," in our parachute pants and the blue-and-pink faux fur coats her mom, June, made, drawing double takes from old-time ranchers, and other teenagers, who couldn't appreciate our "eclectic" sense of style. We weren't looking for attention: we just loved the idea of wearing something that made us feel different and creative.

My high school graduating class—all nine of us—mostly consisted of the same people I'd gone to kindergarten with. Before kindergarten, I beelined across the street one summer morning with my mom in tow the moment I noticed two boys in our neighbor's yard. Those boys were twins—Kurt and Kyle. Today, Kurt and I call each other our first friend.

In a place like Denton, it's an occasion whenever new kids move into town. One day the Coltons arrived from nearby Lewistown.

With a population of roughly six thousand, Lewistown seemed like a big city to us. Shane had a mop of blond hair, a wide smile, and, even more important, a truly fantastic collection of T-shirts. There was a rebelliousness to him that I found amusing. Shane never apologized for anything. I seemed to apologize for everything.

Soon after moving into town, Shane asked me to accompany him to one of the high school plays. Sitting there in those uncomfortable wooden auditorium seats, he held my hand for the entire play — only occasionally letting go so we could wipe the sweat onto our pants.

It took a few years for that relationship to fully blossom, but we officially became a couple during our last few months of high school. Teenage hormones played a part in that, of course, but it turned out that his family life didn't necessarily match the Norman Rockwell imagery on the walls, either, and that brought us together. I knew I could call him, crying, when the adults in the house were screaming and he would be there to distract me for a while.

Despite my rocky high school transcripts, education for its own sake was always important to me. Even before my senior year in high school, in 1986, I enrolled in a pair of college courses at Montana State University, in nearby Bozeman. I lived for the summer with my brother, who by then worked at the school's plant pathology lab as a researcher. I volunteered in the lab, charting plant growth, and took a communications class and a psychology class. After I received my final grade, my psychology professor suggested I take the GED so that I could start college courses right away in the fall and skip my last year of high school. That was an exciting proposition, but on the other hand, I was looking forward to the social part of being a high school senior. After giving it much thought, I stuck to the traditional route — but returned to MSU as a freshman in 1987. MSU offered a skiing course in the nearby Bridger Mountains as well as a colt-breaking class as part of its nationally recognized equine science program, and that pretty much sealed the deal.

Soon after arriving on campus, I joined three dozen other women in the Alpha Omicron Pi (AOΠ) sorority, mainly because I'm an extroverted introvert and I thought it would mean an immediate group of people to socialize with. People have occasionally been surprised in the years since to hear that I was a "sorority girl." I've never fit the preconception people have of that bubbly stock character; I've also always taken pride in defying pigeonholing, and that sorority did, too. It was full of artists, graphic designers, and future engineers and scientists. I learned very quickly how important that sort of old-fashioned social network could be.

One Monday night in mid-October, just weeks after starting my freshman year at MSU, three sorority sisters and I drove from AOΠ's "big brick house" headquarters, at the corner of Fifth Avenue and West Garfield Street, through the leafy off-campus suburbs surrounding Montana State and over to the Sigma Chi fraternity. Shane — who'd enrolled in college in Utah — and I had agreed to put our relationship on hold for at least our freshman year in college, and Sigma Chi was known for having some of the nicest guys on campus.

There was an electricity in the air as I parked the car across the street from the fraternity and headed off on foot across South Willson Avenue, a simple two-lane road that draws its fair share of lead-footed motorists speeding north and south along Bozeman's eastern edge. We were talking about our outfits and anticipating what the night might have in store. And then memories stop.

According to eyewitness and police reports, a blocky white Ford Bronco II sport utility vehicle came flying around the corner. It swerved hard to the left, careened across the street, and slammed directly into us. I can't imagine we had any time to react; I apparently took the driver's-side mirror off with my head. There are some thirty minutes of my life that have been almost completely blacked out in my mind, save the image of my friend Heidi's long blond hair splayed out next to me in a pool of blood. I wanted to yell her name, not knowing if she was dead, but I blacked out again. The next thing I do remember after the accident is hearing an EMT, kneeling next to the parked car I'd been thrown into, yelling to bring me back into consciousness. Heidi was in the same ambulance, and they told me she was going to be okay.

Kurt, my childhood friend from across the street, was one of the first people to make it to the emergency room at Bozeman Deaconess Hospital after I woke up. He took one look at my swollen eyes and nose — and at the open wounds on my face from skidding across the street — and fainted. That was my first indication that things were pretty rough.

But another thing I remember still powerfully: the AOΠ sisters were incredibly supportive, and so were many of the men of Sigma Chi. Several arrived at the hospital before even my family could make it. On that day, I formed a bond that has carried across decades — through marriages, divorce, health scares, and more. It's one I've sought to re-create in the circles of women I would later meet on teams everywhere from Langley to Baghdad. In particular, Vicki Sherick, my big sister in the house, was my anchor of stability for much of that first year after the accident. Without her positivity and gentle care for a person she'd met only days earlier, I'm not sure how things would have gone.

That support was even more significant because the doctors at the hospital seemed less than engaged with my case. They clearly felt I was some neurasthenic creature complaining about pain. For five days I recovered there with little medical assistance beyond a leg brace to alleviate the pressure on my right knee, even though I was regularly coughing up blood. It wasn't until weeks later that my aunt drove me to a specialist who took a few X-rays and said, "You've suffered internal bleeding as well as torn ligaments and cartilage in your knee. I am not sure what damage the internal bleeding has done."

Unfortunately, the legal recourse I sought didn't go much better. The night of the accident, the driver had tried to flee the scene, but a crew of Sigma Chi brothers had surrounded the Bronco to block his path until Bozeman police arrived. The authorities, however, didn't give him a Breathalyzer test for something like eight hours, and by then the booze had worn off. He eventually walked away with a "careless driving" citation.

————

A year after the accident, Shane, my high school boyfriend, transferred to Montana State, and he found an apartment near campus. Some of that likely had to do with being there for me, but at the same time Shane was narrowing his sights on a career and MSU offered more options for him than the junior college he attended in Utah did. I'd never really dated anyone seriously except Shane, and I felt conflicted about the decision. I loved the camaraderie of the sisters at AOΠ. And by then, Shane had begun to feel more like a great roommate than a boyfriend. He may have felt the same way, though at the age of twenty-one, neither of us understood the difference. Still, I did miss him, and it was nice to have someone to think through the future with.

I raced to catch up on credits I missed after a freshman year cut short by the accident and the subsequent surgery and rehabilitation I underwent to repair my knee. Ultimately I decided to transfer to the University of Utah, in Salt Lake City, for my senior year. By then I'd become an economics major, and Montana State offered only an agricultural economics degree at the time, which seemed far too narrow a focus and far too similar to the life I'd already lived. I wanted to learn about whatever it was that existed outside my comfort zone, and Utah offered an economics program with an international focus. Shane, being at that point a year ahead of me academically, had recently graduated, which meant that he would be free to follow me to our new home in Salt Lake City, Utah. It would be the grand start of our new life together.

Days prior, on a sweltering August Saturday in 1991, Shane and I had stood in the basement of Denton's tiny Methodist church—the one for which my great-grandfather had built the pews, altar, and baptismal font. Shane looked dashing in his tan tuxedo; I wore a silk wedding dress my grandmother had bought for me in Lewistown. Shane had just turned twenty-two. I'd turned twenty-two the day after he did.

Standing in that church basement playing with our black two-year-old Saint Bernard–Lab mix, Nixon, who was wearing a white bow tie, we'd listened as seemingly the entire town arrived at the church and found their seats in the pews above us. I was antsy. The back door was open on that boiling summer Saturday; we both walked toward it to catch a bit of the early afternoon breeze.

He cast a nervous glance at me. "Should we get out of here?" he said.

"Oh, God, can we?" I said. "With all these people here?"

Shane and I stood quietly in that doorway until we eventually turned and walked upstairs together. After the wedding we moved to Salt Lake City, and I prepared for my senior year.

Soon after starting at the University of Utah, I met an economics professor, Dr. Rajani Kanth, who influenced my next path, after college; in the years since I took his courses, Dr. Kanth has held visiting professorships at Duke, Harvard, Oxford, and Tufts. I was so taken with his classes that I blew right past my required graduation credits, moving on to graduate-level economics classes before ever receiving my degree. Thanks to that drive—and because in 1992, I graduated right into the tail end of a recession—Dr. Kanth suggested that I continue my studies at one of his previous teaching locations: Jawaharlal Nehru University, or JNU, in New Delhi,

India. With his help, I enrolled in one of JNU's yearlong graduate programs, focusing on a burgeoning agricultural-feminist movement flourishing in the northern part of the country. Shane, who was still settling on what his future would hold for a career, decided to join me on this adventure.

At the time, my international travel experience was limited to one college spring break in Mexico and a few trips to Canada, so in retrospect, I'm really not sure how I expected things to go. To the uninitiated, New Delhi is a climate of extremes: scorching summers lead to blinding monsoons before autumn tumbles into dreary, foggy winters. Montana had prepared me for unpredictable weather. The stray dogs were a nuisance, the wild monkeys were highly entertaining and feisty—and the bureaucracy throughout the nation at the time had very little to offer in terms of clarity. The best example of that was when JNU "mismanaged" its enrollment list for the coming semester. Two days before classes were to start, my admissions status was unclear, though they happily offered to rectify their error for a gargantuan fee. There was no way I could, or would, pay, so I asked to audit courses until the enrollment issue was resolved. Eventually they allowed that. I was mesmerized by the colors of India and the engaging landscape. I was hoping to make this work, but it seemed increasingly less likely.

With all the potential for culture shock, I thought I might be completely overwhelmed. But I wasn't. I was interested in the cultural dynamics and the everyday patterns of the locals: where they shopped, how they got around, how women bargained with merchants and kept men from bothering them. I wanted to appear local, to fit into an urban landscape I had never experienced before. I was slowly cracking the code of the city's inner logic, and except for the snafu at the university and a food-borne illness, I loved *almost* every minute of it.

Shane, however, never felt the same way. He longed to be back in

Montana, starting his own career. I knew how he felt. His frustration turned into bitterness, which then became resentfulness.

———————

Finally, the tension—coupled with my dwindling faith that the administrative issues at JNU would ever be resolved—became too much to bear. We gave up on India, and we spent the money we'd saved for our time abroad bouncing around Europe. We eventually settled back in Missoula, Montana, where Shane enrolled at the School of Law at the University of Montana.

When we'd headed off to New Delhi, I'd had lofty visions of a nonprofit career spent helping to improve the lives of women and children in agrarian and rural societies around the world. Back in Missoula, however, a different sort of reality set in, and to help pay for our house, my horses, and our expenses, I took a nine-to-five job at a local bank. At least I had a bachelor's degree in economics. I felt confident that I could do the work of an entry-level loan officer. But those were the jobs being given to equally qualified male applicants.

Instead the bank offered me a position as a teller. I worked behind the drive-through window listening to the *whoosh* of the pneumatic tube, spending my days cashing checks and telling people how to fill out a deposit slip.

I became resentful. I didn't want to live in Montana at this point in my life, and I certainly didn't want to work the pneumatic tube. I still had dreams of a life overseas, and every day at the bank I began to feel like the walls were closing in on me. In my restlessness, I took a job in organizational development in human resources at a nearby metals-mining company. Somehow, seven years melted away.

By then Shane and I fought more often than not—about past frustrations we couldn't let go of and about a future that seemed increasingly hard to picture. And in April of 1998, we had to let our dog, Nixon, go after he suffered a bout with cancer and underwent a thirty-day experimental treatment at Colorado State University. Nixon was the glue that kept us together for a while. He seemed wiser than both of us put together. Shane began staying out late with the friends he'd made in law school. I put in long hours at the office. We saw each other and spoke to each other less than we ever had. Eventually, and yet somehow suddenly at all once, we realized there was nothing left to be said.

———

I'm still sad to think that our marriage almost permanently ruined a great friendship. I know that at the age of twenty-two neither of us had any real grasp of who we were or of the sacrifices and compromises marriage entailed or of the pitfalls that might lie ahead. Thankfully, our divorce was amicable. He even officially requested annual "visitation rights" to my grandmother's farm for her famous raspberry-rhubarb pie.

We divided our debt, and I quit my job. I packed my Ford F-150 with no plan other than a destination: Washington, DC. I was sure I could find a job there that would let me make a difference in the world, that would take me overseas — that would do the things I'd felt I wasn't accomplishing in Montana.

———

I started the ignition and aimed for the East Coast. Thirty hours later, I arrived at a one-bedroom "English basement" apartment in the bottom of a row house on the north side of Dupont Circle. My rent cost nearly twice as much as I'd paid each month for our mortgage in Montana. But that holiday season in 1999, I forgot all about those things during my evening walks along Massachusetts Avenue, with its blocks of lights and holiday decorations sparkling along Embassy Row.

I had no job in hand when I arrived and no particular job in mind. I had just turned thirty and wasn't entirely sure what I could parlay my résumé into. But I knew the nation's capital was the nerve center for the State Department and was home to nonprofits such as Amnesty International and the Washington delegation of the International Committee of the Red Cross. Any of those seemed like great places to work. Even just exploring the city, I found myself inspired by overhearing work conversations on the Metro. The city seemed like the perfect place to relaunch my career, this time with a global focus.

One particular organization stuck out in my mind. By the time I'd moved, my mom had remarried, and as I papered DC with my résumé, I remembered an ad her husband had shown me in the *Economist*. It announced an upcoming hiring spree at the Central Intelligence Agency. "Don't think," he had said. "Just apply. Why not?"

On the Agency's website, I found an opening for an organizational development analyst, focusing on internal institutional design and supporting "data-driven management strategies and strategic workforce planning objectives." It had significant crossover with organizational development work; the Agency was looking for someone with a business background to devise and implement an organizational strategy inside a massive bureaucratic government entity. It was a job I was qualified for, and at the very least, I figured, it was a gateway to an organization I'd been fascinated with for some time. If I could get my foot in the door, I figured, I could get a great overview of how things work there and then carve out my own path.

That was an invaluable thread of optimism to cling to during an otherwise unsettled time. My grandmother had advised me not to make too many grand life changes at once, yet in the previous few months I'd gotten divorced, quit my job, and moved across the country to a city where I knew hardly anyone—and then, soon after my arrival in DC, Grandpa had a stroke. Days after I submitted my application to the CIA, I got a call from my mother telling me that if I wanted to say goodbye, I had to come right away.

I landed that night at Billings Logan International Airport and drove ninety minutes in a rental car to the hospital. I wasn't entirely sure what I'd say when I saw my grandfather. For most of my childhood, he'd been the only real male role model I'd had. Peering into his hospital room, I felt helpless at the site of that large, forceful man struggling to breathe. My mom, her sisters, and my grandmother had gathered around his bedside. Noticing me in the hall, my mother motioned for me to join them.

I walked over to my grandfather's bed and wrapped my hands around his. Even in his old age, they remained toughened from decades of farming. I thought about those hands on the combine steering wheel next to mine decades earlier, when he'd taught me how to drive it. My grandfather's eyes were closed; I watched his chest rise and fall. "I love you and it's okay if you want to go, Grandpa. We will be okay," I said. Ten minutes later, he drew in one last deep breath and was gone. My grandmother hugged me. "I think he was waiting until you got here," she said.

Amid that backdrop, any response to my CIA application would have been a welcome surprise. I was back home in DC a few days later, sitting in front of my laptop computer, reading the news and devouring a tray of takeout sushi, when the phone call came. I glanced at the caller ID as I propped the phone on my shoulder. It read BLOCKED.

"Hello?" I said.

The caller said she was from the Agency recruiting office. I leaped to my feet—and dumped wasabi and soy sauce all over my keyboard.

"Shit!" I mouthed. Or at least I think I mouthed it, because the caller went silent for a moment. Then she picked back up with a few preliminary interview questions. A few minutes later she asked, "Can you come in for a formal interview?"

I flipped the laptop over and tried to shake the soy sauce out of the keyboard.

"Sure," I said.

A week later, a package of paperwork in a plain brown envelope with a return address of "Recruitment Center" arrived in the mail. I noticed that it came from the Agency's telltale 20505 zip code, and I tore it open. Inside I found a giant application, various other forms to complete, and even a suggested reading list featuring memoirs by prior directors of the Agency. I'd never been simultaneously so excited and terrified to fill out paperwork. The opportunity represented everything I'd hoped for when I'd left Montana.

A few days later I was driving to a nondescript office park in Virginia, more nervous than I'd ever been for a job interview. I'd spent the last of my savings on a navy pantsuit from Brooks Brothers, just for this meeting — I wanted to look the part.

I had no frame of reference for what to expect. They say six degrees of separation can connect any two people in the world, but coming from Denton, I'm not sure that would have been enough to connect me to anyone who'd ever worked for the CIA. It was an organization I'd read about and seen in the movies — far more an abstract concept than a real place. Reading through the packet, I was amused, thinking mine would be the quickest background check they ever did: around noon on any given day, they could find at least a handful of people who knew me at the Denton Café and finish the interviews all in one shot. But my smile faded as my mind kept settling back on the same aching question: What if I'm not smart enough?

After I arrived at the office park, my first interview was with the senior-level officer I would report to, Jim. He was quirky and brilliant, with a PhD in chemistry, and he said all the right things about charting my own path at the Agency. I liked him immediately. Within moments of starting that conversation, I wanted the job — and the Agency apparently wanted me, too. A few weeks later, more paperwork arrived in the mail from 20505. Again I tore the envelope open; this time, it was a conditional offer of employment, contingent upon my passing a background check and returning to the office park for a battery of tests.

My confidence grew with every step I advanced in the process. The pressure was higher at the second interview, but I felt somehow more collected as I walked back into the visitor center. Around a dozen fellow applicants were there that day; no one spoke as we all made our way up a side stairway to the second floor. We barely even looked at one another.

In the applicant-processing office, I approached the check-in counter to register. The administrator handed me a pen. "First name only," she said. I was called into a back room shortly thereafter.

There a doctor administered a basic medical test, including a hearing and vision check. A technician drew a vial of blood and requested a urine sample.

Then came a ninety-minute psychological evaluation using a personality test. That questionnaire is made up of 567 seemingly nonsensical true-false statements, including "I believe I am being followed," "I drink an unusually large amount of water every day," and "I like to talk about sex." I could almost swear I saw "Do you ever dream about setting your mom on fire?" on there. Once completed, my answers were compared to a database of prior results from test takers who are known to have psychological disorders. Happily, our answer patterns didn't match.

Next up were the IQ and knowledge tests, and evidently I did fine on those.

Finally I was ushered into a tiny office for a polygraph test. What I presumed was a two-way mirror ran nearly the length of one entire wall. A friendly-seeming technician asked me how my day was going and pointed toward a chair directly across from a small camera positioned in the upper corner of the room. The setup didn't look anything like the bulky polygraph machines I'd seen in movies, with skittering arms dancing across a readout. Instead, all that sat on the table beside me was a laptop and a machine the size of a few old VHS tapes with various tubes and sensors attached. The technician strapped a corrugated tube around my chest to gauge any changes in my breathing patterns and tightened a blood pressure cuff around my upper arm.

"On this piece of paper, I need you to write down a number between one and five," he said. "Then lie when I guess it. Ready?"

"Yup," I said.

"Four."

"*No*," I said, making my best sincere-looking face.

He glanced at his computer screen. "Okay," he said. "Let's begin. "Are we in Virginia?"

"Yes," I said.

"Have you ever tried to overthrow the US government?"

"No."

On we went for at least an hour, and unlike so many people who wring their hands before taking the test, wondering what it must be like, I found that my first experience came with unexpectedly little stress. I even fessed up to trying marijuana in college.

A few weeks after the testing, in the spring of 2000, I was officially brought into the Agency at the General Schedule, or GS, level 13. Those grades form the US Office of Personnel Management's government-wide pay classification system for just about all white-collar federal employees. There are only fifteen levels in total — though each of the levels is broken down into ten individual pay grades — so entering the CIA at GS-13 made for a semilivable salary. It also covered the new computer I needed now that my laptop keys were either completely stuck or squished whenever I typed.

My first day was scheduled for later that summer. It was time to start over.

CHAPTER 3

Career Analyst Program X

The organizational development work at the CIA proved to be an easy transition into an opaque bureaucracy. The Agency was restructuring some of its departments prior to 9/11, and not long after starting I was tasked with leading a steering committee to reshape hierarchies between officers at headquarters and those in the field. It hadn't taken many meetings, however, before I realized how intractable those established hierarchies had become over the decades, and I wondered just how many ensuing generations it would take to shift that paradigm.

Nonetheless, the job gave me the opportunity to work with, and make a good impression upon, some of the Agency's top executives in the vaunted halls of the headquarters' seventh floor. And there were other pluses to the job—particularly the travel.

In the late summer of 2001, roughly a year after I'd started at the Agency, a coworker and I were sent on a weeks-long European fact-finding tour to discuss some of our realignment ideas with US government officers overseas. Those meetings proved to be informative enough, but what I distinctly remember was the Agency culture, and the sense of adventure—at times gritty, at times urbane—that influenced the way we did business.

One memorable stop was a town in the province of Kosovo, then part of Serbia, which was slowly regaining its footing after NATO had bombed the country two years earlier. Those air strikes had ended awful human rights abuses against the Kosovars at the hands of the occupying Yugoslavs—and it was only once we'd left that someone explained to me why entire portions of the hotel had been roped off to guests. The hotel's garage was the site of a prison prior to the war.

At a work stop in neighboring Albania, where an Italian influence still reigned, my coworker and I agreed that nothing put a long day of meetings behind us like a bottle or two of a dry red wine inside the walled compound where we stayed, alone except for a couple of local guards. The entire experience seemed to validate my decision to move to DC and as that trip wrapped up, in early August of 2001, I felt energized about returning to the Langley campus. I felt like I wanted to do every job the Agency could offer.

Then, a few weeks later, I was at my cubicle in the organizational development office. It was 8:46 a.m. on September 11, 2001. There, I watched the streaming news footage from Manhattan on my computer.

The impact of the first airliner crashing into the North Tower of the World Trade Center silenced everyone around me. I mumbled to myself, "This has to be al Qaida."

Five years earlier, I knew, Usama bin Ladin had published a thirty-page fatwa in the independent London newspaper *Al Quds al Arabi* entitled "Declaration of War Against the Americans Occupying the Land of the Two Holy Places." That religious decree asserted that "the people of Islam had suffered from aggression, iniquity, and injustice imposed on them by the Zionist-Crusaders alliance and their collaborators" and that there was "no more important duty than pushing the American enemy out of the holy land."

Bin Ladin had expanded the battlefield with a second fatwa in February of 1998, concluding, "The ruling to kill the Americans and their allies—civilians and military—is an individual duty for every Muslim who can do it in any country in which it is possible to do it." Six months later, on August 7, 1998, bin Ladin coordinated the bombing of two US embassies — in Nairobi, Kenya, and in Dar es Salaam, Tanzania — killing 224 people. The date marked the eighth anniversary of US troop deployment to Saudi Arabia.

By the morning of September 11, bin Ladin's name was familiar to everyone in Langley. And by the time United Airlines flight 175 ripped into the South Tower, nearly twenty minutes after the North Tower was hit, talk in the office had already shifted from who was responsible to what would come next.

Pictures and video footage of the towers ran for days in newspapers and on news broadcasts around the world. Today, however, I don't so much remember the planes hitting the towers or the ensuing scramble in my office. Instead I remember tears running down my face as I sat at my desk, watching as people jumped from the towers' windows. The questions it forced me to ponder — about hate and fear, courage and mortality — were far too awful to digest.

Just over half an hour after the South Tower was hit, American Airlines flight 77 slammed into the Pentagon. Within the hour, the Agency began evacuating nonessential personnel. I hurried out to my car, then out to Tysons Corner, Virginia, roughly six miles away. That route was the long way home, but it wasn't clear if the Capital Beltway — DC's monolithic, sixty-four-mile interstate, which wraps around the city — was open. This route also let me make a quick stop.

A few months earlier, I had moved out of the English basement into a three-bedroom apartment on a leafy street in DC's Cleveland Park neighborhood. It came with more space and more sunlight and an eclectic pair of roommates. One of them, Laurie Lindsay, had become my first real friend in the city, and she was working in Tysons that day. "They might end up closing the bridges," Laurie said as we met up inside her office. "We should head home."

As it happened, my mom was visiting DC and staying with us that week. I'd tried calling her several times before leaving work, and when I finally got through I told her to simply turn on the TV and wait by the phone. "I'll be home as soon as I can," I said.

Laurie and I found that the Beltway was still open — but also eerily quiet minus the military vehicles as we headed northwest around the Beltway. We dialed each other's cell phones and laid them on the passenger seats next to us. We barely spoke, but even that silent connection was comforting.

Once through Bethesda, Maryland, we hit the interchange for Route 185, which led us toward our apartment. As we turned south, an ashen cloud appeared on the horizon, billowing up over the Pentagon. Suddenly the quiet was broken by the staccato chop of an army medevac helicopter roaring overhead and then off into the distance.

Arriving home, I found my mom struggling to make sense of the events and the disjointed news coverage. I told her what little I knew; then we all retreated to a familiar place: the Park Bench Pub, a now-defunct underground watering hole a few blocks from our apartment. It had become a reliable spot for first dates, a trusty last stop on ladies' nights out, and now it was just the sort of comfortable place where we could think through a day that seemed unthinkable.

That new reality was only underscored when, as we neared the bar, a fleet of armored military vehicles raced past on Connecticut Avenue heading downtown. Laurie and I just stared. "What is this?" she finally said. "Northern Ireland?"

Over the following days, I realized that I felt out of sync around the office. When I walked across that giant CIA seal on my first trip to Langley, I felt like I'd been welcomed into Oz. But it occurred to me that it hadn't taken too many weeks of analyzing and organizing data in spreadsheets before my mind began drifting off toward new roles at the CIA, roles that would put me at the center of the action.

I wanted to be challenged. I wanted to make a *difference*. That's why I'd left Montana.

Every day I felt honored to be a part of the CIA, but I wondered if everyone else in the office could tell I was eager to leave the HR department. Once the shock of the attacks had worn off, I applied for work in the Directorate of Intelligence, or DI — the land of the analysts.

It was somewhat unprecedented for a person to transfer from an administrative position to a substantive position at the pointy end of a spear. I knew that at the DI I would be viewed as an outsider initially — or, perhaps more succinctly, not the "Ivy League" version of an analyst. I was so set on getting the job and trying to become part of the substantive work that I didn't focus on the perception. I just wanted to get going.

My favorite part of working at the Agency was the ability to create my own career path and to continually reinvent myself. There was never a lack of amazing things to research and study — particularly outside the HR department — and I'd spent my share of lunch breaks surfing the Agency's internal job-postings database. As in any organization, the best jobs at the CIA are found through connections, which means that there are definite rewards for applying yourself in ways that don't necessarily get discussed at an annual review. That "hall file" — the reputation that precedes you among your coworkers — is often as important in hiring decisions as the tangible things you've accomplished. In my case, I wasn't sure how my organizational development experience translated to the DI, but I hoped my hall file would help clear any early hurdles on the way out of HR.

The Directorate of Intelligence — or the Directorate of Analysis, as it is now called — employs analysts to anticipate and quickly assess rapidly evolving international developments and their impact on US policy concerns. Analysts provide written products and briefings to the White House, the cabinet, Congress, and other leaders.

Thanks to my background as an international economics major, DI coordinators placed me in the Office of Transnational Issues, making me an analyst in the illicit finance wing. I was "following the money," mapping out relationships among illicit organizations and foreign threats, which was at times incredibly cool. Which is not always the same as exciting.

As much as the CIA cultivates its mystique, its aura of secrecy — as do many of its employees — a lot of what you read in the newspapers and hear on TV is, frankly, bullshit. The Agency is an unusual bureaucracy, perhaps — but there are some decidedly routine things about the actual work. They just come with a twist.

There's an overpriced company cafeteria, for instance, that offers Chinese food and has a Burger King within it, and on nice days, you can eat outside in the central courtyard. It reminded me of any other white-collar environment except for the sign by the door reminding you not to take classified material outside.

And, as at every other company I'd worked for, training seminars pinballed between stress- and snark-inducing at a moment's notice — especially among a workforce that's capable of being a little too smart for its own good. I saw that firsthand in May of 2002, a few months after being reassigned to Transnational Issues, when I was sent to CAP, the Agency's Career Analyst Program.

At some point during the first year on the job, every analyst is pulled away from his or her department and sent to the sixteen-week-long CAP. The course, held in a sprawling office building not far from headquarters officially known as the Sherman Kent School for Intelligence Analysis, aims to provide "the basic thinking, writing, and briefing skills needed for a successful career," according to the Agency description. At first blush, the underpinnings felt unmistakably like spy school, including one teaching module called "Fundamentals of Denial and Deception." Inside the classroom, my two dozen classmates and I wore special blue name badges that authorized us to access computers labeled TOP SECRET.

So yes, the place crackled with energy. But instead of being newly minted college grads, most of my classmates and I were midcareer professionals with outside experience. A majority of people in the room probably had graduate degrees and PhDs. We weren't shy about pointing out to our instructors when the hit-or-miss curriculum, still evolving at the time, really seemed to miss.

One day, to practice drafting memos and briefing products for lawmakers, the class was broken into teams and given hyperexaggerated Middle East rainfall data to thumb through. We were told to draft a "bottom-line assessment"—basically, what middle schoolers know as a topic sentence—that anchors the inverted-pyramid, bottom-line-up-front writing style demanded of analysts. The style is so standard that fellow analysts just call it BLUF. Our hypothetical subject matter for the exercise: the geopolitical implications of heavy rainfall in Iraq.

Sitting in that classroom, I couldn't get past the fact that I knew you could count most of the country's inches of annual rainfall on two hands, if not one. This is silly, I thought. There was no realistic example we could have used? I rolled my eyes.

The instructor soon went around the room, asking teams for their assessments. "Factoring in projected population growth by 2030," one said, "climate change that produces more rain in Iraq will likely forestall the impending rise in poverty and malnutrition that would have been expected under current environmental conditions."

"More rain will lead to increased political stability in the region, as enhanced water infrastructure will better facilitate industry, municipal water quality, and sanitation for the general population," another said.

The teacher looked at us.

"After examining all the available outside evidence," our team concluded, "it turns out that vast swaths of Iraq are actually still just desert."

The instructor pretended to smile. "Why don't you try again," she said. It wasn't a question.

We thumbed through our list of rejected bottom-line assessments. "Oh!" we said. "Prospects still iffy for Saddam's new 'Mother of All Waterslides.'"

There was no smile that time. Then, as the newness of the experience and our nervousness wore off, the tension escalated.

One day a professor played a clip from the 1956 film *The Man Who Never Was*. The movie was based on an actual benchmark operation from the tail end of World War II known as Operation Mincemeat. That mission involved a spy unlike any the British had ever used before: a dead one, pulled from a London morgue. Intelligence officers invented a fake identity for the guy, then dressed him up, stuck fake plans for a Greek invasion in his briefcase, and dumped his body on a beach for the Germans to find. Voilà: denial and deception.

In fact the damn thing worked perfectly. Word of the Allies' "official" plans made it back to Berlin, and Hitler sent German troops to the wrong place. It was indeed an operation worth studying—except that a CAP class of students who grew up on Monty Python and *Mystery Science Theater 3000* couldn't help ad-libbing on behalf of the poor "Royal Marine" who was being unceremoniously poked and prodded by confused Germans.

"Please, I've been swimming for days—I'm not actually dead."

"Really, I'm alive, but I'm in a great deal of pain."

"Hey, that's my wallet! If I could move, I'd kick your ass!"

We also made up our own fake assignment on official letterhead, then dropped it into the bowl from which class teams drew their morning exercises. The first one read: "A leading radical Islamic cleric is being recruited by the CIA." Then came the pièce de résistance:

"Write a bottom-line assessment of his value to the Agency. Then fold the paper three times, walk to the room with the instructors, stop at their table, and pull on your ear. The instructor who tasked this assignment will look at you funny. Hand said instructor the paper; he will confirm receipt by saying, 'What's this?' To complete the exercise, wink at him and respond, 'My phone number.'"

Soon enough, we watched another analyst fold his paper three times and march straight out of the classroom.

We laughed hysterically—which is how the poor analyst knew whom to yell at when he came back four minutes later looking ready to break things.

Of all the troublemakers on our team, Dennis Gleeson, with dark hair and broad shoulders, whose affability belied the mischievousness of which he was capable coupled with a healthy skepticism of authority, might have been the most brazen about it. Of course, I immediately wanted to be fast friends. For one class briefing on opportunity analysis, or OA—analysis that goes beyond looking at ground conditions to highlight ways to advance US interests in a particular place—we bet Dennis he wouldn't brief the class as Dr. Seuss. We should have known better.

"You can do OA on a plane," he triumphantly declared. "You can do it on a train! You can do OA on a bus—without a fuss! Even next to Gus, and that's a plus, because do OA you must, must, MUST!"

"Very clever," the instructor shot back. "What rhymes with 'fail'?"

Dennis said later that he was smart enough not to respond, "Sail, pail, whale..."

So okay, we were probably a little pompous. But what we were really after was to be challenged, and hypotheticals about Iraqi rainfall didn't cut it. Nor did CAP instructors making us perform trustfalls with our teammates (I have another story Dennis won't let me tell about that). The students were appreciative to work for an organization dedicated to the safety and security of our country — a place where the phrase "the best and the brightest" was a common refrain, whether or not it was actually true. There were very real threats the United States was grappling with: in May of 2002, al Qaida remained a looming and insidious threat. People in the intelligence community are constantly exposed to possible threats, and we had to examine their validity with intense scrutiny. But for my CAP classmates and me, most of whom had become analysts in the months following 9/11, those potential dangers felt much more imminent. We were there specifically because we wanted to help make things safer — even if it didn't always seem that way. I understand that our now infamous CAP class number 10 may have been the most recalcitrant group ever to graduate. But regardless of a little goofing around, none of us ever forgot why we had joined the Agency — or sought out the DI.

———

CAP had been instituted only two years before I attended, despite the fact that Sherman Kent — the school's namesake and a man the CIA often describes as the father of intelligence analysis — had proposed creating a training school as far back as 1953.

The immersive training session we attended was a vast departure from the more general approach of the mid-1990s, which saw new analysts given a week or two of briefings on procedural housekeeping before they were put right to work. "They don't do a lot of training," Mark Lowenthal, a former staff director of the House intelligence committee, told the *New York Times* at the time. "They say, 'Congratulations, you're the Mali analyst, have a nice day.'" By the time we attended CAP, everyone there understood that a lack of codified standards had led to headline-generating misses.

At its best, our CAP course prepared us for the rigor of the analytic work we would soon be responsible for.

I'll never forget our introduction to a crisis task force. My classmates and I were fed some of the original data from the Rwandan genocide, which had taken place a few years earlier, in 1994. In April of that year, a plane carrying President Juvénal Habyarimana, an ethnic Hutu, was shot down as it came in for a landing in the country's capital. In response, Hutu extremists sought revenge against the rival Tutsi population, whom they blamed for the attack. In the weeks following the presidential assassination, some eight hundred thousand Tutsi men, women, and children were slaughtered, entire families at a time.

Our assignment was to put ourselves in the shoes of those earlier Agency analysts, writing products and delivering briefings just as if the events in East Africa were unfolding in real time. The exercise was meant to give students a sense of the pressures that come with filtering and analyzing such a relentless torrent of incoming data—which today seems almost quaint in retrospect. A Rwandan child with a smartphone today has access to more information than anyone at the CIA did in 1994. Regardless, for that CAP assignment, I loved imagining being in the middle of a major world event, helping to define for a fictional policy maker what course of action the United States could and even *should* take. I dove into the exercise. But I had no idea how the first satellite image I saw from the conflict would rock me.

To substantiate reports the Agency had received about conditions on the ground in Rwanda, my team zeroed in on the turbulent Kagera River, which forms a natural border with Tanzania to the east and funnels water from the majority of Rwanda's rivers onward to Lake Victoria. We pinpointed the river's Rusumo Falls, sitting where the shoreline pinches together above a gorge and the water swells before spilling over the edge and crashing down onto the rocks fifty feet below. At that waterfall, branches, elephant grass, and other detritus from the river basin pooled. And in the spring of 1994, the same was true of mutilated bodies—one Tutsi after another, many with their hands still tied behind their backs, ultimately collecting there from whichever tributary their executioners had chosen to dump the bodies into. There was nothing hypothetical about those grisly pictures.

"Remember," one of the instructors said solemnly, "a picture is worth a thousand words. But it's still just a photo without any context." Counting those dismembered bodies formed the basis for our initial casualty figures. As an analyst assigned to study illicit finance and money laundering, I'd never thought about being confronted with death on a daily basis or the toll such work can take on the people who do it. I understood immediately why some of the analysts who'd first scoured those images in 1994 quit soon afterward. I didn't suspect at the time that it might have foreshadowed my career ahead.

Our CAP graduation was held on November 8, 2002—the fiftieth anniversary of the founding of the Agency's Directorate of Intelligence. As part of the semicentennial celebration at headquarters, our diplomas were presented by Vice President Cheney. "The men and women receiving diplomas today are following a long line of excellence and faithful service to the country," he said in his address. "In your line of work, the greatest contributions are also the hardest to quantify....In national security, the long-time horizon often means that the wisest judgments and the best work go unrecognized until many years after the fact."

It was a day of celebration for our class. We were finally done. "Hey," Dennis said, elbowing me in line as we waited for our diplomas. "Don't scuff your feet on the carpet before you get up onstage."

"Why not?" I said.

"You'll shake Cheney's hand and fry his pacemaker."

Which was, of course, the only thing I could think of as I received my diploma—and why, unfortunately, the first time I met the vice president of the United States, it was all I could do to not laugh and look slightly horrified at the thought.

Following that ceremony, however, I was all business as I settled back into my role on the illicit finance team. I helped identify key players in smuggling rings, international drug cartels, and most any other industry that fell into the multibillion-dollar-a-year underground economy. But for the next several months, I couldn't shake the memory of that grim Rwanda exercise, in part because of the very point Cheney had made at our graduation: "The wisest judgments and the best work go unrecognized until many years after the fact." I was finding quickly that Transnational Issues was a great place to learn, but the products I wrote there basically planted seeds for lawmakers that said, "This isn't on your radar now, but you should know it's floating out there." It was a department described as "strategic."

Granted, that's important work. But it also means that analysts only know if their assessments hit the mark a few months or years after the fact. That struck me as a long time to wait for a payoff—and even then, there was no guarantee that anyone would actually look at what I'd spent all that time working on. After all, as I was periodically reminded, the president's day is typically planned out in five-minute increments. The most precious commodity in Washington isn't money or access but time. When lawmakers are bouncing from one political fire to the next, who has time to plant seeds? And if an analyst slaves away on a product but no one ever reads it, does it really make a sound?

The Rwanda exercise, on the other hand, was the exact opposite: tactical. Political. Immediate. And in the aftermath of the 9/11 attacks, it was clear where that kind of work was being done at the Agency. In mid-2002, after several months as an analyst on the illicit finance team, I noticed another posting on the internal job board: a new CTC unit dedicated to examining extremism in Iraq was looking for an analyst. I applied—and felt like I'd just begged to dive into a shark tank. Policy-maker interest in CTC's work was intense, and that meant they had a vested interest in the products being created there.

Transitioning into CTC required taking a few new classes at the Sherman Kent School to bolster the original training I'd received in analytical methodology with substance-based training that was specific to the region I'd be studying. But that was straightforward enough. And soon I was swept up into the chaotic center and placed with the Iraq unit. With no time to hesitate, I dove in and rushed to catch up.

In the summer of 2002, Abu Musab al-Zarqawi arrived in Iraq to lie in wait for the United States to invade. At that point, Zarqawi's followers were a loose network of men from the Levant, North Africa, and a smattering of other countries who were attracted to his brazen ideas. Unlike al Qaida, Zarqawi wasn't requiring immediate allegiance—he merely asked for cooperation and support for his loosely connected group.

By late 2002, we had determined that Zarqawi held roughly a dozen different passports. On a given day, he could be Jan Ellie Louise from Britain or Ibrahim Kasimi Ridah or Abdal Rahman Hasan al-Tahihi from Iran—or one of a number of other characters the governments of Iraq, Syria, Jordan, Turkey, and beyond legally acknowledged. As I joined the Iraq unit, he was using those identities to crisscross the Middle East, recruiting foot soldiers for a holy war he'd first envisioned more than a decade earlier.

It took almost as many years for us to compile his full dossier, collecting scattershot bits of information from various sources, gradually piecing them together to get a full understanding of his personality, his operational strategies, and his background.

Born in the al-Masoum neighborhood of Zarqa's "old town" in October of 1966, Ahmad Fadil al-Nazal al-Khalayleh was one of ten children in a very poor family. His hometown—Jordan's third-largest city, with a population of some 850,000—sits on the eastern edge of the country seventeen miles north of Amman. It is sometimes described as "the Chicago of the Middle East" because of its poverty and crime. Khalayleh knew both: his father, Fadil, worked as a farmer and herbal medicine salesman but couldn't provide enough for his family, which, I always presumed, was why Khalayleh dropped out of high school at the age of seventeen. He had few educational aspirations anyway; his former schoolteachers later told me he spent most of his time gazing out the window at the nearby Palestinian refugee camp.

Fadil died the year after Khalayleh dropped out, and at that point, any sense of direction the teenager might have had crumbled. He was fired from whatever odd jobs he could get. He became a drunk and a thug, holding court in the garbage-strewn Masoum cemetery across the street from his two-story concrete-block family home, periodically sticking up passersby so he could collect the cash to buy more alcohol. Sexual assault became a key tool in Khalayleh's quest for power. He raped local women to assert his dominance; he raped other men to establish control.

Before long, locals referred to Khalayleh as the green man because of the growing number of tattoos that covered his upper body, including an anchor on his right arm and three dots—a mark of the gang he'd joined—at the base of his left thumb. I always figured those were no more than simply signs of impulsive teenage rebelliousness; the booze and body art flew directly in the face of the orthodox Islam that Khalayleh's mother, Dallah Ibrahim Moham-med al-Khalayleh, encouraged at home.

In 1987, the wayward young man was arrested for drug posses-sion and sexual assault and sent to prison for two months. It was, ironically, the worst thing that could have happened. I learned quickly in CTC that nowhere do casual crime and revolutionary Islam intermingle better than in detention centers—and that's especially true in Zarqa, a city that produced more foreign fighters than just about anyplace else in Jordan. Many Americans first heard of the city in 1993 as the hometown of Mohammed Salameh—the Islamic extremist who rented the van that accomplices loaded with explosives and drove into the parking garage beneath the World Trade Center. That blast killed six people and injured one thousand more—but by then those detention centers in Zarqa had long acted as fanatical breeding grounds for people like Khalayleh.

Aimless and angry, with no educational underpinning to chal-lenge the fanciful tales of jihad he had heard on the streets and in prison, Khalayleh served his first prison stint, which marked a turn-ing point in his life. Upon his release, I later found out, Khalayleh's mother insisted that a rigorous religious education could be his path to salvation, and suddenly Khalayleh seemed eager. She arranged a marriage for him—to his first cousin Intisar Baqr al Umari—and led Khalayleh to Zarqa's Al Hussein bin Ali mosque, where he became a fixture.

I've always wondered if Dallah al-Khalayleh understood the kinds of sermons that were being delivered there, because for months her son was steeped in fiery frontline reports from Jordanian mujahideen who had returned from Afghanistan. There they had joined the flood of Arab fighters who were helping Afghans battle back against the Russians, who had invaded nine years earlier. The ghastly conflict had claimed roughly one million civilian lives, but ultimately the outgunned Afghans prevailed against the Red Army—a sign from God, the returning mujahideen said, if ever there was one.

In no time Khalayleh devoted himself fully to jihad — partly, I've always believed, for its larger sense of calling and purpose but also for the simple macho adrenaline fix. He gave up alcohol and tried to carve off or burn his tattoos, a key identifier in the photos of him we'd later collect. Then, in 1989, Khalayleh himself headed off to fight — stopping first in Peshawar, Pakistan, then traveling on to Afghanistan. However, the squat young would-be *mujahid* arrived in Herat, in far western Afghanistan, just as the Russians vacated that final stronghold in the country, and suddenly there was no one left to kill. Khalayleh spent the next three years with a pen instead, acting as a roving reporter and interviewing other jihadists about their experiences in and around Afghanistan for the radical Islamist magazine *Al Bunyan al Marsus* (The well-ordered structure).

During Khalayleh's years as a reporter, we later discovered, his radical ideologies were further shaped by a man who would soon become his spiritual leader: Abu Muhammad al-Maqdisi, an ideologue and central cleric in the growing, ultraconservative Sunni Muslim doctrine of Salafism. While the most common form of Salafi dogma preached a return to Sharia law and the ways of Prophet Muhammad, Maqdisi's was a particularly virulent strain that came to be known as Salafi-jihadism, which encourages violent extremism to achieve those ends.

Khalayleh and Maqdisi formed an instant connection. The Salafi scholar, seven years Khalayleh's elder, had lived for a time in the Palestinian refugee camp the troubled teenager had seen through his schoolhouse window. Maqdisi found in Khalayleh an eager student who soaked up every word of his sermons: the idea that God, not man, was the source of power, and that His word was the one true law; that a nonbeliever, including a Muslim who does not fully apply Sharia law, is a heretic — a *kuffar*, in extremist slang — and that the pursuit of a pure Islamic caliphate is justified.

Those principles spoke directly to Khalayleh's sense of black-and-white righteousness. I've always thought the impressionable extremist probably saw Maqdisi as the father figure he'd long been lacking. With that inspiration, Khalayleh renamed himself in honor of Musab bin Umayer, an ancient warrior for Prophet Muhammad whom extremists consider a patron saint of suicide bombers. Khalayleh then adopted a surname that paid homage to his blue-collar breeding ground, Zarqa. He became the literal and figurative Abu Musab al Zarqawi.

———

In 1991, Zarqawi and a handful of other mujahideen fighters skirmished with Afghan government troops in towns throughout the country's eastern provinces. The battles weren't complex or significant, but they did allow Zarqawi to return home a combat veteran in 1993.

Once he and Maqdisi reached Zarqa, Zarqawi was eager to proselytize. He had apparently taken to wandering the dirty streets, reprimanding women for clothing he didn't find suitably conservative. "It was not easy with him [once he returned]," Zarqawi's brother-in-law Salih al-Hami later told a German reporter. "When you spend so much time with jihad, it's like oxygen. It gets hard to do without it." In Zarqa, Zarqawi helped Maqdisi round up a handful of veteran Arab-Afghan fighters and form a militant group that came to be known as Bayat al-Imam (loyalty to the Imam). They began smuggling weapons into the country and plotting to overthrow the Jordanian government.

But theirs was a poorly crafted operation. I was later told that their first mission called for a group member to blow up a local theater that showed pornographic films—sinful material, in their interpretation of Islam. The jihadist became so enthralled by the movie that he lost track of time, forgetting about his bomb, and blew his own legs off.

Then, in 1994, Jordanian intelligence—which had been monitoring fighters returning from the Afghan war and had kept a casual eye on Zarqawi since his days as a street thug—caught Zarqawi stashing weapons in his basement in advance of potential attacks inside the country. When he was arrested, Zarqawi claimed he'd stumbled upon the weapons while walking down the street. "He never struck me as intelligent," the extremist's lawyer, Mohammed al-Dweik, later recalled.

Both Zarqawi and Maqdisi were sentenced to fifteen years in prison for plotting against the government. They were ultimately locked up together at al-Jafr prison, one of Jordan's harshest maximum-security penitentiaries, located on the edge of the country's south-eastern desert some fifty miles from the Saudi Arabian border. But again, Zarqawi flourished in confinement. His tenure was split between the communal cell in the prison's high-security wing, which he shared with a dozen other inmates, and the scorching solitary confinement cells he was thrown into whenever he talked back to the wrong guards. During my early days in CTC, I read reports of his physical transformation behind bars: when he wasn't trying to memorize the Koran, Zarqawi was known to kill time by bench-pressing buckets of rocks. Never exactly one for small talk or lofty ideas, Zarqawi became the perfect henchman-accomplice for Maqdisi, the stoic philosopher.

In his role as the muscle at Jafr, Zarqawi embraced his former gang mentality. He doled out prison chores to other inmates—this one does laundry; that one reads the Koran aloud. Zarqawi sent a fellow inmate a threatening note after he caught him reading *Crime and Punishment,* by Christian author Fyodor Dostoyevsky, whom he considered a heretic. "He spelled Dostoyevsky 'Doseefski,' " the inmate, Khalid Abu Duma, later recalled. "The note was full of bad Arabic, like a child wrote it." Zarqawi even reportedly covered the ward's TV sets with black cloth so the other inmates couldn't be tempted by shapely women on the screens. They were only allowed to *listen* to TV.

Zarqawi basically became a mob boss at Jafr—and I've long

thought that "boss" was the important part. In that prison, he truly learned to lead and to protect the men who fell in line behind him. He acted as an intermediary between the guards and the inmates, who have since insisted that Zarqawi was repeatedly tortured by prison officials. In turn, Zarqawi once personally bathed an inmate who was dumped back in their collective pen after a torture session.

The men in the cell at Jafr grew to love Zarqawi as much as they feared him. "He was tough, difficult to deal with," Sami al Majaali, former head of the prison authority in Jordan, later acknowledged to author Loretta Napoleoni. "We were always careful in approaching him, especially because he was a real leader, a 'prince,' as the inmates called him. All the dealings with any of those convicts had to go through him. If he cooperated, the others would follow suit." Zarqawi's popularity began to rise while in Jafr with Maqdisi, whose influence among the inmates remained strong as a spiritual leader.

With the help of other inmates' wives and mothers, Maqdisi had managed to smuggle his own religious writings out of prison and arranged for them to be uploaded onto Salafi websites. Scarred by torture, driven by extremism, and emboldened by a zealous following, Zarqawi was born again. No longer did he scribble his name at the bottom of the flowery letters he sent his mother; instead he used a nickname he picked up as a fighter in the Afghan civil war, "al-Gharib" — the stranger.

Then, in May of 1999, five years after Zarqawi was sent to prison, Jordan's King Hussein died. As a gesture of governmental reconciliation, the newly enthroned King Abdullah II granted a royal pardon for political prisoners, a blessing not only for Zarqawi but also for another organization that had noted his rising influence: al Qaida.

Years later, a book by Jordanian journalist Fuad Hussein, *Zarqawi: jeel al-Qaeda al-thani* (Zarqawi: the second generation of Al Qaida), would shed further light on Zarqawi's backstory for our team — evidence that high-value government intelligence gathering can sometimes be done in the most pedestrian of ways. The author interviewed Sayf al-Adl, a former Egyptian army colonel and top military coordinator for al Qaida, via a series of handwritten letters that were folded to the size of cigarettes and smuggled back and forth, a level of access even the Agency never had. Adl told Fuad Hussein that at the time of Zarqawi's pardon, Usama bin Ladin— who was based at the time in Kandahar, in eastern Afghanistan— had been hunting for updates on former Arab-Afghan fighters. They had spread out across the Middle East once the Soviets retreated, he knew. Often aimless and adrift, they would make obvious recruits for a growing terrorist organization with global ambitions.

Among extremist networks, Zarqawi's reputation preceded him. "We were therefore very pleased early in 1999 when we heard that [Zarqawi] had been released," Adl later recalled. Just a few months after that, as we in the Iraq unit later discovered, Zarqawi was sitting in a safe house in Kandahar, awaiting a meeting with bin Ladin.

But that meeting never happened. Many in al Qaida didn't want anything to do with Zarqawi.

Moreover, bin Ladin was suspicious that Jordanian intelligence might have infiltrated Zarqawi's prison network and that Zarqawi could inadvertently lead them directly to him. Finally, the more scholarly among al Qaida's higher-ups found Zarqawi to be something of a filterless punk, an impression that was underscored by the Jordanian's unapologetic stance concerning Shia Muslims: they were *kuffars* who deserved to be executed—a group that would have included bin Ladin's Shia mother.

I'm sure the disdain was mutual. It was clear that Zarqawi found al Qaida's approach to jihad far too moderate. He even disagreed with its targets. Bin Ladin's holy war focused on the "far enemy," including the United States and its Western allies. Zarqawi was content to try toppling what he and Maqdisi thought of as the "near enemy"—Middle Eastern governments such as Jordan's. Partly because of that, Zarqawi was distrustful of bin Ladin's longtime familial connections to Saudi Arabia's royal House of Saud. Finally, Zarqawi's ego had been inflated by his time in prison. He fancied himself a genuine leader, and he wasn't interested in paying *bayat,* or swearing allegiance, to anyone—a condition of formal cooperation with bin Ladin.

Still, some in al Qaida, including Adl, believed there was a place for Zarqawi in the larger movement. After letting Zarqawi languish for two weeks in that Kandahar safe house, bin Ladin permitted Adl to pay him a visit. There, Adl later recalled, he found a man "with poor rhetorical skills, who expressed what was on his mind bluntly."

"But," he added, "his ambition was great, his objectives clear."

Bin Ladin was deeply unenthusiastic about allying with Zarqawi, but the upstart was connected. If his name alone—much less his background in Zarqa—could bring recruits to his jihad, that was worth something. With Adl's encouragement, the al Qaida leader acquiesced.

Bin Ladin authorized $5,000 in seed money for Zarqawi and granted him the use of a training base outside Herat—on the far western edge of Afghanistan, near the border with Iran. Whether because of distrust or simple dislike, bin Ladin was keeping Zarqawi as far away as possible. Al Qaida's leader didn't demand *bayat*, just that Zarqawi assist in "coordination and cooperation in the service of our common goals," Adl recalled. Inside the CIA, analysts would later describe Zarqawi's role at the time as a "senior associate and collaborator" with al Qaida, but nothing more. As a result of Adl's encouragement, bin Ladin left it to him to keep Zarqawi in line.

Not long after, the former street thug moved into his small camp in western Afghanistan with a dozen or so followers. It's not hard to imagine the sick, triumphal pride he must have felt as he first strung up a flag above the base emblazoned with his new group's name, al-Tawhid wal-Jihad—unity and holy war.

That camp is where Zarqawi awoke on September 11, 2001.

Completely unbeknownst to him, bin Ladin and his al Qaida foot soldiers were about to unleash the worst international terrorist attack in history. It would be more than a year later when President Bush and then secretary of state Colin Powell tied Zarqawi to those attacks. That moment must have surprised Zarqawi as much as anyone.

CHAPTER 4

No Room for Ambiguity

Soon after the October 2002 speech in Cincinnati in which President Bush implicated Zarqawi in the 9/11 plot, the pace in our office reached a fevered pitch. My dinners were often reduced to leftover bags of tortilla chips from some happy hour we'd planned for the branch, rescheduled, then simply forgotten about. Many days, that was the only food around, as lunch just sort of blended into dinner, which sometimes blended into a second dinner. Even when I arrived on the team, a few months earlier, some members were already leaving, either to return to their original assignments or because the pace was a frantic mess. There simply wasn't time to coddle anyone.

I was determined to excel at my work in the Iraq unit. Much of the Agency's analytical ranks are populated with PhDs and Ivy League degrees, as you would find at think tanks and research facilities. My previous role had given me insight into ways I could benefit the team in spite of my less traditional qualifications, but there are very few people who start in HR at the CIA and later find themselves on one of the fast-paced analytical teams in the building. In the Iraq unit, my fear of failure drove me to almost obsessive ends; I was always scared I might screw something up.

That was particularly true because no politician cared what I, Nada, thought about a given issue. Politicians cared deeply, however, about how the *CIA* assessed critical situations—and I never forgot that in those unbylined products, my word stood as the official Agency position. Doing something wrong wouldn't ever just be *my* screwup; it would tarnish the Agency brand to provide expert, objective analysis. Protecting that brand was crucial to me.

I've never forgotten the blunt truth I first heard from Martin Petersen, a forty-year veteran of the Directorate of Intelligence: analysts are forced to write everything down. There is no room in the DI for ambiguity or, later, coy selective memory. "One can fight over what was said in a briefing, but the written word is in black and white," Petersen said. "It is the paper product that gets held up at a congressional hearing or eviscerated on an editorial page."

As one of the newest members of the Iraq unit, I still had much to learn about the issues—starting with where and how Zarqawi came to be in Iraq at all.

I knew that in the weeks after 9/11, the United States set its sights on toppling al Qaida and, in turn, the Taliban in Afghanistan. To help accomplish that, US Special Operations Forces had been inserted by helicopter near Herat—the general location of Zarqawi's private terrorist training camp. There, those US soldiers had met up with Northern Alliance leader Ismail Khan and some five thousand of his militiamen. Soon those allied forces poured into the city, and by the following day they had sent al Qaida and some of the Taliban fleeing west into the mountains along the border with Iran.

Zarqawi and his men had interest in taking part in the fighting—at the time we heard reports that he may have been wounded in his chest or leg in a November 2001 airstrike—but he escaped with a few broken ribs.

By December of 2001, Zarqawi was in Iran, setting up a network of safe houses. One was in Tehran; another was in Zahedan, just inside the Afghan border; and another was in Isfahan Province, in the south of the country. That last location was on Bahar Street, block number 27, in Kuhak, right along the border with Pakistan. It was registered to one "Ahmad Abdul Salam." But by then, we learned, Zarqawi had nearly as many pieces of contact information as he did aliases: 0041-793686306 was his Swisscom satellite phone number at the time, and 0098-9135153994 was the number for one of his Iranian cell phones. He could sometimes be reached at alzabh@yahoo.com.

From there, using a list of his various passports, we systematically mapped Zarqawi's travels to Syria, then to a Palestinian refugee camp in Lebanon, then back to Jordan in an effort to recruit militants. Whatever loose cooperation Zarqawi had had with al Qaida appeared to be severed after the retreat from Herat, though we couldn't be certain of that at the time.

We later figured out that in the spring of 2002, Zarqawi went west, across "the wall," the jihadist nickname for the Iran-Iraq border, and after he had received medical treatment for broken ribs in Baghdad from sympathetic Islamists (according to some disputed reports), he settled in the northern mountain town of Khurmal, in Iraq's autonomous region of Kurdistan. Without much of a team to speak of, Zarqawi was traveling light, presumably subsisting on whatever generosity and meager financial donations he could pick up along the way. Still, those things were enough to allow him to plan and finance a low-budget mission that proved to be one of the first successful attacks of his life—one that further intensified the administration's focus upon him: he paid two men to gun down an unlikely victim, Laurence Foley, a representative for USAID (the United States Agency for International Development), in Amman, Jordan.

Early on October 28, 2002, sixty-year-old Laurence Foley—a veteran of government development posts in Bolivia, Peru, and Zimbabwe—left his two-story limestone villa in Abdoun, an upscale neighborhood in central Amman periodically compared to

Beverly Hills. The former resident of Oakland, California, had come to the country with his wife, Virginia, two years earlier, acting as the chief administrative officer for America's assistance programs in Jordan. He had eschewed life in a diplomatic compound; although a government security detail conducted periodic drive-bys of the home, there was no twenty-four-hour guard in place. Just the ever-present pink bougainvillea spreading across the tops of the walls surrounding the home and a burgundy Mercedes-Benz with diplomatic plates sitting in the Foleys' driveway.

Around 7:15 a.m. that October day, as Foley walked to his car, Libyan national Salem bin Suweid darted out from behind the sedan holding a 7mm pistol equipped with a silencer. Foley was shot eight times in the head, chest, and abdomen. Suweid fled in a getaway rental car driven by Jordanian Yasser Freihat; soon afterward, Virginia found her dead husband crumpled on the driveway.

Suweid and Freihat were quickly arrested by Jordanian authorities and ultimately hanged for the murder in the same prison where Zarqawi had earlier done time. Before his execution, Suweid told Jordanian police that Zarqawi had personally handed him the gun, ammunition, and silencer used in Foley's killing and that Zarqawi had transferred tens of thousands of dollars to him to finance other terrorist plots in Jordan. Zarqawi was found guilty of participation in the plot by Jordan's State Security Court and sentenced to death in absentia. Back in Washington, the administration believed even more fully that Zarqawi was a rising menace who should be taken out of the picture.

A few months after that attack, following discussions with the vice president and other administration officials at Langley, a senior colleague in our branch agreed to draft the portion of Secretary Powell's February 5, 2003, presentation to the United Nations that was to center on Zarqawi. Those remarks went through a number of edits by higher-ups in our unit, CIA management, and then a predictable back-and-forth with the White House. Finally the remarks were approved by all, and everyone in our unit clutched a copy of the speech in our hands as we crowded into an office to watch it on TV. "Iraq today harbors a deadly terrorist network headed by Abu Musab Zarqawi," Secretary Powell said, "an associate and collaborator of Osama bin Laden and his al Qaeda lieutenants."

That was the first time most Americans had heard Zarqawi's name. In the Iraq unit, it was the first time we'd heard that line.

At once, we all looked down at our copies of the speech. The sound of papers rustling filled the silence — everyone was scouring their documents to see what page Powell was on. In fact he wasn't giving the remarks we'd carefully edited at all. Powell underscored his assessment with a PowerPoint slide showing a chart purportedly linking Iraq to al Qaida, with Zarqawi's photo prominently displayed in the top-line kingpin spot.

"What the hell is that?!" someone blurted out.

Days later, President Bush made a similar proclamation in his weekly radio address: "Iraq has also provided Al Qaeda with chemical and biological weapons training. We also know that Iraq is harboring a terrorist network, headed by a senior Al Qaeda terrorist planner. This network runs a poison and explosive training camp in northeast Iraq and many of its leaders are known to be in Baghdad."

I couldn't believe what I was hearing. Even with the limited information we had at the time, those assertions were impossible for me to digest. The Kurds in northern Iraq among whom Zarqawi had been living had long been marginalized enemies of Hussein's regime. In 1988, the dictator had gone so far as to drop bombs full of sarin and mustard gas on the Kurdish city Halabja, killing some five thousand civilians. That area would have been the last place for an ally of Hussein's to set up shop, and those extremists would have been the last people to whom Iraq's regime would offer chemical weapons training. It was clear, to me, that Zarqawi chose Khurmal for a very different reason: it was where Ansar al-Islam (supporters of Islam), or AI, had set up shop.

———————

Ansar al-Islam, a Sunni extremist organization mostly made up of Iraqi Kurds, had been formed in 2001, prior to Zarqawi's move into Iraq, when various regional terror groups consolidated their power. Those groups' general aim had been to establish one true Islamic caliphate, and they concluded that working together would give them greater strength and a wider recruiting network than working alone would. AI welcomed fighters fleeing Afghanistan after the US invasion — and that included Zarqawi, provided he aligned his forces with theirs.

At the time, Zarqawi was on the run. Once US forces overran Herat, he fled west with a small band of loyal followers into the border towns of Iran. We surmised that the Iranian government was cracking down on al Qaida refugees, setting Zarqawi on the move once more. Aligning with AI in their mountain stronghold of northern Iraq, therefore, might have been a move born of necessity for Zarqawi — or maybe it simply accelerated his larger plan.

The Jordanian had long believed that "sooner or later, the Americans were sure to make the mistake of invading Iraq," according to Sayf al-Adl, Zarqawi's former al Qaida handler. Once the coalition tore down Hussein's regime, Zarqawi thought, he would tear apart the rebuilding efforts — and from the ashes of Iraq, the caliphate could rise. So he agreed to align with AI and focus on northern Iraq. "The choice was not arbitrary," Adl said, "but well considered."

Relocating Zarqawi's training enterprise was an elaborate undertaking, however. For assistance, he called upon a friend and key facilitator we would later identify as twenty-nine-year-old Luay Muhammad Hajj Bakr al-Saqa. The son of a wealthy factory owner in Aleppo, Syria, Saqa had affiliated himself with Zarqawi in Herat, Afghanistan. Within a few years he had established himself as an experienced facilitator, doling out fake passports and acting as an intermediary between terror cells along the Syrian-Turkey-Iraq border area.

In that role, he'd invited Zarqawi to join al Qaida's plan to blow up hotels and tourist landmarks in Amman on January 1, 2000. The millennium bombing plot was disrupted by Jordanian authorities in November of 1999, and both Saqa and Zarqawi were sentenced in absentia to fifteen years in prison. Foiled or not, that plan began a long professional connection for the two men. In 2002, when Zarqawi had his sights set on northern Iraq in anticipation of a US invasion, he clearly reconnected with Saqa, and soon Saqa began coordinating logistics to help Zarqawi establish a new camp in AI's mountain stronghold. In no time at all, a steady drip of new fighters and equipment began flowing along the rat lines, as the military called them, to Khurmal from Algeria, Morocco, Pakistan, Libya, and two dozen other countries throughout Europe and the Middle East.

The full scope and capabilities of that training camp remain to this day a topic of debate, inside the government and out.

Our team received Agency reports from the field at the time saying that Zarqawi and his growing band of fighters had established a crude toxins laboratory in Khurmal, where they began toying with rudimentary biological weapons such as cyanide gas and aerosolized ricin. We knew that because the CIA knew exactly where Zarqawi was at the time. A small team of Agency operatives had infiltrated northern Iraq prior to the US invasion for a counterterrorism mission from July 2002 to May 2003. In the process, they found Zarqawi's new home, right as he was becoming a household name in the intelligence community.

Thanks to ongoing feedback from the field, Jim, an Agency

colleague in CTC's Weapons of Mass Destruction department, was able to follow Zarqawi's increased testing of those contact toxins throughout 2002. First, the Jordanian and his AI associates set up a ramshackle operation to tinker with blocks of cyanide salt. The common mining chemical could have been dangerous had they mixed it with another substance to create a toxic vapor, but instead they almost entirely defanged it by mixing it with aloe and horse liniments, hoping someone might fall ill after slathering it on in large quantities.

Then the group tried the same with ricin, a poison that occurs naturally in castor beans. But like cyanide, ricin's molecules are too large to be absorbed through unbroken skin. Zarqawi's dabbling in chemistry simply made no sense. As one Agency analyst pointed out to me, "Zarqawi was a dropout, a drug dealer, and a thug. At no point in there do we think he became a chemist."

Stray dogs and miscellaneous barnyard animals had become unwitting subjects for the terrorists' toxin tests. I thought back to those sunny mornings on my grandparents' farm and my horses. It's funny what resonates with each of us: Zarqawi's torturing of a donkey and other animals might have marked the first time I wanted to eliminate the man myself.

One group that took exceptional interest in Zarqawi's chemical testing, however, was the Bush administration, an interest that continued into early 2003.

"Well if you're focused specifically on the question of the links between the Saddam Hussein regime and al-Qaeda," Douglas Feith, then the under secretary of defense for policy, told Australia's ABC News on February 21, 2003, "people who do not see the link are just not familiar with the evidence." The connection, he said, included "combined operations regarding bomb making and chemical and biological weapons."

Soon after, on March 9, 2003, the White House national security advisor, Condoleezza Rice, said on *Face the Nation*: "The strongest link of Saddam Hussein to al Qaeda...first of all, [is] a poisons master named Al Zarqawi." She added, "And secondly, [there is] a very strong link to training al Qaeda in chemical and biological weapons techniques."

The general idea that Zarqawi was pursuing chemical weapons was indeed real, even if the framing was markedly off. Yet the framing raised an obvious question, considering the intelligence pouring in from the field, which was perhaps best articulated by then Senator Joe Biden, Democrat of Delaware, the day after Powell discussed the Khurmal camp in his presentation before the UN. "Why have we not taken it out?" Biden asked the secretary during a Senate foreign relations committee hearing. "Why have we let it sit there if it's such a dangerous plant producing these toxins?"

Powell said he could not discuss the decision-making process in public. Our unit in Langley still hoped a swift strike on the Khurmal camp might be coming in the wake of Powell's UN presentation and Senate appearance, but weeks went by without any military response at all. NBC News would later report that the US military had drawn up possible plans to hit the site with cruise missiles, but "the plan was debated to death in the National Security Council." After that, the administration returned to its talking points and the talk-show circuit.

In the Global War on Terror, Cheney said on *Meet the Press* on March 16, 2003, "we also must address the questions of where might these terrorists acquire weapons of mass destruction, chemical weapons, biological weapons, nuclear weapons. Saddam Hussein becomes a prime suspect in that regard."

Cheney concluded with the infamous observation "I think things have gotten so bad inside Iraq from the standpoint of the Iraqi people, my belief is we will, in fact, be greeted as liberators."

"Seriously?" I muttered to myself.

By early 2003, I'd taken to watching those Sunday shows regularly because I saw that the tough questions administration officials fumbled during the discussions invariably became research topics for the team days ahead. At times, they'd quite literally make me scream. I became so fixated on the Sunday-morning circuit that I pleaded with Roger—he and I had begun our relationship in earnest at that point, and I was at his row house when the infamous Cheney segment aired—to buy his first TV set in years so we wouldn't have to cut our Saturday date nights short. But even though he bought the TV, he usually let me watch those shows alone. I can't say that I blame him.

In retrospect, I think online dating was my first act of targeting.

I was single for a few years after moving to DC, choosing instead to focus on friends and finding a job. I made a few friends at the Agency on my winding path to CTC, and they invited me to wine-and-knitting parties, which was actually a thing that thirty-year-old cosmopolitan women did at the time. But I was always hesitant about dating any of the men I worked with.

For a time, part of me hoped for some celestial Hollywood moment when a stranger and I would lament the endless wait for a Red Line train or a guy with an accent would say something charming while we were standing in line at the bagel place—but that didn't seem to be getting me anywhere. It surely didn't help that the north Dupont Circle neighborhood, where I rented my first apartment, wasn't exactly a hotbed of straight men at the time. I think it was the annual 17th Street High Heel Race, featuring a wave of cross-dressers roaring past my place, that really tipped me off.

That's not to say I didn't have fun being single in a big city for the first time in my adult life. There may have been a first date or two that started at the Park Bench Pub and ended after breakfast. And I laugh at the memory of one New Year's Eve when my friend Sara and I bought tickets for a party at a DC hotel. We each flirted just enough to find a guy to kiss at midnight a few minutes later; then we strolled out by ourselves to grab some falafel in Adams Morgan. But in terms of an actual relationship, it didn't take long to realize how insular DC's cliquishness is when you're working sixty-five-hour weeks. So I turned to Match.com—an admission that practically feels old-fashioned today but that I would make to absolutely no one in 2002.

I must have rewritten my bio three dozen times; it's hard to imagine there is anything more awkward than writing a dating profile. I uploaded a photo taken from a distance, which presumably hurt my prospects, but it felt like the smartest move for a woman, let alone someone in the CIA. Besides, I thought, I'm smart, funny, and engaged with world events—that'll come through, and that's got nothing to do with my photo. And hey, I'm just looking for someone with a job who'd be fun to hang out with. How hard can that be?

Answer? Pretty freaking hard.

For the following few weeks, I checked my e-mail at night over takeout sushi and practically lost my appetite. Or maybe just a little of my will to live.

Strangers called me babe, chick, and honey. Guys asked what size bra I wore and how often I slept with a man on a first date. Two-thirds of the first e-mails I got were clearly copied and pasted—and a stunning number of those were vulgar.

When it wasn't blatantly ridiculous or demeaning, the whole thing felt like a slog, especially when I was clicking through photos of men who spent way too much time in the bathroom. Before long my standards were falling so fast that I was just hoping to find a guy who didn't have more crap in his hair than I did. *"A normal guy!"* I wanted to scream. *"That's all I'm asking for!"*

On the few occasions I did meet a guy through the site, my general hope was that he'd either be really amazing or batshit insane. Because three hours after the fact, one made almost as good a story as the other. In the years since, it's become clear I wasn't alone in that regard.

I've heard about guys who randomly stopped a conversation mid-sentence to snort coke off the bar. A guy who spent the first thirty minutes talking about his pet chinchilla—which, not coincidentally, was exactly how long the date lasted. (Apparently chinchillas can jump really high.) The guy who showed up to the date three drinks in, spilled his beer on the woman, and then instead of apologizing waved the bartender over to refill his glass. Then there was the guy who *probably* wasn't the one who stole his date's purse that night, though we're still not positive. The guy who cried in the restaurant over his prior failed "relationship," which gets quotation marks because he'd been catfished and was still in love with a woman who didn't exist. The handful of guys who told me they were in their thirties, then showed up actually pushing sixty and wondered why I cut our date short.

So it was for me for a few months—a surreal experience followed by lame conversation followed by an actual sweet guy who stopped returning my correspondence only to pop back up months later and ask if I was still single.

There was an important lesson I took from that, though. A girlfriend pointed out that our dating challenge didn't lie in looking for Mr. Right. He never existed anyway. The challenge for us was making the best choices we could based on profiles and initial communication. Once we avoided the extremes, we had to let ourselves be open to recognizing someone we could build a real foundation with.

Waiting for that guy to find me clearly wasn't working, so I went on the offensive. I updated my profile with a photo of my Saint Bernard, who was living with my mother back in Montana, and took matters into my own hands, scouring profiles and targeting men who seemed like they could be datable. That wasn't exactly a high bar, but Match.com hadn't given me a whole lot of hope, either.

Then one evening, the sight of a hat made me pause on a profile.

The man in the photo was clearly on a river someplace, holding two steelhead trout. His broken-in baseball cap had been jostled around, and on it, in big white letters, were the words POWDER HORN — the massive sporting goods store that's stood for decades in downtown Bozeman. I sent him a short note that night.

Over a few e-mails through the site, Roger told me he was a DC transplant originally from Buffalo and a telecom engineer with an outdoorsy streak. His last name, Bakos, sounded a whole lot like Bacchus, the name of my Saint Bernard, which made me wonder about kismet. Until he stopped e-mailing me. Roger later told me that he'd been living in Baltimore at the time and thought he couldn't sustain a relationship with someone who was in DC. It was too far away. A few months later he e-mailed me a mea culpa, however, asking for another try. I responded, "Why do you suddenly think I'm all that and a cup of coffee?" He said the right things, though, after I made him explain it a few more times to convince me he was worth it; then we agreed to meet.

We arrived that fateful Saturday evening at the now-shuttered Zebra Lounge in northern DC, both with friends in tow on the way to other plans.

To this day I'm not sure that Roger had any real idea what he was doing that night. He was deeply earnest and just slightly awkward enough to be endearing. I loved that about him. I immediately felt safe around him — and his friend Grant was amusing, which was good, because Grant ended up as something like the Cyrano de Bergerac of Cleveland Park that night.

"So what made you respond to my e-mail?" I asked Roger early on.

And then there was a pause. A long one. Eventually, my eyes drifted over the crowded room, then back to Roger, who seemed to be thinking pretty hard. At that point, Grant leaned over and whispered something to him, and Roger replied, "I thought you looked smart and interesting."

I laughed.

Prompted by Grant, Roger walked me to my car later that evening. He called the next day. We've been together ever since.

Not that it's always been easy, mind you—no relationship ever is. As unhinged as life can seem for Agency personnel caught in a work maelstrom, that lifestyle exacts a stiff toll on their partners, too. Trust often feels like an elusive thing. Spouses generally have to lie about what their loved ones do for work—to the extent that they truly understand it at all. I waited weeks to tell Roger even the basics of what I did all day in the Iraq unit, even though at the time I was an analyst and not undercover—so I could tell him where I worked.

The culture and peculiarities of an Agency life are difficult to describe to anyone who hasn't experienced them firsthand. There's a reason so many CIA employees marry other CIA employees—then in many cases get divorced and marry different CIA employees. Roger and I were both learning all that for the first time.

One of my clearest memories of our early relationship was Roger arriving at my apartment one evening in late 2002, once the tempo in the Iraq unit had become fully frantic. I was working the "briefer shift" at the time, arriving by 4:00 a.m. to digest all the information on Iraq before the president's and cabinet-level briefers arrived at Langley. The work created a level of stress that manifested itself differently for everyone on the team—and I've learned over the years that I have a pretty telltale sign, which Roger had picked up on. When he arrived at my apartment, he was clearly troubled and clearly having trouble figuring out how to talk about it.

Roger led me over to the couch in the living room and sat down.

"Nada," Roger said. "The thing is..."

He shuffled his hands and sighed.

"You gained weight."

I shot up in my seat. My mouth fell open.

"I mean," he continued, which was a real mistake, "I've been telling myself you're the same girl I fell for. And you are!"

I jumped up from the couch. "Are you fucking kidding me?" I snapped. "The stuff I do for this country every day, and you're shaming me for gaining weight?" I was really ramping up. *"Who does that?"*

He had tapped into my profoundly anti–body shaming streak, and not in a good way. Define me and reward me based on my merit — that's all I've ever asked. But to do it by pants size? At that moment, I thought back to the gross Match.com e-mails I'd gotten from guys who wrote "I only date women smaller than a size 2" and "I'm really looking for a fellow *ectomorph*."

I wanted to write back to those guys: "Oh, yeah? Well, I'm looking for a guy who isn't a narcissist." But I didn't. It seemed clear those men had self-esteem issues — and that my size, depending on the time of year and the selection of baked goods nearby, really wasn't the problem.

I have never understood vanity, for better or worse. While I have certainly had my fair share of angst over my weight, it wasn't a priority for me. I wasn't obsessing over achieving Barbie's thigh gap; as a young girl I was more disgusted by the fact that Barbie couldn't sit on my plastic horses without splitting off a leg. I also realized fairly quickly that the men who obsess over the idea of physically perfect women have self-esteem issues of their own and aren't likely to be genuine. I had zero interest in even entertaining that possibility, no mental bandwidth for that kind of shallow obsession. I know that broaching the topic of weight only invites strangers to scrutinize me. But if the size of my thighs matters to some people, then it does.

Roger, of course, meant way more to me than those men who wrote to me. I was shocked that he'd say what he did, and it stung.

He left before digging himself in any further. My cell phone rang two minutes later.

I recognized Roger's number and hit the End Call button, several times. I marched across the living room, threw open the bathroom door, and climbed onto the scale.

Standing there alone, I realized that I had actually put on fifteen pounds. Quickly.

Oh.

My phone rang again. I stood there clenching my jaw at the scale, men, and my life.

There was still no reason for Roger to have said what he did. I can't imagine his reaction if I'd ever said the same to him. He wasn't exactly svelte at the time either. But at least *technically* speaking, I suppose his assessment hadn't been entirely inaccurate. Clearly, stress-eating and a few too many second breakfasts during the night shift at work did have some downsides.

Once he found the right words to apologize, I forgave him.

In truth, that was merely the most obvious example of the fact that my friends and family understood only the broadest strokes of what I did all day and the impact it had on me. They never knew many details; I really couldn't talk about it. So by the start of 2003, Roger mostly came to know my vacant stare into the middle distance as I sat at home in the evenings, trying to make sense of some late-breaking news and wishing I had more sleep.

In the Iraq unit, I couldn't physically take classified work home with me, but I found quickly that it was never far from my mind.

———————

In hopes of making myself invaluable around the office, I said yes to everything. Did a policy maker need an assessment of the Iraqi Intelligence Service's force protection capabilities in the event of an American invasion? "I'll do it," I said.

Someone to take on the 4:00 a.m. briefer shift? "No problem."

And in early May of 2003, two months after the US-led invasion, I became the second member of my team to volunteer for a temporary-duty assignment in Iraq. I thought it might be something like my brief time in Kosovo, only more raw. A few weeks later, I boarded a late-night commercial flight at Dulles International Airport bound for a transit point in the Middle East. At 5:00

a.m. the next day, a driver picked me up at my hotel and delivered me to a nearby private runway, where airmen were finishing driving a white Toyota truck up the tail ramp of a one-hundred-foot-long air force C-130 cargo plane.

Looking at the plane, I thought back to CAP training. Our class, escorted by a representative for George Tenet, then the director of Central Intelligence, had flown out to Offutt Air Force Base, near Omaha, Nebraska, the home of US Strategic Command. That office was first established by the Department of Defense to oversee US nuclear defenses in the aftermath of the World War II bombings of Hiroshima and Nagasaki. Over the years, Strategic Command grew to have a hand in cyberwarfare, missile defense, and reconnaissance and surveillance, among other things. Our class had visited to understand the key interplay and cooperation that were possible between the military and the CIA.

An air force sergeant gave us the tour. Walking along the empty tarmac, he began to tell us about the military's unmanned aircraft capabilities and the air force's latest intelligence collection mission. Then he stopped. "I'm not sure you guys are actually cleared to hear this," he said.

"Sergeant," Tenet's rep had said plainly, "these analysts have more security clearances than you do, your commanding officer does, and his commanding officer does beyond that. Finish your story."

The sergeant paused for a moment, then continued. Dennis and I glanced at each other.

Almost two years later, standing on the moonlit Middle Eastern tarmac at 5:00 a.m. en route to Baghdad, I could have used a dose of that rookie confidence. At the front of the C-130, I climbed the four metal steps of the fold-down crew entry door. Inside the plane, rows of orange nylon seats ran down the spartan sidewalls of the aircraft, flanking the truck and a dozen pallets of miscellaneous gear strapped to the floor. I never found out what that bundled material was; it could have been anything from weapons to watermelons. Outsiders call the C-130 "Hercules"; they also have the nickname "trash haulers." They aren't exactly built for comfort.

By sunrise we were off the ground. I made quick introductions with the handful of other Agency personnel who were belted in beside me. They were officers from the Agency's other main branch, the Directorate of Operations — the spies and case officers who help gather intelligence on the ground. They didn't offer last names, and I presume none of them used their real first names, either.

I spoke as little as possible. Confident as I was by then in my abilities back in the Iraq unit, being a thirty-two-year-old woman who wasn't an operations officer in a cargo plane full of experienced officers, heading to my first war zone, felt very different. Pretty much by definition, analysts aren't often sent to the front lines. But in the aftermath of the US invasion, a shift in protocol was rapidly becoming necessary.

In the year after President Bush's May 2003 declaration that major combat operations had ended in Iraq, some twelve thousand Iraqis were taken into custody by American forces for a whole host of offenses, both real and — at times — imagined. Once those detainees arrived back at US bases, however, the military often had no good way of interpreting or verifying the information that came from prisoner interrogations, nor did the officers necessarily understand where new leads might come from. They had enough trouble positively identifying insurgents, who weren't in the habit of telling their captors their real names. To help, the military needed Agency analysts who had come to understand the enemy and its network better than anyone else in the world. But there in the Hercules, peering through the orange mesh behind me, watching the desert unspool through a tiny porthole, I began to realize just what I'd gotten myself into.

First, I couldn't remember my proof-of-life statement. That's on a form I'd filled out when I was first hired. It contains a predetermined set of words the Agency keeps on file in case employees in the field are abducted. In the event of a kidnapping in Iraq, I'd inevitably be paraded in front of a video camera. If there was any way to manage communicating with the outside world, I could say those exact words, and Agency personnel would trust that I was actually still alive and would continue hunting for me. Forgetting those words wasn't ideal, let's put it that way.

On the other hand, the so-called Green Zone was just beginning to coalesce in Baghdad as a placeholder for the Coalition Provisional Authority — the government that was slated to temporarily govern Iraq after Hussein was deposed. The Agency will probably just stick me in some walled compound, I told myself, and that will be that.

Doubt, however, crept in again. It occurred to me in that C-130 that I had no real clue how to fire a handgun. This is a war zone, I thought. Shouldn't I know how to do that?

Unfortunately, handgun training had fallen by the wayside in my initial predeployment preparation. Going down the Agency's checklist, I'd gotten all my necessary documentation, attended a few short courses on field tradecraft in the region, and even managed an Agency-sponsored shopping spree at the massive REI store near Langley. But all that prep meant being out of the office at a time when I was becoming an ever-larger contributor in our unit. So when I tried to schedule myself at the CIA's weeklong weapons training program, our team's group chief, whom we will refer to as Cornelius — an overworked Agency long-timer one rung above Katherine in command — nixed the request. "I'd rather have you come back in a body bag than let you miss more time for that," he muttered. He was the boss, so I didn't push back. At times he could be intimidating as he rounded the corner heading to Katherine's office with his blocky jaw and starched white shirts that always billowed around his towering frame, but he was also capable of real persuasiveness and charm.

Staring out the window at the desert, I hoped he wasn't about to get his wish.

But as the hours rolled by and I reflected on all the coffee I'd had that morning, a more pressing concern hit me in the C-130: *I really have to pee.*

"Honey bucket's in the aft of the plane, ma'am," one airman said.

"Oh, okay?" I said.

I unhooked my belt and clambered around the white pickup to the rear of the cargo hold. There, seeing no other option, I slid aside a matte-gray shower curtain clipped to some piping overhead. Behind it, I found a little step that led to a five-gallon stainless steel pot bolted to the wall: the honey bucket, as generations of airmen have called it.

I spun in a circle to see if the curtain was securely closed. Turning back to the pot, I noted the multicolored bungee cord lashed diagonally across the front of it — which suddenly made sense as a rattle of turbulence almost knocked me off my feet.

Under the bucket's lid, I found a frigid metal seat with little hooks underneath where the user could hang a plastic bag. (I certainly hadn't thought to bring one of those.) A spent roll of toilet paper hung nearby. I stood there, staring at the whole thing, then checked my watch and tried to guess how much longer I could hold it.

Later, I learned that everyone has a favorite honey-bucket story — from under-the-weather pilots who couldn't free themselves from their flight suits in time to passengers who were dumped on the floor with their pants around their ankles, frantically clutching for the curtain. Or maybe for their self-esteem. In that moment, though, I just sighed.

That mantra proved prescient for my time in Iraq, particularly when it came to aircraft. Flight plans during my time in theater would consistently be disrupted and rescheduled. I would eventually make my peace with the landing maneuver planes used on their final approach to the Baghdad airport to evade possible enemy small-arms fire. For a moment, every time, I could swear we were weightless and in free fall. In helicopters, I even got used to seeing what appeared to be glowing cinders knifing over the cockpit and arcing off into the distance.

"What was that?" I asked the first time it happened.

"Tracer fire," the copilot had said. "They're shootin' at us."

CHAPTER 5

Looking for Unicorns

The cargo ramp of the C-130 opened into a broiler.

It must have been 110 degrees by the time we landed at Baghdad International Airport—my first day in a war zone. Around me, a handful of the CIA's logistics crew scrambled to offload the gear.

Military trucks roared by in the distance. Beyond them, a collection of tandem-rotor Chinook helicopters fluttered on the horizon like chubby hummingbirds. In May of 2003, that airport was home to many of the 150,000 US troops in Iraq at the time, and it was the transit hub for almost all of them.

I stood motionless for a moment on the ramp, taking it all in. Even with my sunglasses on, I thought the entire tableau appeared white, as though someone had mishandled the exposure on a photograph.

Behind me, the white truck rolled out of the tail of the plane and came to a stop nearby. I jumped into the bed of the truck with my other colleagues from the flight, and one of the Agency's logistics officers drove us through the dusty haze to a Baghdad terminal at the airport, my new home.

Like the rest of the country, Baghdad International, or BIAP, was itself at a crossroads. In the early 1980s, when the French built the airport, Iraqi leaders had hoped the civilian terminal there would handle 7.5 million passengers a year. But then Iraq invaded Kuwait in 1990, and the United Nations responded by grounding most of the civilian flights. So by the time I arrived, that terminal was mostly a tacky homage to a bygone era, with its arcing silver rafters and funky green hues mirroring the palm trees outside.

The scale of US military operations on those six square miles of airport grounds, however, was staggering to me. Cruising across it in the pickup, I knew we were driving through the heart of a growing constellation of military camps that would be built on and directly around BIAP, which together came to be known as the Victory Base Complex.

Among that cluster was Camp Sather, on the western side of the airport, named after Staff Sergeant Scott Sather, who a month earlier had become the first airman killed in the war. Even at a quick glance, I recognized how unique that air force outpost was: the edges of the property were well-groomed, with flags lining the driveway. The 132-tent camp acted largely as a conduit for virtually all personnel and materiel transiting through BIAP. Planes such as my C-130 landed, were serviced, and were reloaded there by the air force, then promptly sent on their way again.

We soon pulled up outside the terminal, which had none of the tidiness of Camp Sather. I hopped off the back of the pickup and grabbed my backpack. Suddenly another logistics officer appeared at the tailgate and said he'd be glad to move my bags into my housing quarters. Wow, I thought. That's unexpected service.

Outside the door to the terminal, I noticed a brown metal barrel that looked like a deep umbrella stand. A sign on it read: LONG GUNS TO BE PLACED HERE. PROHIBITED INSIDE THE TERMINAL. "Long guns" essentially meant anything bigger than a handgun. On the other side of the doorway was a second metal barrel. The sign on that one read: CHEMICAL SUITS.

Suddenly the logistics worker tapped me on the shoulder. "Nada," he said, "your bags are in your quarters, next to your husband's."

I was confused. "I don't have a husband that I know of," I said. I tried a little levity. "Unless that's my cover?"

"You are Nada?" he replied, adding a surname that wasn't mine.

"Oh, no," I said, offering up something I don't think I'd ever said before. "That's a different Nada."

I soon wished I had her private room. As I walked through the terminal, I could see that the marble floor was dusty. Supply boxes and meals ready to eat, or MREs, lined the walls, and sleeping cots were wedged into just about every empty space. I followed a hallway that led into a larger building, just one of Hussein's seventy-five or so former palaces. At least our terminal was simple in comparison: most of Saddam's opulent structures came with garish names, such as the Victory over Iran Palace, commemorating the disastrous eight-year war he began with neighboring Iran in the 1980s, and the Victory over America Palace, in honor of the first Gulf War. As one US military historian drily put it, "Any war that Saddam survived was a victory."

Like those other palaces, however, our terminal was a sight to behold—and that was true even after American forces had shot their way through it. I made my way beneath its grand, arching doorways of deep brown wood and down hallways whose walls and floors had been lined with two-foot-by-two-foot white marble slabs. There were black-and-red marble inlays in the floor, spaced just so to mirror the horizontal lines of the Iraqi flag. The ornate green light fixtures mounted high on the walls mirrored the green *Allahu akbar* inscription Hussein had ordered put on the flag in 1991. I marveled at how skilled the craftsmen must have been who built this place and how wasted their talents were in building it for some-one like Hussein.

The invasion, of course, had done the palace no favors. Walking down the hall, I saw one window after another shattered or duct-taped, shot out by soldiers or blown out by blasts in the assault on the airport. There were shell casings and broken furniture in heaps on the floor of one room I passed. A stack of picked-over MREs in their grayish-brown pouches sat in another. I stuck my head in; a military veteran had told me to look for the vegetarian variety, so I grabbed one of those. I would soon learn, though, that regardless of what the label said, all MREs taste about the same anyway.

The palace plumbing had been blasted into oblivion, but the Agency's logistics team had been able to magically hook up a shower trailer that worked most of the time. If nothing else, there was a pump out back where I could collect water for a sponge bath and for filling a little washing machine. I never took for granted even those rudimentary creature comforts; many of the Marines there were sleeping on the hoods of their Humvees and keeping up their hygiene however they could. Outside the airport grounds, it was even worse. Bombing and combat — followed by opportunistic looting by locals — had devastated Baghdad's already antiquated sewage and water infrastructure. Electricity was hardly a given. The Iraqis had it far worse than we did.

In the middle of the terminal, I found my cot. There were at least forty others just like it in the same room, heads against the wall, feet pointing toward the center. I set my backpack on an empty one fairly near the door.

The close quarters were one thing. But suddenly my ears pricked up with the sound of metallic *clinks* and scrapes echoing off the walls. Behind me, a handful of soldiers on cots were cleaning the long guns they hadn't left in the barrel outside. If a round discharges in here, I thought, it will ricochet like a pinball.

———

Before long, my self-guided tour took me back outside the terminal, to my "office" for the next three months.

A row of unmarked double-wide trailers anchored in the packed dirt. That handful of SCIFs, or sensitive compartmented information facilities, was the equivalent of vaults back at Agency headquarters. The trailers, which had been configured with a dozen or more workstations in each, featured high-tech soundproofing and were impermeable to radio frequencies; there were bars over the ductwork, multiple door locks, and an assortment of highly regimented safety measures. I'd been in Baghdad only a few hours, but I was already impressed by the Agency's infrastructure.

I picked a trailer and climbed the metal stairway to the door. I stepped inside and was greeted by several heads immediately swiveling around and popping up over their monitors to see who'd entered.

"Hi," I said sheepishly. "I'm the CTC analyst who just arrived. Do you know which SCIF I should be in?"

"Hi," said an upbeat young woman. She greeted me with the widest smile I had seen in a while. "You're in the right place," she said and held out her hand. "I'm Eve."

"Nada," I said. "But not that one."

I sat down at an empty computer terminal next to Eve, toward the front of the trailer, and grabbed from my bag the assigned temporary-duty hard drive I'd been given before I deployed. I inserted it into the computer and pressed the Power button. Almost instantly, I was patched into the appropriate networks.

Eve, like everyone else in the trailer, was an operations officer, a.k.a. case officer, tasked with recruiting and developing local sources who could secretly provide the US government with valuable intelligence.

The operations side of the Agency's work is a direct descendant of the Office of Strategic Services (OSS), which William "Wild Bill" Donovan established in 1942, in the wake of the attack on Pearl Harbor. True to Donovan's nickname, an action-oriented cowboy ethos has always permeated the operations ranks. Exude confidence, the thinking goes. Always confidence. Operations officers recruit agents to spy on behalf of the United States. There are other jobs within the Directorate of Operations, but operations officers form the business end of the human intelligence collection pipeline.

In my mind, that swagger was best embodied by Marty Martin, an Agency colleague who began his career in special operations forces before climbing the ranks at the CIA as an operations officer. He ultimately oversaw the entire operations side of the hunt for high-ranking al Qaida personnel following 9/11. Marty was the one who chose the publicly released photo of 9/11 mastermind Khalid Sheikh Mohammed, which showed the terrorist not in one of his "Arab yuppie" outfits, as Marty called them, but rather in the dirty white T-shirt that left KSM looking like he'd spent the previous two days without sleep or a shower. A muscular fiftysomething with swept-back hair, Marty always had a decisive view of his work: "My job was to kill al Qaida," he would later say. "Get with us, or get out of the way."

To be fair, that work requires a bit of bravado. Being on the front lines jeopardizes lives every day, be they the agents' own, their sources', or, on especially bad days, those of their sources' families. I saw quickly in the Counterterrorism Center that it was better for an officer to be decisive rather than the opposite.

Beyond the aggressive mind-set, or perhaps because of it, there was another obvious difference between the Agency's Directorate of Intelligence and Directorate of Operations, or DO. The operations side was the men's world at the CIA, especially at that time, a situation that had been acknowledged by no less than Nora Slatkin, the Agency's executive director from 1995 to 1997. "Women in the DO have often been delegated to jobs writing reports, doing research, or other support work," she told the Chicago Council on Foreign Relations in 1996. "Even war-seasoned [female] OSS veterans . . . found themselves doing largely office work when they got to the CIA, rather than recruiting spies."

That trend was so pervasive that it led to a bruising 1986 class-action lawsuit filed by several hundred women who'd worked on the operations side. The suit alleged that women in the DO had been routinely denied promotions, overseas assignments, and supervisory positions because of what lawyers for the women described as the CIA's "pervasive culture of sexual discrimination." Nearly a decade later, the Agency quietly settled with the women, providing them $940,000 in back pay and granting twenty-five retroactive promotions to the victims. "We all know that James Bond is a fantasy," Slatkin told the council, "and Bond women are a fantasy of a different sort."

Clearly, in that era, women on the operations side faced steep hurdles in working their way up to the senior ranks. In the DI, thankfully, people were mostly judged by the substantive knowledge they brought to their work and their ability to do their jobs.

Looking back at my time in the CIA, I think the simplest difference in approaches comes from the way women tend to balance risk and reward. I know this veers toward armchair theorizing, but there's a scientific underpinning for it. In a 1999 meta-analysis of 150 studies comparing risk-taking tendencies of males and females, entitled "Gender Differences in Risk Taking," researchers James Byrnes, David Miller, and William Schafer concluded that "clearly . . . male participants are more likely to take risks than female participants." Other studies built upon those findings, including the 2006 "Gender, Financial Risk, and Probability Weights," by Swiss researchers Helga Fehr-Duda, Manuele de Gennaro, and Renate Schubert, which found that females weigh probabilities differently from males and that women are more pessimistic about potential significant gains. Taken together, researchers found, "women's relative insensitivity to probabilities combined with pessimism may indeed lead to higher risk aversion."

I don't think it's risk aversion; I think it's measuring risk. Women incorporate measuring risk into their daily lives in ways that many men don't even consider. We make sure our toddlers are drinking from BPA-free sippy cups and surreptitiously slip vegetables into family meals to guard against disease. Risk is, of course, a fundamental component of growth and innovation, something to be embraced in the appropriate contexts. Women may tend to calculate the dangers more judiciously than some men—and the failure of work environments, including high-level government bureaucracies, to recognize that does a disservice to everyone.

Ambitious women shouldn't have to adopt stereotypically male behaviors or character traits. Yet even today, when inroads into the upper echelons of management still feel like a form of cultural success, many women take the path of least resistance—acting like a man. This demoralizes women employees and kneecaps the effectiveness of the overall organization. Because often, even if only in hindsight, it seems clear that thinking like a woman is sometimes the better option. To be clear, I think the argument that you might be better at one job or the other based on gender is false, be it man or woman. This is why diversity is so important; if everyone has the same background and thinks the same way, it's no better than a giant self-licking ice cream cone.

The baseline for our work in the Counterterrorism Center was the first strategic warning delivered to US government policy makers about bin Ladin. It had been written in August of 1993, as thousands of Saudi guerrilla fighters had finished campaigns against the Soviets in Afghanistan and were spreading out across the Middle East. In response to that notable trend, a young analyst who was at the time in the State Department's Bureau of Intelligence and Research, Gina Bennett, drew up a product entitled "The Wandering Mujahidin: Armed and Dangerous." She called special attention to a benefactor of the movement living at the time in the capital of Sudan: "Among private donors to the new generation, Usama Bin Ladin is particularly famous for his religious zeal and financial largess," she wrote. "Bin Ladin's money has enabled hundreds of Arab veterans to return to safehavens and bases in Yemen and Sudan, where they are training new fighters." Bennett later moved to the CIA to continue her work.

Bennett's work received little attention at the time, and in the following years, other analysts in the intelligence community would quietly toil away on the same case. Barbara Sude, one of the pioneering counterterrorism analysts, has said that in the mid-1990s, "I remember one senior analyst from another account saying at some conference, 'Terrorism people are just tracking things. That's not real analysis.'"

The subject was so amorphous, and such a departure from the traditional topics being analyzed in Langley, that it was difficult to garner attention for it. This continued even after the 1998 US embassy bombings in Nairobi and Tanzania, when George Tenet said that "we must now enter a new phase in our effort against bin Ladin. . . . We are at war." He concluded, "I want no resources or people spared in this effort, either inside CIA or the [intelligence] Community."

Later, a joint congressional task force investigating intelligence lapses prior to 9/11 would find that "despite the DCI's declaration of war in 1998, there was no massive shift in budget or reassignment of personnel to counterterrorism until after September 11, 2001." A further cutting report by the CIA's own inspector general recommended that Tenet and other senior officers face an "accountability board" because they "did not discharge their responsibilities in a satisfactory manner" in enabling the CIA to battle al Qaida.

My earliest days in Iraq were spent poring over information brought back to base by the Pentagon's special operations units. That included units from the army's special operations force and the navy's special operations force deployed to Baghdad. It was similar to the work I'd done in Langley, though from Iraq I wasn't contributing directly to products for policy makers. Instead I had a closer look at the tactical perspective of ongoing operations, something impossible to do back at the office.

My boss at Baghdad Station, the term for the CIA's main operating facility in a foreign location, was a man I'll call Charley, a former operations officer. Back in 1986, in an era when the Islamist threats largely consisted of kidnappings and bombings in and around Beirut, Lebanon, he had helped create the Agency's precursor to the Counterterrorism Center. Just shy of six feet tall, he had gray hair and the semistocky build of a man who'd spent his career in the field focused on terrorist organizations and al Qaida. I was relieved to be working under someone who understood my unit's counterterrorism mission so well — in large part because everyone else in those BIAP trailers was focused on an entirely different sort of hunt.

The Bush administration's rationale for invading Iraq had contained a few pillars. A big one was Hussein's potential support for terrorism, which I was dutifully pursuing from my temporary workspace. But perhaps an even larger justification for the war had been the supposed need to rid Iraq of chemical and biological weapons once and for all. "The truth is that for reasons that have a lot to do with the U.S. government bureaucracy," Deputy Defense Secretary Paul Wolfowitz later acknowledged, "we settled on the one issue that everyone could agree on which was weapons of mass destruction as the core reason."

Logic dictated that once Hussein was overthrown, the administration actually had to locate those weapons. And already, by the time I arrived in Iraq, the search had not found anything to support Saddam's having WMD.

I settled in at BIAP just as the Pentagon's Seventy-Fifth Exploitation Task Force wrapped up seven frustrating weeks of work. The six hundred or so people comprising the task force — including experts in everything from biology to computer science to special operations forces combat — had visited all the nineteen top suspected WMD sites identified prior to the invasion. These locations also generally happened to be targets the coalition had bombed, however, and that looters had subsequently ransacked. If there had been anything to find prior to the invasion, it wasn't there afterward.

I saw weapons investigators wandering the airport grounds some evenings, back from their latest wild-goose chase through some charred office building. Their shoulders were perpetually hunched. The task force leaders no longer thought they were going to "find chemical rounds sitting next to a gun," Army colonel Robert Smith told the *Washington Post* at the time. "That's what we came here for, but we're past that." I could tell they couldn't wait to get back on a plane to the States.

Just as the team rotated out, another team arrived to fill its shoes. With a key pretext for the war on the precipice of complete invalidation, the Pentagon nearly tripled-down on its hunt for WMD with a new fifteen-hundred-person task force. Known as the Iraq Survey Group, or ISG, the multinational, multiagency team fell under the general command of the Pentagon's Defense Intelligence Agency. Unlike the previous task force, however, this new one was headed by CIA director Tenet's handpicked special adviser, David Kay, who had served as a United Nations weapons inspector in Iraq after the first Gulf War. It was immediately clear to me, as his team mounted an expanding array of missions across the Iraqi countryside, that Kay had the full might and resources of the Agency behind him. It was less clear whether even that would be enough.

I wasn't privy to the details of the WMD case, but there was an overwhelming skepticism among my coworkers that any major stockpiles of weapons existed. Sitting next to Kay at lunch one day, I asked him.

"Do you think you'll find anything?" I said.

His outlook seemed upbeat, if somewhat restrained. "If there is anything there to find," he said, "we'll find it."

To help in Kay's efforts, it seemed like a stream of new CIA officers began arriving every day. Eventually the growth of Agency operations with the ISG would necessitate that they move from our living quarters and workspace to an airport camp of their own, full of gaudy marble guesthouses, lakeside villas, and a central palace that was allegedly a former brothel. WELCOME TO CAMP SLAYER, a sign outside their outpost would soon read. ANOTHER DAY IN PARADISE. But during my first few weeks at BIAP I shared quarters with the growing team of weapons hunters at the Baghdad Station's SCIF. If they knew who Zarqawi was, they didn't especially care.

Charley, thankfully, did. He understood the nuances that exist, perhaps paradoxically, at the nexus of extremist groups, and he had his own skepticism about al Qaida's supposed connection to Hussein's regime and the ensuing invasion. I decided early on that those must have been the reasons for the fierce scowl he usually wore. Charley was clearly the sort of coworker whose good side you wanted to be on — not someone you wanted to bother unnecessarily. But fortunately, we clicked. When I arrived, he was instrumental in facilitating the handoff of information from the Iraq unit analyst who'd held the seat in Baghdad before I did. As I settled into a groove there, he offered a willing second set of eyes for the cables I wrote about extremists operating in Iraq. And after I'd been in country for a few weeks, it was Charley who first offered me an overview of the right way to interview detainees.

If I was going to properly investigate the administration's question — What role, if any, might the Iraqi Intelligence Service have played in cooperating with terrorists such as Zarqawi? — I needed to ferret out information myself. Training in interview and interrogation techniques is par for the course among CIA operations officers, but analysts back at Langley are rarely called upon to cull fresh intelligence from sources. Questioning detainees was something I'd simply never done before.

Sitting across from me in the dusty space that was formerly Saddam's personal airport conference room, Charley walked me through "Debriefing 101." In practice, he said, the difference between an interview and an interrogation is largely one of art — particularly to the person wearing the handcuffs. But at its simplest, an interview is direct and efficient. Where was the detainee on this particular date? How did he know that other individual? Who is this person in the photograph? I was looking for information, Charley said, not necessarily to catch someone in a lie. That applied to "high-value detainees" as well as to the lowliest shopkeeper. Besides, if someone were innocent, this would quickly clarify that, too.

"Gain their respect and their trust," he said. "Be patient, and try to be unimposing. Then they'll talk."

Interrogating, however, is something different. It's directly confrontational, and it's built on the certitude that a detainee is guilty of something. The end goal is to convince him that a confession is in his best interests. That wasn't my job, Charley pointed out, but it was useful to understand the difference. And what a difference it was.

After Charley's debriefing tutorial, I needed to calm my nerves. The next day I would be heading to the detention center. So I climbed under the mosquito netting enveloping my cot at my terminal and thumbed through the one book I'd thrown into my bag before leaving Washington: Stephen Batchelor's *Buddhism Without Beliefs*.

I appreciate now the irony of preparing to question high-value radical detainees by reading about a religion in which Four Noble Truths revolve around understanding suffering and the path to enlightenment. But I'd packed the book simply because it was slim and full of short essays on subjects such as culture, integrity, and emptiness. I figured it might take my mind off living in a war zone with new acquaintances, trying to digest my role in all of it.

Lying on my cot that night at BIAP, I grabbed a pen and underlined this, from Batchelor's essay on compassion: "A compassionate heart still feels anger, greed, jealousy, and other such emotions. But it accepts them for what they are with equanimity, and cultivates the strength of mind to let them arise and pass without identifying with or acting upon them."

That seemed like a valuable ethos for an interviewer. Little did I know how many times I would need to repeat this to myself in the coming weeks.

If the detention facility on the western edge of the BIAP grounds had a proper name at the time, I never knew it. Later, news reports and investigations would refer to it as Camp Cropper, but at least in the summer of 2003, Cropper was a "camp" in the same way Alcatraz might have once been. As a colleague and I drove through the late-morning haze the next day, those endless spools of razor wire surrounding the facility were just the most obvious hint that Cropper wasn't there to house Americans.

The camp wasn't the largest prison, or "theater internment facility," the US government would build in Iraq. That honor goes to the isolated Camp Bucca, in the country's southeastern desert, which was swelling steadily by the time I arrived in Iraq and would grow to hold as many as twenty-six thousand inmates. Cropper isn't the most notorious Iraqi detention center, either. For most Americans, Abu Ghraib likely holds that distinction, thanks to what a 2004 army internal report described as the "sadistic, blatant, and wanton criminal abuses" of inmates there. But in the United States' war on terror, Camp Cropper just might have been the most important internment facility. It's where the high-value detainees were held.

By the time I arrived, Cropper's ranks included Huda Salih Mahdi Ammash, the head of Iraq's biological weapons development program, whom everyone in the Agency referred to as Anthrax Annie. Humam Abd al-Khaliq Abd al-Ghafur, the former head of Iraq's nuclear program, was also in a cell in Cropper. Former Iraqi foreign minister and deputy prime minister Tariq Aziz, who oversaw the killing of forty-two Iraqi merchants the government accused of price fixing, was there as well.

Not long after I arrived, Ali Hassan al-Majid, better known as Chemical Ali because of the horrific gas attacks he orchestrated against the Kurds in 1988, was apprehended and sent to Cropper—and if and when the coalition tracked down Hussein himself, I knew he'd go there, too. Basically anyone who appeared on one of the Bush administration's deck of fifty-five terrorist Personality Identification Playing Cards got sent to Camp Cropper.

I was hoping to interview the comical Baghdad Bob—the Iraqi information minister, Mohammed Saeed al-Sahaf, who denied the presence of US troops on television even as tanks were rolling in the background behind him. He was detained but then immediately released because he was low on the hierarchy of power. Given that he stated on television, "They are trying to say that the Iraqi is easy to capture, in order to deceive the world that it is a picnic....One day, they [will] start facing bitter facts," I thought he might be an interesting guy to talk to.

Outside the camp's perimeter row of twelve-foot-high steel-reinforced concrete T-walls, designed for blast protection, I was met by a sergeant in no mood for small talk. His M4 carbine was slung over his shoulder, and I could see an MP tag on his shoulder as he leaned over and peered into the car window. The patch under his tag, depicting a crossed pair of spears, signified the 320th Military Police Company, based in Saint Petersburg, Florida. I'd heard about those MPs trailing the war effort back in March, setting up prisons to hold the Iraqis captured during the coalition's initial advance. But I mentioned to him that I thought those reservists were supposed to have been sent home when President Bush had declared combat operations over.

"Orders changed," he said, barely concealing his frustration.

It turned out that the detainees weren't the only ones who didn't care for the prisons. At the time, the US Army had half a million soldiers on active duty, the sergeant said, but only a few thousand of those were military police. Only a subset of *those* MPs had undergone the special training necessary to become prison guards—which is a niche assignment, perhaps, but not a job you can simply throw at an everyday soldier and expect to have it go well. In no other place in the army would a private be in charge of nearly one hundred people, particularly people who might be hostile toward him. The MPs in Iraq who had the composure, judgment, and training to manage a prison proved far too valuable to rotate home—especially as the Pentagon's detention plan began to unravel.

That airport facility, I'd been told, had originally been designed as a central processing place for the Defense Department's network of Iraqi prisons. Insurgents in and around Baghdad would be brought to BIAP, cataloged, then distributed among various internment facilities around the country—many of which, like Abu Ghraib, had originally been built by the Iraqis. But this plan presumed that existing prison facilities would be in working order, and yet as Iraqi military forces retreated, they pillaged and neglected many of them. Suddenly the internment options were far more limited. By the time I first visited Cropper, which was built to house around two hundred people, it held somewhere between five hundred and one thousand.

The sergeant pointed us toward a makeshift parking area up ahead. I drove through the gate and stopped by a large blown-out airplane hangar. The giant corrugated metal sheets on its roof flapped whenever there was a sharp gust of wind. My colleague, who'd been to the camp before, hopped out and headed for the door. I hurried to keep up.

Walking through the searing sunshine, down a fenced corridor toward the special housing unit, I saw groups of male detainees, in whatever clothes they'd been wearing the moment they were arrested, milling about inside a giant pen. To battle the heat, many had taken off their shirts and wrapped them over their heads. At the edges of the courtyard was more elaborate fencing, delimiting the female-only section of the jail as well as the juveniles' section. The whole setup looked more to me like livestock pens than a detention center for humans.

The original Pentagon plan had anticipated that these men would have all cycled through Cropper and gone on to other facilities within three days. In reality, most of them would be detained there for more than three hundred days. The men glared at me as we walked—and to be sure, some of the animosity was mutual. A percentage of the detainees, I had been told, had been an active part of the brief conflict. Others had been arrested while plotting attacks against US personnel and infrastructure in Iraq. A reminder of what some of these detainees were capable of was delivered a few weeks earlier, when an army convoy had taken a wrong turn on the road to Baghdad. Insurgents attacked the caravan, killing eleven soldiers and kidnapping seven others, including Private First Class Jessica Lynch, then nineteen years old. When the West Virginia native was rescued eleven days later, special operations forces found her right arm shattered, her spine fractured, her left leg splintered, and indications of sexual assault. They thanked God she couldn't remember that.

Inside the facility, we stopped briefly among the rows of yellow metal walls that made up Cropper's solitary confinement wing. Former Iraqi government officials and other high-value detainees were brought here. If they were cooperative, some of them were allowed more than one hour of sunlight per day.

From there the tour continued on to the detainment area for the general population. We stopped into the makeshift intake office, where three MPs stood next to a few computers and several clipboards full of the names and numbers of the detainees. I ran my finger down the list, reading through the notes about why each detainee was arrested—the start of a task that soon became part of my daily routine. Up ahead, an MP led us into that same blown-out airplane hangar we'd parked next to. There I could interview detainees.

I made a sweeping circle of the place with my eyes. The flapping metal roof offered a modicum of shade over the dirt-and-gravel floor, but that was it. A row of adjoining plywood rooms, each maybe a dozen feet square, stood off to the right. The MP gestured us over to one of them.

There were no ceilings on the rooms and little in the way of privacy. But they each had a small table, a few plastic chairs, and a door.

"Your office," the MP said.

CHAPTER 6

Long Guns to Be Placed Here

It was an early afternoon at the end of May when MPs led a man I'll call Mahmoud to my plywood shack. He was the sixth detainee I'd questioned at Cropper that day, and I had been told that he had only been in Iraq for a few weeks before he'd been arrested by US forces. Like the other people I'd questioned, Mahmoud was clearly no Iraqi freedom fighter or devout Hussein loyalist. Yet he was being described by the military as an enemy combatant.

Mahmoud sat down in the salvaged plastic chair with a thud and threw his restrained hands up on the tabletop in front of him. His right leg twitched in his dirty clothes. He scanned the tiny room.

To my left sat a man named Percy. Nearly forty years old, he was born in the Middle East, then immigrated to the United States as a teenager. He'd earned scholarships to college, then caught on at the Agency as an invaluable interpreter. His knowledge of local customs and nuances was almost impossible to replicate, even by the best-trained American-born Arabic speaker. Percy's beliefs were not vague, ingrained platitudes about American superiority; his passion for the US intelligence mission came from a deep appreciation for the opportunities he had in his adopted homeland. I trusted him fully and was glad to have him sitting there silently by my side in the shack, staring right back at Mahmoud.

The detainee craned his neck and glanced behind him. Leaning against the back wall was an analyst in his mid-thirties named Ron.

He wore a white button-down shirt and khakis, and he worked for the Pentagon's intelligence wing, the Defense Intelligence Agency.

That Ron was even in the room was something of a coup and a testament to the idea that the CIA and the Pentagon could set aside their rancorous history of petty squabbling in service of the larger mission. I hadn't exactly been searching for help when I'd met him a few days earlier, but there were few of us in Iraq at the time who were focusing on Hussein's potential connection to extremism. I could tell Ron was savvy about his work, and we both agreed that two heads were better than one. Besides, I sensed from our first conversation that Ron was a kindred spirit because of the way he viewed the whole misbegotten enterprise in Iraq. To that end, I could vent with him when the days got particularly long.

The work was a free-for-all: you could either sit idly by in the trailer SCIF or do something, and Ron and I both chose to do something, and that meant looking for our own leads. So there was Ron with his arms folded, leaning against the back of the shack as I began with Mahmoud.

"Do you know Zarqawi?" I said calmly.

Percy turned to the detainee and repeated the question.

"I don't —" Mahmoud said; then Percy cut him off.

"She asked you the question," Percy said flatly. "Direct your answers to her."

Mahmoud was taken aback, then turned to me. "I don't know what you're talking about," he said.

Through his indignation, I sensed that Mahmoud might be telling the truth. And after a long day of asking the same scripted questions from headquarters, probing for the same weak links between Hussein's regime and possible al Qaida fighters, even I was a little bored of talking about the Iraqi Intelligence Service. I felt like that path was a dead end. So I changed the subject.

"You got here through Syria, right?" I said. "Did Darwish facilitate your travel or Saqa?"

Mahmoud's eyes darted around the room. He seemed surprised by the question.

The truth was, I didn't know the answer myself; they seemed to be the logical choice to help foreigners who enter Iraq by way of Syria and soon get labeled as "enemy combatants." Maybe he had something to do with Zarqawi's network. Maybe he didn't.

"Zarqawi and Darwish," I repeated. "What can you tell me?"

Mahmoud again took stock of his situation. "I don't know who that is," he finally said. "I came here to visit my family."

That instantly felt to me like a lie, but there was no way for me to prove it; I had zero information or background on this guy. So I asked him a few more questions, then sent him off with the MPs, back to the general population.

"Zarqawi, huh?" Ron said to me as we watched Mahmoud walk back through the hangar doors.

"Thought I might as well ask," I said.

Before the coalition's March invasion, Zarqawi had said goodbye to Sayf al-Adl, his main al Qaida contact in Iran, to set up a camp with Ansar al-Islam in northern Iraq. Some of his followers from Herat, Afghanistan, moved with him, and eventually other foreign fighters would join his ranks. Ron and I only understood this in the broadest strokes when we sat down with Mahmoud.

From researching the Iraqi Intelligence Service, I knew that in the years preceding 9/11, Hussein had taken a decidedly conservative turn. While he'd always been a dictator, he'd begun his presidency in 1979 advocating a surprising amount of separation between church and state. Following a Shia uprising, he had declared that his Sunni party must "oppose the institutionalization of religion in the state and society....Let us return to the roots of our religion, glorifying them—but not introduce it into politics."

By 1988, however, Hussein sought to rebuild support following his disastrous war with Iran, which killed more than a million people. In a naked appeal to the country's hard-line, conservative

Muslims, Hussein opened an Islamic university in Baghdad. He introduced compulsory religious education into Iraqi schools. He shuttered nightclubs with seedy reputations, and he even made an unsuccessful appeal to Saudi Arabia to unfreeze funds held in Saudi banks so Baghdad could import ten million copies of the Koran. The more support those moves gained, the more pious the dictator tried to appear. Meanwhile, his geopolitical blunders only amplified the impact of religion on the Iraqi people.

By 1994, as Iraq faced chronic shortages of food and medicine, thanks to international economic embargoes, desperate men and women turned toward a higher power than even Hussein: Allah. More men began praying five times a day. More women veiled themselves. "We are really against this," Ihssan Hassan, a University of Baghdad sociology professor and adviser to Hussein, told the *Los Angeles Times*. "It is a backward thing. If we could ban it, we would. We can't."

But Hussein steered into that curve. Among other things, he banned alcohol from restaurants, a move publicly criticized by no less than his son Udai, who saw it as a marked turn toward Islamic fundamentalism. Hussein added the words *Allahu akbar*—God is great—to the Iraqi flag, in script modeled on his own handwriting. By 2001, my research showed, construction crews had finished the first of three gigantic Baghdad-area mosques that the dictator commissioned. Named the Mother of All Battles, with minarets shaped like Scud missiles, the mosque housed a six-hundred-page Koran encased in glass. The text was written with fifty pints of Hussein's blood, which he'd donated over the course of two years.

Perhaps, I thought as Ron and I stood there in the doorway of the plywood shack, Hussein's gestures to hard-line Islamists really had resonated with the Sunni fighters now entering the country. Maybe it was that simple.

But my gut wasn't buying it. And if those foreign fighters entering Iraq had no allegiance to Hussein or his supporters, they would introduce a nasty new element into the war. The coalition would suddenly be facing an enemy more networked than the fragments of Hussein's deposed regime and more unpredictable than guerrilla warriors defending their homeland. These would be rogue opportunists, hell-bent on sheer destruction, from which their caliphate could rise from the ashes.

Ron turned to me. "So what do we make of today?" he said.

"No clue," I said, watching Mahmoud disappear back into the detention center. "But now I'm really afraid of what Zarqawi might be up to."

———

Ron and I fell into an easy rhythm with those debriefs, speaking with as many as ten run-of-the-mill detainees a day. Most of those conversations failed to move the intelligence needle in any real way, but around 20 percent of them provided some useful information that expanded our knowledge base. After those conversations, as well any debriefs of high-value detainees, which were considered important no matter what they said, I headed over to a secure trailer to quickly think through what we'd heard and to send an encrypted cable back to Agency headquarters. Ron, too, was allowed into the trailer as long as he was with me.

Typing those cables was the most tedious part of being in Iraq. They all followed a standard template: names of the people involved, date and location of the debrief, then a little background context to go along with any new information, listed in three or four neatly numbered paragraphs. It just seemed like an awful lot of words for bite-size nuggets of information. Having been on the Agency-based receiving end of cables from Iraq, I obviously understood how important that steady drip of useful details was, though I admit there were times, as workdays in Iraq stretched to sixteen and seventeen hours, when I questioned my earlier assessment of "useful."

There was another reason I didn't particularly enjoy working out of those trailers, and it was one entirely foreign to my experience behind a desk in Langley: the trailers were located in the general area where mortars were landing.

By the summer of 2003, that simple piece of weaponry was becoming a staple for anyone looking to take a potshot at coalition forces. Mortars are just metal tubes that are closed on one end, are usually planted in the ground, and have an explosive charge inside — a mobile version of the cannons first used to blast away at medieval castle walls. Drop in a metal mortar shell — or one of the thousands of tiny Iraqi Army rockets that went missing after the dismantling of Hussein's government — light the figurative fuse, and you have a weapon that can fire upon American positions a few miles away. The insurgents didn't even have to have a direct line of sight to the target.

Anyone who's played *Angry Birds* understands the trickiness of aiming a projectile along a simple parabola. Add to that the pressure of having to scramble away from the mortar before coalition forces pinpoint the origin of the shot and return fire, and it's safe to say that accuracy isn't the weapon's strong suit. That was only doubly so, as the rumor went, because the person firing the mortar often wasn't a trained former member of Saddam's military. American troops periodically found the empty mortar tubes stuffed in hay bales. Guerrilla fighters had mitigated their own risk by paying local farmers to lob a round in the general direction of the nearest US base.

That's not to diminish the mortar's potential lethality: if one hit you, you would be instantly killed or maimed. Then again, a bolt of lightning could do the same thing. Walking around BIAP, I'd occasionally hear their faint thump in the distance, often followed by someone yelling, "Incoming!" and maybe a little return gunfire. In general I thought of those mortars as full of sound and potential fury but signifying very little.

On one occasion it was getting late in the day, and I'd just wrapped up a debrief that warranted a cable. There in the trailer, near the airport's western perimeter, a half dozen of us were all realizing we'd be working through dinner. Suddenly there was an explosion outside.

This was no muffled pop on the horizon, however. This one hit with a bang, then echoed. I remember the feeling most of all: the nearby blast rattled the trailer and caught everyone off guard. That had never happened before. Instantly everyone was silent.

"So, uh, that one was close," someone finally said with a forced chuckle. Tepid laughter filled the room.

Just then, a second rocket slammed into the ground outside. This one sizzled on the way in, then rocked the trailer with its blast waves. Around me, binders were knocked off the shelves. "Holy shit!" someone blurted out.

I'd experienced a few earthquakes in my life, but those were nothing like a mortar round detonating mere feet away. In that moment, I'd have believed some giant had grabbed the trailer by the corners and started shaking it. Even more to the point, a second rocket landing in the same general spot as the first indicated that the shooters were actually dialing in their range.

Most of us stood frozen in anticipation of what might happen next. The Agency's Baghdad chief at the time, who just happened to be with us in the trailer, continued his conversation with another Agency officer. I wrapped my arms around a few of the binders I'd caught as they fell off the shelves and sat down in my chair near the door. Really, there was nothing else I could think to do. Inside the trailer seemed like the safest place to be, but it was hardly fortified against a rocket attack. If a mortar shell landed on us, I assumed I'd have typed my last cable.

And that, more than anything, is what my mind settled on in that eerie silence, as I waited out one of the closest things to combat I would ever experience: the sheer nonsensical luck of war. I was sitting there helplessly, clutching those binders, anticipating the worst, and the end was about to come—or it wasn't. There didn't seem to be much I could do about it either way.

Not that everyone was so stoic about the situation. Soon after I sat down, the door to our trailer was flung open by one of the Agency's communications workers. "They're shooting at us!" he announced. Josh, pudgy and bespectacled, was practically vibrating with energy. "It came from over there!"

All eyes turned to the silhouette in the doorway, draped in a Kevlar vest, wearing a helmet, and holding his M4 carbine. Officially a communications officer, Josh was an IT wiz and exactly the sort of guy you'd want to help build a war-zone communications infrastructure from baling wire and three pieces of duct tape. And exactly the opposite of anyone you'd want to do any actual fighting.

But just like that, Josh was back out the door, running in a dozen different directions all at once. I could swear I heard him yell, "I'll save you!" but I might be misremembering that. Either way, I leaned back in my chair to peek out the doorway and watch his Gomer Pyle helmet zigzagging across the gravel parking lot.

The station chief walked past my chair to the door. "Are you trying to make yourself a target?" he yelled at the intrepid communications officer. "Get back to your trailer! Now!"

"Okay!" Josh said, then rattled and clanked his way back to his trailer. Additional mortars fell over the next half hour, but thankfully the explosions got fainter and farther away and eventually petered out altogether. At some point I finished my cable. We ended up no worse for wear after that assault, even if no one said much for the rest of the afternoon. Josh had even managed to get a little jog in.

"How would these guys even know Zarqawi?" I asked out loud to no one in particular. Back in the air-conditioned trailer on yet another sweltering morning, I aimlessly flipped through a sheaf of my past cables, hoping inspiration might strike. "Do they even think he's a real person? Would that even matter?"

Ron looked up from his own notes. "Abdul knows something," he said. "You can just tell. It's all over his face."

I was sure Ron was right. The array of ideologues we debriefed in that camp fell into a few categories. Many of them opposed the US occupation but lacked any real religious underpinning or radical drive behind their anger. Some of them had simply been in the wrong place at the wrong time and gotten scooped up in a group arrest. But the nearly forty-year-old detainee whom I'll call Abdul fell into the truly hardened category.

Years earlier, he'd done time in Hussein's prison system for plotting attacks against Iraqi security forces and had been grabbed by US Special Operations Forces soon after the invasion because he was suspected of turning those plots against coalition peacekeepers. Abdul sincerely believed that Americans were *kuffars*, or infidels denying Allah's holy truth, who deserved the full fury of righteous extermination in His name.

Perhaps not surprisingly, Abdul wasn't cooperative during our interviews. I hadn't been naive enough to believe that my friendly demeanor would cause detainees to instantly open up, but in general I felt like I was getting pretty good at those conversations. I'd even found a sneaky cultural benefit in being a woman. To those Islamic extremists, being questioned by a woman was simultaneously shocking and shameful. The jihadists couldn't believe that a woman — someone inferior to them, in their eyes — would dare question them. Or even be *chosen* to question them. That gave me an advantage: anything that rattled a detainee out of delivering rote answers offered us a better path to the truth.

Even as my confidence grew, however, trying to get information from Abdul had become a source of frustration — particularly at a time when conditions in Iraq were taking a noticeable turn.

Throughout the late spring and early summer of 2003, the coalition had seen a slow but steady increase in violence across the country; Abdul had been arrested when the US military started trying to stem that tide. The uptick in violence could have been merely opportunistic, but maybe there was something else to it. At around that same time, the Pentagon finally bombed Zarqawi's Khurmal site. The strike killed a smattering of foot soldiers, but thanks to all the publicity the camp had generated prior to the war, Zarqawi and a number of his followers had long since gone. Were they still in Iraq at all? Might Abdul, a hardened extremist who bore no allegiance to his earlier torturers in the Hussein regime, have been one of them? He was our best chance to understand the growing number of attacks against coalition targets, yet he was giving us nothing.

"I'm really starting to hate that guy," I said to Ron.

A head popped up behind me.

"Trouble?" said a floppy-haired case officer who stood up from his desk at the other end of the trailer. I'll call him Brandon. "What's the problem?" he asked.

I looked over, half in surprise. Though I'd been in the trailer with Brandon a number of times, we'd never said more than a passing hello to one another.

"We're not getting anywhere with a detainee," I said cautiously.

If there was a cookie-cutter young case officer, Brandon was it. Six feet tall, with blond hair and blue eyes, he probably went to Yale and had a master's degree in foreign something-or-other from a school like Columbia, which he'd probably earned within the previous five years. He had probably been told he was "a real go-getter." Most of all, Brandon had the confidence of a man who didn't know how much he didn't know.

"I'd be glad to take a run at him for you," he said.

I immediately suspected Brandon had offered to help because case officers are graded internally by how many foreign sources they can recruit and the sheer volume of intelligence reports they produce. If he was having a slow day, swooping in to capitalize on someone else's potential source of intelligence could put an easy feather in his cap. As much as I was skeptical of Brandon's motives, however, Baghdad at the time seemed like no place for an analyst like me to be territorial—and this was no time to risk missing out on valuable intelligence because I wanted some sort of brownie points for cracking a detainee myself. I was under no delusion that a few weeks of questioning prisoners had somehow made me an expert at it. If Brandon could actually get something from Abdul, he was welcome to brag—I was more focused on the fact that Abdul surely knew *something*, and I desperately wanted to know what it was. Besides, I sensed that if Brandon was so eager, this might end up being fun.

"Okay, sure," I told him. "Thanks."

Ron, Brandon, and I hopped into a pickup and drove over to Cropper. Along the way, I mentioned, "You know, we've talked to this guy three times already."

"Right," Brandon said. "But as an analyst, you can't really solicit information from these people if you haven't had the training, you know? There's just a . . ." He flapped his hand back and forth to signify a meeting of the minds. I think.

"Right, okay," I said, offering a little nod.

"I mean, that's not your fault," he added. "We couldn't do what we do without you guys doing what you do, and vice versa. That's just how it works, you know? But I've got a few ideas."

Ron and I looked at each other. He smirked. This *was* going to be fun.

Percy met us at the hangar. The four of us split up among a pair of adjoining plywood shacks—Ron and I standing on the dirt floor in one, positioned to overhear everything that transpired; Brandon and Percy in the room next door. Without any ceilings, eavesdropping would be easy.

Above us, tin siding rattled when the hot breeze blew through the disintegrating hangar. The whole place had begun smelling like dirty laundry. Ron pointed to the metal folding chairs in the shack, which seemed practically luxurious, and we made a mental note to swap them for the junky plastic ones in ours the next morning. Moments later, we heard Brandon tell a nearby guard to bring in the detainee.

Soon there was the familiar sound of the plywood door being opened, then slamming shut on its own. We could hear Abdul taking his seat a foot or two from us, on the other side of the plywood. Ron had a pen and a pad of paper at the ready. I glanced at my watch; it was just after 10:00 a.m.

"I'm Brandon," our colleague said in halting Arabic. "I know you've been speaking with other people, but I've got a few more questions."

There was no response from Abdul. I could imagine the glare he must be giving Brandon by then; I'd seen it many times myself.

"Oh, so I guess you like it in here," Brandon said, switching to a blunter tactic. "I could arrange for you to stay a lot longer."

"So what?" Abdul muttered in Arabic. I'm sure he rolled his eyes.

"You know, you could make this easy on yourself," Brandon shot back. The young case officer was becoming agitated. "Just tell me what I need to know, and I'll be on my way."

On Brandon pressed. Twenty-five minutes drained off the clock, then forty-five. Abdul simply toyed with him—a matador parrying a charging bull—and more than once Ron and I had to put our hands to our mouths to keep from laughing. Finally, even the jihadist got bored with the gamesmanship.

"You see this?" Abdul suddenly said in perfectly passable English. We could hear him slap his right arm down on the little metal table. He'd done it in front of us, too, early on. With Ron and me, Abdul had begun slowly rolling up his shirtsleeve with his left hand. Each new fold had exposed another winding, blotchy scar. Some were from burns, I'd guessed, and others must have been from garish slashes with an assortment of blades. Some wounds had clearly been closed with staples.

"Saddam's men did this to me," Abdul said, switching back to Arabic. Now his temperature was rising as well. "Who are you? What can you do to me that would even matter?"

With that, Percy told us, Brandon took the bait. He leaped to his feet. The sound of a chair being slammed back from the table echoed through the hangar, and suddenly the young case officer was yelling. "You want to know who I am?"

This was young Brandon's *"I want the truth!"* moment. He actually pounded on the table, which made Ron and me jump and bang into the plywood wall.

"I can make you hate life!" he screamed.

Abdul laughed at him. Ron's shoulders shook as he tried to muffle his laugh. I couldn't control my laughter. Tears started rolling down my face from holding it in — and with that, the interrogation was clearly over. I knocked on Brandon's door, and in my most authoritative-sounding voice said, "Officer, you're needed out here for a moment."

Abdul was soon led back to his pen, where he remained in detention for the rest of my time there.

Driving back to the terminal that afternoon, once the laughter had subsided, I furrowed my brow. Debriefing Abdul had been like talking to a brick wall for all of us. Brandon threatening him with a longer prison stay? Of course that wouldn't rattle a guy like Abdul, but I didn't have any great ideas, either. This man was a potential murderer, and I had important questions — about Zarqawi's plans, about the mobilization of dangerous elements in the country — I believed he could answer. But there was no way for American debriefers to *force* Abdul to tell us anything. There were limits to our interactions, and he knew it.

"What if someone just kicked his ass one time?" I finally wondered. "I'll bet he wouldn't be expecting that."

I soon came to understand that I wasn't the only person struggling with that question.

As the world would later learn in graphic detail, by the summer of 2003 the methods CIA interrogators used to keep terrorism suspects off-balance varied widely. What the Agency authorized as "enhanced" techniques could be physically abusive, and many have described some methods as outright torture. The pushing of those limits in black-site prisons around the world was something I heard vague stories about as it was happening. There were, however, none of those black sites in Iraq for me to visit so I could personally verify the whispers about Agency techniques — and it wasn't until a congressional investigation took place a decade later that many of us working for the CIA at the time truly understood the tactics being unleashed.

In addition, I know from some experience that morality and righteousness can become surprisingly fluid things in a war zone. As I reflect on questioning detainees in Baghdad, and what I might have been hypothetically willing to authorize in order to learn what an enemy combatant knew, the lines aren't clean, and they can't be distilled onto a bumper sticker. I know that the individual interrogation techniques I heard about at the time were of less interest to me than whether or not they generated actionable intelligence.

There in Iraq, the Agency questioners I interacted with were either debriefers, as I was, or polygrapher-interrogators. I have always been skeptical of the polygraph's validity, but it was a useful tool for keeping detainees off guard, especially if they were hiding something. Often, being confronted by "truthiness" from a machine was more valuable than whatever appeared on the readout. The traditional process of gathering intelligence from prisoners rarely if ever came with a dramatic breakthrough or a Hollywood-style revelation. It was far more often a methodical slog, in which a larger picture came into focus only a piece at a time. And we went to some unusual ends to gather those pieces — most memorably, in my experience, with a walking, talking mountain named Evil Hagrid. He'd been a key player within the former Iraqi Intelligence Service.

Colloquially known as the Mukhabarat, the IIS under Hussein comprised twenty-four different directorates, each designated with an *M*, so the offices were known as M1, M2, M3, and so forth. Another nine smaller regional offices helped fulfill the government's demands for foreign intelligence collection, domestic counterintelligence, and clandestine operations. Those were the usual duties of an intelligence service. As a high-ranking intelligence officer, however, Evil Hagrid had a specific role that made him stand out: his department performed Iraqi government–sanctioned assassinations inside and outside the country.

After dozens of conversations with detainees, I was refocusing on the lingering question at hand from the administration: Was there any evidence that Hussein had united with al Qaida or Zarqawi? In the summer of 2003, I accepted the fact that my job in Iraq was to run down any threads that *might* have tied them together — and I knew that any cooperation Hussein's government extended to those extremists might have gone through Evil Hagrid's office. That made the former intel officer valuable enough to be one of the first regime officials arrested by US forces after the invasion and an important enough source of intelligence for my colleagues and me to try something extraordinary.

I'd heard that Evil Hagrid had been uncooperative with the

Agency questioners who came before me in Baghdad, both the interrogators and the preceding analyst. I'd never spoken to him myself, but it seemed clear enough that the regular routine wasn't working. So a specially trained CIA polygrapher-interrogator and I began thinking outside the box. Or, rather, outside the prison.

Our plan was for Percy and the interrogator to grab Evil Hagrid from his cell, then create some confusion in the prisoner's mind as to why he needed to be immediately removed from Cropper. Ideally, that would be "for his safety." One option was to tell him they'd uncovered an urgent plot among other detainees to murder former Iraqi officials in prison and that moving him was the only way to protect him—but I left the details to them. At the very least, we hoped, the unexpected change of venue would rattle Evil Hagrid a little before our interview—and if he seemed grateful for what he thought was our saving his life, all the better.

The next day at Cropper, Percy, the interrogator, and I—along with a CIA case officer who'd asked to tag along—were told by MPs that the only available space in which to speak with Evil Hagrid was an old bomb shelter located across a gravel lot from the detention center. That was actually perfect, because it avoided any messy storytelling on our part as to why we wanted to waltz one of the MPs' highest-value detainees straight out of prison.

Inside the pyramid-shaped shelter, we found a series of dark stone passageways that wove around a single central room and led off to a series of side exits. That was great, too, we decided, because it meant that the case officer and I could listen from the shadows as Percy and the interrogator talked with Evil Hagrid. Slowly, the interrogator would turn the psychological screws, and because I knew the general roles and responsibilities inside the IIS, I could later call foul on any claims Evil Hagrid made about not being privy to various bits of information.

The whole plan struck us as a little *Scooby-Doo,* but I was eager to try anything that might make Evil Hagrid more cooperative. I felt like we were finally showing real initiative. So Percy and the interrogator headed into the prison to collect him, and the case officer and I took our places in a side passageway of the bomb shelter.

Soon after, Percy and the interrogator arrived at the shelter with a guard and Evil Hagrid in tow. Ankle shackles scuffed along the dirt floor. I peered around the corner from my passageway as the group flowed toward a set of plastic chairs sitting beneath a single overhead light. Then, as they fanned out, my first glimpse of the prisoner made me rethink everything.

Evil Hagrid was tall, with broad shoulders and large hands, resting there on the arms of his chair. The former IIS officer was relatively clean-shaven, but his overall hairiness was apparent from the greasy tufts that popped up around the sweat-stained collar of his shirt. That's what an assassin and murderer looks like, I thought, recalling his role in the IIS. Suddenly, as I watched the guard leave the shelter, I was glad I wasn't in that cramped central room with Evil Hagrid and the others.

Not that the passageway in that bomb shelter was my idea of fun, either. It was pitch black and for the vast majority of the time uninhabited. That meant it had likely become a den for every bug, animal, and snake found in the Iraqi desert. I really don't care for most reptiles when they are within arm's reach, and I *really* don't care for spiders—yet the case officer and I could hardly take a step without clearing out cobwebs with our faces. There in the shadows, I did my best to focus on the conversation with Evil Hagrid, but I was regularly distracted by the sound of something scurrying or slithering nearby.

Thankfully, every so often, the interrogator would take a break from the conversation with Evil Hagrid "to check on the situation in the prison," he said. He'd pop out the front door of the bomb shelter, then swing around to one of its side exits, where I'd emerge from the passageway to meet him. Then, after a good shakedown to be sure I wasn't covered in scorpions, I'd suggest a few questions for Evil Hagrid to help the interrogator home in on various details, and we'd both head back to our spots in the shelter.

And then, suddenly, in the middle of one round of questioning, the interrogator simply got up and walked out. He left the shelter entirely, with no warning, no explanation, no anything. My jaw dropped. Was he ill? Was that a mind game he was playing with Evil Hagrid?

As quickly as we could, the case officer and I slipped out the side exit of the shelter and raced around front to see what was going on. The interrogator was already well across the gravel lot, heading into another nearby building. "Be right back," he yelled.

"Oh," the interrogator added, with a gesture in Evil Hagrid's general direction, "don't let him leave." Then he turned and kept walking.

I froze in my tracks. The MP who'd escorted Evil Hagrid into the shelter was nowhere to be found. I glanced at the spindly case officer and guessed that he and I were the same weight — and that even combined, we might equal Evil Hagrid's size. There had been nothing inside the shelter to chain that giant to. How on earth would we stop him if he wanted to leave?

"Do you have a gun?" I asked the case officer.

"No," he said. "You?"

"Uh-uh."

We looked back at the pyramidal bomb shelter.

"Okay," the officer said. He ran to the outside of the shelter and walked up one side of the pyramid. Then he shimmied his wispy frame out to the edge of the stone header above the main entranceway.

"If he comes out," the officer said, "tell me and I will jump on him." He made a gesture that looked like a high dive. I couldn't tell if he was joking. I think we were both being sarcastic at first, then realized this really was our only option to slow him down, which was all we really needed to do.

I thought for a minute. "Maybe Percy —"

Then I caught myself. I'd completely forgotten about our loyal translator sitting there alone in the bomb shelter with a murderer. Oh, God, I thought.

I sneaked back through the side exit into the dirty passageway. I took a quick glance into the central room, where Evil Hagrid was still seated with his back to the door. I could see that Percy, seated in front of him, farthest from me, was managing to act like this was routine. They were even chatting a little, although given their size difference, Percy had to have felt far more like the captive at that point. An eternity seemed to tick by. I couldn't imagine what was going through our translator's mind.

Seeing no way to help in there, I hustled back out the side door of the shelter, did my anti-scorpion shimmy, then raced around to the front, waving my arms the whole time to keep "Spider-Man" — the case officer — from jumping on my head. Thankfully, when I got there, I saw the interrogator heading back to the shelter.

"All right," he said nonchalantly as he walked past me. "I'm back."

He offered no explanation, and I was too frenzied to ask.

"Okay," I said. The case officer climbed down from atop the doorway.

I'm still not sure exactly what Percy said to Evil Hagrid during those harried few minutes when they were alone, but it seemed to have worked, at least relatively speaking. Evil Hagrid soon offered the most relaxed account of his intelligence work that any of us had heard to that point. Whether he was rattled by the change of scenery, felt some sense of gratitude to us for protecting him from a made-up prison riot, or just enjoyed the one-on-one conversation with a fellow native Arabic speaker, we felt he was being honest. As was typical, Evil Hagrid offered no grand revelations, but the quest to gather a few new pieces of intelligence and corroborate a few working theories had been a success.

For me, it marked an interesting interlude in the former IIS officer's time in detention, which continued long after I left Iraq. Following that day in the bomb shelter, Evil Hagrid repeatedly told other Agency questioners just what he'd told us: he had no knowledge of any relationship between Iraq and al Qaida or of WMD stockpiles. Those answers continually contradicted the narrative being put forth by the White House, apparently frustrating the administration no end.

Evil Hagrid may have been evil, and possibly a murderer, but he was in prison for being a former Baath Party official.

CHAPTER 7

Strategy, What Strategy?

Walking back to my cot late that night, after sending a cable about Evil Hagrid, I couldn't let go of the White House fixation on him and figures like him. Why were we wasting our time with those guys?

Sure, I understood that the coalition needed to be comfortable that former IIS elements didn't have a dangerous counterattack waiting up their sleeves. But outside the airport perimeter during May and June of 2003, more than one US soldier was killed each day. Pressing former government officers for historical information was quintessential backward-looking analysis at a time when the seeds of chaos in Iraq were already being sown—whether anyone in the administration wanted to acknowledge it or not. That was the forward-looking component I felt was missing from the conversation.

I had not been privy to the five-phase plan the Pentagon had sketched out before the war, but entering the terminal that night, I tried to put myself in the position of a war strategist. The US government's initial planning and decision making (Phase 0) had led seamlessly to the positioning of initial coalition forces in the region (Phase I), which had enabled the attack on Hussein's regime (Phase II). Phase III, the complete and systematic destruction of the regime, was then under way—both militarily and administratively. And that's where I stopped following the logic.

I later had a conversation with a military officer who was assigned to US Central Command days before the invasion. When he arrived, he walked into the middle of a Hawaiian-themed party—complete with Hawaiian shirts—hosted by General Tommy Franks. His first questions were: Where are the war plans? And what is our strategy afterward? He was met with a blank stare.

With Iraq's dictatorship overthrown, the Coalition Provisional Authority, or CPA, had been established in Baghdad in its place. The CPA was the placeholder government tasked with keeping Iraq together long enough to enable democratic elections and the transfer of power to its elected leader. The head of the CPA was effectively Iraq's temporary president—US diplomat L. Paul Bremer III, whose appointment may have had more to do with his longtime friendship with Scooter Libby than his experience as former ambassador to the Netherlands and chairman of the bipartisan National Commission on Terrorism. Regardless, just as I had arrived in Iraq, Bremer had enacted his first two administrative orders, which hit Iraq as hard as any mortar rounds.

In an effort to fully cleanse the new government of Hussein's legacy, CPA Order Number 1 decreed that former Baath officials could not have roles in Iraq's future unified government. "Noting the grave concern of Iraqi society regarding the threat posed by the continuation of Ba'ath Party networks and personnel in the administration of Iraq," the order read, "members of the Ba'ath Party...are her[e]by removed from their positions and banned from future employment in the public sector."

I later came to realize that Doug Feith was the architect of this plan. It was quickly blessed by Rumsfeld without allowing time for consideration by the National Security Council.

I had been stunned by what seemed like such a cavalier dismissal of roughly eighty-five thousand government workers—including the leadership of ministries that oversaw the hospitals as well as communications, electrical, and transportation infrastructure, and more. Most of us at the CIA, including then director Tenet, had been shocked by the move. "We knew nothing about it until *de-Baathification* was a fait accompli," Tenet later wrote. "Clearly, this was a critical policy decision, yet there was no [National Security Council] Principals meeting to debate the move." But Bremer felt strongly that those party members were the "true believers" in Hussein's regime, he later wrote in his memoir, and thus they needed to go. Clearly, I decided as I walked past another taped-off restroom in our terminal, the CIA would just have to forget about hiring someone to fix our plumbing.

CPA Order Number 2 completely disbanded the Iraqi security forces, as Washington decided that Baghdad should build new ones from scratch. Suddenly the ranks of the unemployed included some 385,000 former Iraqi soldiers; 285,000 workers from the Ministry of Interior, including police officers and other domestic security officers; and 50,000 guards from Hussein's presidential security units, including the Republican Guard. Almost overnight, a half million Iraqis were without jobs. Most were in desperate need of a paycheck, and all seemed very angry.

The sad irony was that those orders made in the name of stability virtually guaranteed the opposite. They alienated hundreds of thousands of Iraqis while simultaneously collapsing their social and economic infrastructure and crippling their everyday security. The CPA's first two orders directly created the potential for the kinds of rogue former-Iraqi-government elements the White House had been fixated upon. Whether their anger might lead aggrieved former soldiers to align with the rising tide of foreign fighters in Iraq was of decided interest to me.

I could tell at the time that those everyday security considerations resonated with me more than they did with some of my coworkers in Iraq. By July of that year, two months after the CPA decrees, I could sense a shift in attitudes on the ground. On my periodic drives from BIAP into Baghdad, I saw fewer people on the streets. On the sidewalks, passersby glared at me rather than glanced. That included Iraqi women, who when I first arrived in country had been generous and friendly to me. By then, they were traveling only in groups, and it appeared that they went about on foot as little as possible.

The reason for that development, I feared, had to do with the sharp increase in anecdotal reports we'd been receiving of sexual assaults and abductions of women and children. The CPA-mandated disbanding of Iraqi police and investigative units, which preceded the apparent spike in violence, also guaranteed that there would be little comprehensive documentation of it. Identifying the perpetrators was equally hard to do. But the toll on the victims was becoming immense. I read one Human Rights Watch report, released in July, that detailed the cases of two dozen women and children who'd been raped during the previous few weeks. That growing trend, Human Rights Watch concluded, was "keeping [women] in their homes, out of schools, and away from work and looking for employment."

Unfortunately, I found, as much as the US government focused on interdicting and eliminating obvious weapons of war in Iraq, it seemed to pay little mind to the prevalence of sexualized violence there. In the hypermasculine business of war, where combatants' masculinity is always insecure, rape offers a brutal avenue through which men can assert their physical superiority. That horrific tool of war generates far fewer headlines, yet its ramifications can be similarly destructive. In Iraq, where the women I passed on the sidewalk were largely responsible for the day-to-day well-being of the children and the elderly, abuses and fears that disrupted their daily lives also tore at the larger fabric of their families, affecting fathers and husbands as well. I'm sure none of the male war architects back in Washington had thought to factor female engagement into their plans for Iraq—but I'm convinced that by the summer of 2003, it was one obvious reason why US forces weren't actually being greeted as liberators.

On a more tangible level, I was also convinced at the time that overlooking those assaults allowed us to miss tactical clues about the road ahead. The sheer numbers of and sudden increase in sexualized assaults in Iraq, I was hearing, were far outside the norm for the country's cultured, largely well-educated society. The trend seemed to me far more reminiscent of the endless assaults that were seen as mere patriarchal privilege throughout the tribal areas of Afghanistan and other foreign extremist strongholds. That it was now happening in Iraq, I thought, might be a real indicator of whom, exactly, the coalition was up against.

I knew rape had the potential to become a grotesque recruiting tool for an extremist group. Wayward men might be attracted to the cause, thanks in part to the perverse theology that encouraged them to assault non-Muslim women. Meanwhile, for Muslim women victims, who were believed to have brought shame on their families, there was an even more harrowing possibility: becoming weapons themselves. Many raped women believed that under strict Sharia law, their families' "honor" could be restored through their holy martyrdom.

———

Back at our terminal following the Evil Hagrid fiasco, I finally made it to the "bedroom." It was dark at that hour — 1:00 a.m. Sitting on my cot with a late-night "mystery" MRE in hand, I realized how clearly my frustration with the government's blind spots in Iraq was beginning to color my attitude on a daily basis.

———

In a literal sense, by the summer of 2003, almost six months after the invasion, the military operation in Iraq no longer featured the battle lines and face-to-face opposition that defined traditional large-scale engagements. We had won that part of the fight; the Pentagon was no longer worried about whether it could take and hold ground. To complete the final push to eradicate Hussein's regime and other tricky individual targets, military planners had decided that small, nimble units would be free to organize raids and crash through doors with blinding efficiency in small-scale battles the American public would rarely know anything about. Achieving that vision, however, required following through on a collaborative combat structure three decades in the making—one that would cast a long shadow over my career with the CIA.

When I arrived in Iraq, that secretive collection of special operators was made up of members of the army special operators, navy special operators, and other units, including coalition forces. The task force that encompassed all the units was also based at BIAP. The Chinooks I heard flying low over the terminal in the wee hours of the morning almost certainly served as transportation for their missions.

The task force operators had been focused on searching out figures from the Bush administration's deck of terrorist playing cards. The US military had proved themselves to be equal-opportunity snatch-and-grab artists, conducting multiple weekly missions to apprehend suspected insurgent bomb makers and handle other high-stakes engagements.

I noticed there were differences between the army special operators and the navy special operators. The army guys had a steely focus about them, emphasizing thorough plans and clear processes for their missions. They were almost aloof at times, and I came to appreciate their quiet professionalism. Talking to navy special operators, on the other hand, tended to feel like being back at a college fraternity party. They were the ones who tended to boast or get in your face. Though as members of perhaps the world's most iconic special operations unit, who'd then been handpicked to join an even more elite combined task force, they had reason to be boastful. And the creative flexibility they demonstrated on the fly was at times remarkable.

Regardless of their origin, the job for the men of the task force was both technically and tactically unconventional. In a technical sense, their focus on surgical strikes and close-quarters combat differentiated them from larger military units that fought conventional battles. In a fight as lopsided as the one between highly trained US special operators and bedraggled insurgents, however, killing and capturing enemy personnel was the easy part. The challenge was finding people and identifying the next target on such an irregular battlefield. "A single person can move around and hide," Defense Secretary Rumsfeld told reporters at the time. "The people on the Ten Most Wanted List for the FBI have been on that list for decades. So it's hard." The thing that made the task force tactically unconventional was that in order to achieve its goals, those men needed outside intelligence specialists to pinpoint which doors to crash through and to help make sense of what they found there. In short, they needed the Agency.

The operation in Iraq took place just as the CIA's collaboration with elite military units under the special operations vision that had been first established in 1980 was being formalized. It was only once a new enemy emerged on September 11, 2001, that the operational collaboration rose to such prominence. For military planners, its effectiveness had been proved in the weeks following 9/11, when Agency personnel working closely with special operations forces, or SOF, in Afghanistan had dealt crippling blows to the Taliban there. Following that success, the model was implemented in Iraq as well.

The task force fell under the authority of the Pentagon's Special Operations Command. The task force didn't actually have to coordinate with the Pentagon on specific missions, unless the target fell outside the list of most-wanted former Iraqi regime members. Otherwise, SOF had control of the "target deck"—our computerized list of people we wanted to apprehend—and the data we could use to find them.

In almost no time, that list expanded to include names the operators gleaned from intelligence sources and brought back from missions. Other times, my interviews at Cropper turned up the name of someone I thought might have ties to Saddam's former regime or Zarqawi's network. Regardless of where the lead came from, as soon as a new figure was highlighted and located, the task force's preparations would be under way for a new surgical strike.

Early on, the cooperation between the CIA and the military was still being worked out. It was the first time I'd had a hand in the front end of the targeting process, identifying people I specifically wanted to debrief as opposed to spending my days in the plywood shack interviewing whomever someone else happened to pick up. From the comfort of my desk back at the terminal, the process was revelatory, the independence and immediacy of it almost addictive. I'd never imagined intelligence could turn into action so fast.

Through it all, however, the Agency and the military remained two distinctly different cultures. And as the wheels of that intelligence strike machine began spinning even faster, two aspects of the process began making me decidedly frustrated.

In war, there is an important concept known as the OODA loop. First mapped out by a former air force pilot who'd flown fighter jets during the Korean War, the loop maps out the observe-orient-decide-act planning process that occurs prior to every mission. In crafting a theory to clarify the situational decision making that unfolds in combat, John Boyd, the former pilot, must have been at least partly inspired by dogfights—rapid, close-quarters engagements among small groups of aircraft. There were at least some parallels to these missions—and parallels to the thinking that underpinned them—in the operations the task force prosecuted on the ground.

I could appreciate that, particularly during manhunts, a quick OODA loop offered a tactical advantage. If we could compress the time the enemy had to reorient itself in response to a task force mission, we had a better chance to drive the action on the battlefield—what military strategists thought of as shaping the environment rather than adapting to it. I wasn't excited about the task force members' plan to achieve that, however: they suggested that even a few hours of intelligence-turnaround time back at BIAP could be shortened if I simply reviewed documents, photographs, and other intelligence being picked up with suspects on the scene, in real time. A couple of operators wanted me to join them during the raids—as a ride-along. If I could *observe* enemy combatants at the moment they were apprehended, they said, the task force could *orient* itself with the newfound information, *decide* on the next target, and *act* on that more quickly—perhaps without even returning to base first.

So on one predawn morning I found myself strapping on a bullet-resistant vest at BIAP and climbing into the back of a Humvee for the first of a half dozen raids. Details of those missions remain classified, but in broad strokes, our target that first night was a former Iraqi Intelligence Service official who was lending his bomb-making prowess to insurgents. At the time, the technician was a priority not so much because of his past but because of the future carnage he might enable. Heavily outgunned insurgents were settling on roadside bombs as the ultimate force multiplier against the coalition, and, we believed, this former official was a key component of that. Disrupting the efforts of technicians such as him was rapidly growing in importance.

By mid-2003, the rudimentary roadside bombs being used by insurgents consisted of charges made from mortar rounds or leftover artillery shells that were lashed together and hidden among the garbage strewn along the sides of the roadways. Sometimes ball bearings were packed in, too, to increase the shrapnel and maximize damage. The bombs all had a power source, usually a tiny battery, that provided just enough power to activate a detonator, which in turn set off the charge. The trickiest part of the devices—really, their Achilles' heel—was the trigger, which goosed that power source to set the chain reaction in motion.

At the time, the bulk of the triggers used by insurgents were still hardwired to the bombs. That meant that once a soldier spotted a device, the bleak so-called fight at the roadside was as straightforward as locating the wire snaking off into the distance, then shooting the person at the other end of it. But as more sophisticated bomb makers integrated into the enemy ranks, the technological prowess spiked. The devices began to include radio receivers that could be triggered wirelessly from a half mile away with garage door openers, wireless doorbells, or remote-controlled toy car controllers, making bombers vastly harder to spot and increasingly difficult to stop.

As those horribly iconic roadside bombs went on to kill thousands of Americans throughout the war, billions of US dollars would be spent engineering vehicles to better withstand the attacks. SOF, however, had a different approach—one that aimed "left of boom" on the timeline: get the bomb makers before the devices are even built. I couldn't argue with that logic. But I could hardly digest what it looked like in practice.

Climbing into a pickup, I packed in among SOF with long guns, side arms strapped to their legs, and extra ammunition bulging the pockets on the outsides of their bulky vests. Folding my hands in my lap, I surveyed the men around me; they appeared almost as if we were headed to get an ice cream cone. My adrenaline nonetheless began to surge. The bomb maker, we believed, was operating out of a nearby neighborhood in a quiet section of Baghdad.

Twenty minutes later, the pickup turned off the main road into the bomb maker's neighborhood, and our driver shut off the vehicle's lights. Someone in a second task force Humvee radioed that he had circled around to the opposite end of the block, walling off the roadway.

There was a last moment of silence as we pulled to a stop; then the doors flew open. The team spread out across the street, then filed forward along the beige brick walls toward a metal doorway outside the technician's house. I crouched low in the backseat, awaiting the all clear to follow. In the moonlight, I could make out a hand signal from the lead task force member in line; then the team burst through the doorway.

Even from a distance, their maneuvers were stunning. The damage those units unleashed on people and property was immediate. Just as in a large OODA loop, they'd explained to me, in a small, close-quarters battle your role can be either proactive or reactive. Proactive is always better.

Soon one of the soldiers emerged from the metal doorway and waved for me to follow. No one was inside the home when we arrived, he said, but someone had clearly been there recently. Inside we found a series of radio controllers. Nearby, a few doctored plastic toy car chassis sat on a workbench, and we found other indications that the technician had been trying to convert them into rolling, guidable bombs. We packed up his devices and equipment to bring with us back to base; if we couldn't grab the bomb maker that night, I took some consolation in the idea that losing all his equipment would at least slow him down.

Days later I joined another late-night raid in Baghdad. The intelligence about the occupants of the residence was more uncertain, but we were trying to move quickly, to be proactive. There we missed our suspected insurgent target as well—but that didn't mean there was nobody home. This time, once the yelling and sounds of shattering glass subsided and I was waved over to enter the house, I found two people sitting on the floor surrounded by special operators. One, we quickly learned, was a male relative of the target, whom we had no indication would be there that night. The other appeared to be his son, whom I saw cowering behind his father's back.

"Are they useful?" one of the operators asked. Heads turned in my direction. My heart sank.

As many disquieting things as I'd seen during my days at Cropper, nothing unsettled me as much as the children's wing of the prison. Most of the kids landed there simply because they happened to be with an adult when that person got arrested. Once back at BIAP, those adults were logged into Cropper, and the children were shuffled into their own large holding pen. In theory, the kids were free to leave when a guardian came to pick them up—but what if their lone guardian was locked inside Cropper? If those kids had other guardians, how were those adults supposed to locate a child who suddenly disappeared in the middle of the night?

In the beginning of my time at the prison, when I recognized that a child had been there for a week or more, I had visited through the wire to make sure he or she was relatively okay. I couldn't get the children out, and I couldn't promise them anything, but maybe a friendly face would be worth something. Anything, I hoped, was better than having them spending endless hours sitting on the packed dirt, waiting. As the population of Cropper's children's wing began ballooning along with its adult population, I visited less and less. Not being able to reverse the course of war became my eventual unraveling.

Soon after, I stopped joining SOF teams on missions. I had no misgivings about trying to stop people who presented a threat to coalition troops, but I was not trained to be on those missions. In other words, I was pretty sure that I would either cost an operator his life or lose my own. I thought I might have more to contribute by trying to piece together intelligence that allowed us to focus on specific targets.

It was starting to become clear that devotion to absolute speed at these raids compressed the OODA loop, thereby de-emphasizing analysis of the intelligence and undervaluing the effectiveness of the mission—and it got innocent people, including children, thrown in prison.

I thought about that one night after my last ride-along as I heard another Chinook disappearing into the distance. I thought about whom those operators were going after. I knew that when they returned, the helicopter would likely be carrying Cropper's newest detainees, and I hoped that in a day or two I'd find myself in the shack with them. Percy, Ron, and I could get to work, generating new leads in the hunt for former Baath officials, Zarqawi's network, or whatever the day's work happened to be.

But I knew all bets were off if they passed through another camp—a place we called purgatory—first. And that would only make everything harder.

For years, a camp on the outpost of the southwestern edge of Baghdad International Airport didn't officially exist. Thirteen years later, it is only begrudgingly acknowledged. But Hussein's former interrogation chamber was always terribly real. Under the command of the task force, it wasn't repurposed, and to many of Cropper's detainees it was purgatory.

With its rows of fencing and permanent guards at the gates, the camp didn't look much different from any other camp at the airport. That it blended in made it an ideal location for the task force's headquarters. But inside, the camp was very different.

The main facility was designed around four interrogation chambers, where SOF sometimes attempted to gather their own intelligence from the detainees they brought back to base. The "soft room," I'd begun hearing by the summer of 2003, which offered couches and even tea service, was held out as a reward for cooperative detainees. The rectangular "red" and "blue" rooms, each about six feet wide by fifteen feet long, were standard, stripped-down chambers where arrested Iraqis were questioned more forcefully.

But the detainees who lied, or who the task force thought sufficiently uncooperative, got dragged to the "black room," a garage-size cell lacquered from floor to ceiling in black paint, as one former interrogator later told Human Rights Watch. There was a table in the center, which held a boom box and a computer, and behind it a token chair or two. Everyone knew those chairs weren't for sitting; more often, handcuffed detainees ended up suspended from the eighteen-inch-long hooks that hung from the ceiling.

Multiple times per week, unmarked helicopters landed at the camp. Task force members dragged shackled detainees, clad in blue jumpsuits and blindfolded by goggles covered in duct tape, through the intake center to be registered. Many were then moved along to Motel 6, as the task force called it—a kennel of some eighty-five plywood holding cells that reeked of excrement. Many of those cells weren't big enough for the prisoners to stand up in.

When coalition forces and SOF members delivered new prisoners to the camp, they never did so alone. They were always accompanied by at least one American soldier, who was officially recorded as having made the capture. The rationale, according to an extensive investigation that later ran in the *Guardian* newspaper, was that the arrangement "enabled the British government to side-step a Geneva convention clause that would have obliged it to demand the return of any prisoner transferred to the US once it became apparent that they were not being treated in accordance with the convention."

By mid-2003, as the Agency and the military disagreed about the pace of SOF missions, those task force personnel began creating their own interrogation tactics on the fly—some an outgrowth of broad-stroke guidance in the *US Army Field Manual on Intelligence Interrogation*. But there was another document, a one-page set of guidelines that was considered a "logical interpretation" of some of the techniques in the field manual. This document listed approaches such as "Fear Up Harsh," "Fear Up Mild," and "Pride and Ego Up." The techniques were loosely modeled on torture tactics employed by the Soviet Union and other Cold War enemies of the United States and included relatively innocuous-sounding things such as dietary manipulation, the use of muzzled dogs, sleep adjustment, and sensory deprivation.

In practice, those techniques led to members of the task force beating prisoners with rifle butts and spitting in their faces. The urgency to organize new missions completely overrode long-standing tenets of effective interrogation, as savviness and subtlety were thrown aside in favor of blunt-force trauma. One former interrogator, later given the pseudonym Jeff Perry by Human Rights Watch, recalled an incident in which a detainee was "stripped naked, put in the mud and sprayed with the hose...[Then] he was taken out of the mud and put next to an air conditioner. It was extremely cold, freezing, and he was put back in the mud and sprayed."

"This happened all night," Perry added. "Everybody [at camp] knew about it."

Other Defense Department personnel reported seeing blotches on detainees' clothing and welts on their bodies. Around that time, the task force began firing paintball guns at detainees and hung a sign referring to it as the High Five Paintball Club. On that same sign, a motto read: NO BLOOD, NO FOUL. *If they don't bleed*, the message was, *they can't prosecute*—not that that message was always adhered to.

When Iraqi major general Hussam Mohammed Amin, the six of clubs in the deck of Personality Identification Playing Cards, rotated through purgatory, he claims he was hooded and beaten with "some kind of special metal stick" while task force interrogators demanded the location of weapons stockpiles. The assault left him with gashes in his face that required stitches.

Medical evaluations would corroborate that detainees at the camp had been punched and kicked and even had baseballs tied into their mouths. I saw task force teams returning to the airport with pickup trucks full of new detainees, stacked like cordwood in the truck bed. Once, I watched a group of detainees, black hoods or burlap sacks drawn tight over their heads, pulled from the back of a SOF truck. Not long before, a group of US forces had been kidnapped nearby and their Humvee stolen; I later learned that vehicle was found in the possession of these detainees — the last of whom spilled from the back of the truck and hit the ground with a sickening thud. I assumed that by then he was dead; the operators led the other detainees inside and just left him in the dirt.

To the extent that I or any other outsider could decipher it, the command structure at the camp was as horizontal as any I've seen in the military. Everyone at the base went by first names, pseudonyms or not, and beyond one or two rotating commanding officers there, ranks were an unnecessary distraction. "It worked better that way," Jeff Perry later told Human Rights Watch. "You didn't have to worry about sucking up to whoever and pleasing this person or that person."

The depths of the depravity at the camp have largely only been revealed by task force interrogators suffering crises of conscience. At the time, investigators weren't allowed inside, including those sent by the International Committee of the Red Cross, who must be permitted under the Geneva Conventions to "visit with prisoners privately, examine conditions of confinement to ensure the Conventions' standards are being met and distribute relief supplies." Yet as Perry told Human Rights Watch, "The commander was insistent that [the Red Cross] wouldn't come, and that they never would come because [camp] was just very secretive." Perry added that interrogators were assured that secrecy "was very necessary for the efficacy of the operation."

Only once, in the summer of 2003, did I ever go inside the camp. I decided immediately not to go back. That decision was soon codified by a mandate from Langley, as stories of detainee abuse at the camp began spreading back to the States. By August of that year, the CIA had become so concerned about goings-on at the camp that it barred its employees from visiting the camp at all. Still, the activities there reverberated on the other side of the airport.

When SOF finished with individuals at the camp, they often moved them over to Cropper for longer-term detention. There I had access to them, and in my little plywood office, I saw men sitting across from me who were almost unrecognizable from their intake mug shots, taken days earlier. I was always told that the bruising and swelling that covered so much of their bodies came from their "resisting arrest."

I was certainly not immune to the urge to force someone to talk. When you're in that moment, looking for a guy building improvised explosive devices specifically to slaughter your friends, you're not full of empathy. I'm confident that most of the members of the task force I worked with weren't running on blood lust but on adrenaline. For the most part, the violence at the camp wasn't born from a desire to hurt people but rather was perpetrated in service of a larger mission to *stop* people from hurting our troops, our allies, and innocent Iraqis. It has been said that the best defense is a good offense, and at the camp, those operators were extraordinarily aggressive in the hopes of saving lives. Bad people provoke bad things out of even good people.

Beyond the stomach-churning sight of a battered victim sitting in my shack at Cropper, however, I couldn't conceal my frustration over the squandered opportunities their mistreatment represented. Those prisoners were physically and psychologically broken, rendering even the most knowledgeable of them unreliable sources of information. Either they would say anything to not be sent back to the camp, or the fear, anger, and battery had robbed them of the kind of nuanced cues in speech and body language that Ron and I might have seized upon to tease out additional information. My concerns about the camp grew as fuzzy, coerced intelligence led to more SOF missions to useless locations and a rise in innocent Iraqis being apprehended. Strictly from a tactical perspective, if we really hoped to get anywhere in the hunt for key individuals in Iraq, beating information out of people wasn't just against the rules; it was a waste of our time.

Even that same army field manual from which the military extrapolated some of its enhanced techniques agreed, explaining that "experience indicates that the use of force is not necessary to gain the cooperation of sources for interrogation." Reading that, I felt validated: even as a relatively new questioner, I might still be doing things the smart way, at least according to that manual. "The direct approach is often called no approach at all," it read, "but it is the most effective of all the approaches."

Over the course of the summer of 2003, it was tough to detail exactly how much progress was being made in either my assigned duties in Iraq or the ones I felt should have taken precedence. Hussein's former government leadership was on the run, and with them went any hope of scouring information about hypothetical secretive plans prior to 9/11. But the high-level detainees I'd already spoken with had dismissed that theory, and the run-of-the-mill insurgent characters I found at Cropper couldn't possibly have that kind of official inside information. Meanwhile, Zarqawi and his close followers had also scattered since the post-invasion missile strikes on his Khurmal compound. Ron and I recognized a marked increase in the number of foreign fighters spilling into Iraq, but even if that was Zarqawi's network reconstituting itself, it didn't seem to have enough solid infrastructure for those foot soldiers I debriefed to map it out.

Suddenly our attention was drawn elsewhere. Out of the blue, in June of 2003, a political firestorm was whipped up back at Langley over rumblings from the Pentagon that a trove of Iraqi government documents had been uncovered and that they cast explosive new light on Hussein's efforts to obtain WMD and to take part in terrorism plots against the United States. Any attention I'd hoped to pay to Zarqawi that week instantly took a backseat as the White House was poised to crow about a paper trail that justified the war. Executives in the Agency eager to play political games and appease the administration would be happy to let them.

The implications in the documents made global news when, a few months later, London's *Sunday Telegraph* ran a front-page exclusive describing supposed documentary evidence that Mohammed Atta, the al Qaida mastermind of 9/11, had received terror training in Baghdad. It announced: "Details of Atta's visit to the Iraqi capital in the summer of 2001, just weeks before he launched the most devastating terrorist attack in US history, are contained in a top secret memo written to Saddam Hussein, the then Iraqi president, by Tahir Jalil Habbush al-Tikriti, the former head of the Iraqi Intelligence Service."

What we came to know as the Habbush letter did indeed contain explosive accusations. The paper was dated July 1, 2001. It said that Atta "displayed extraordinary effort" in his training and had demonstrated his ability to lead a team "responsible for attacking the targets that we have agreed to destroy." To the Bush administration, it represented ironclad evidence of a direct operational link between Iraq, al Qaida, and the 9/11 attacks. Furthermore, if authentic, the

Habbush letter would represent a damning critique of our Iraq unit, which battled against that purported connection at every turn — and even more so for me, because the IIS and figures such as Habbush were my focus.

If real, the letter could have a substantial impact upon the way the Agency approached its work in Baghdad. If those former government officials had a hand in training a 9/11 mastermind, we should have approached them as war criminals instead of merely high-value detainees.

Immediately, Katherine, our unit's no-nonsense chief, and the rest of our Langley branch were skeptical about its authenticity. The letter's fundamental assertions about Atta didn't match up with anything we'd heard before, for one thing. Furthermore, I knew that Iraqi intelligence officials were notoriously conservative; they rarely if ever put anything so brazen and incriminating in writing. On the other hand, if the letter was fake, it would seem to represent a shocking and extreme attempt to defend the war effort and simultaneously discredit our branch at the CIA. That didn't make much sense, either.

In the hope of determining whether the letter was authentic or not, Katherine divvied up the investigative duties. One member of our unit called the FBI, one reached out to the Secret Service — and I drew up a list of the highest-ranking officials detained at BIAP whom I could drag back to my plywood shack.

The FBI was important because their units had compiled detailed records of airline travel, ATM withdrawals, cell-phone usage and hotel stays that indicated Atta was living in Florida and crisscrossing the United States in the summer of 2001, not traveling in the Middle East. One document they passed along to our unit, classified as Law Enforcement Sensitive, showed that during the last few days in June — the time frame in which the Habbush letter asserted Atta was training in Baghdad — he "conducted extensive travel," making stops in Florida, Boston, New York, New Jersey, and Las Vegas. Almost all his movements were accounted for: on June 27, 2001, for instance, the FBI recorded Atta flying from Fort Lauderdale to Boston. The next morning, he flew first class from Boston to San Francisco, switched planes, and ultimately landed in Las Vegas that afternoon at 2:41 p.m. There he rented a Chevrolet Malibu from an Alamo rental-car office, set up an account at an Internet café called the Cyber Zone, and checked into a cheap EconoLodge motel on Las Vegas Boulevard nestled in among a line of seedy strip joints barely two blocks from the local FBI office.

Records were similarly thorough for Atta's movements over the following few weeks. His only international travel that summer occurred on July 7, when he boarded a flight from Boston to Zurich, then transferred on to Spain. He returned to the United States on July 19, 2001. I thought Atta seemed pretty clearly to be casing America's air travel system; the suggestion that he was physically in training eight thousand miles away in Iraq seemed dubious at best.

Meanwhile, in Baghdad, every detainee I questioned suggested the allegations about Atta's training were bogus. The former government officials being held at Cropper pointed out that, among other things, the chain of command described in the letter was fake, down to the incorrect titles. The idea that Habbush, the former head of the IIS, wouldn't know his own official hierarchy strained credulity at best.

Our unit also consulted with the leading government experts in forgery, the United States Secret Service (USSS).

Along with its highest-profile duty—protecting the president— the service has other branches that do everything from detect counterfeit currency to monitor networks of electronic crime. One branch, some 120 men and women strong, collects ink. More than 8,500 samples of ink, in fact, which have been sent to the USSS from manufacturers since the 1920s.

Each new ink formulation prompts a new delivery, with samples arriving from around the world as liquid in a bottle or perhaps a new batch of pens or refills. Each time, the team scribbles a sample of the ink onto Whatman filter paper, grade 2—hence the paper's common nickname, scribble sheets—tucks it into a protective sleeve inside a binder, then stores it in dark cabinets to protect it against degradation from light, temperature, and humidity. The USSS proudly oversees the largest ink library in the world—and we needed their expertise.

That team performs various tests for law enforcement investigations, gauging ink's reaction to ultraviolet and infrared light, even picking it apart at the chemical level to study the multiple color bands that make up something as seemingly simple as black. Our unit requested something more basic: static dating to determine exactly which ink was used in that Habbush letter and when it was created. If the ink used on the memo wasn't available in July of 2001, the note couldn't have been written at that time.

Within days of examining the memo, the Secret Service had concluded that the ink was inconsistent with types manufactured around the note's purported date. The coup de grâce: they found that the piece of paper it was written on wasn't manufactured until after the July 2001 date scribbled on it. Coupled with what the FBI knew of Atta's travels at the time and what I was hearing in Baghdad, there was no way the letter was real.

With all that information, Katherine made a trip to the White House. She told me later that she walked into Vice President Cheney's office. "The letter is fake," she insisted, laying out the details we'd uncovered. I wasn't in the room, but she told me the vice president was gracious and thanked her.

That a week of my time in Iraq was spent on such a backward-looking wild-goose chase was irritating. As I looked ahead, though, I thought the obvious follow-up questions were even more problematic: Who was behind the forgeries? Were they going to try to derail our work again? If so, how? Perhaps the Habbush letter was, we speculated, the product of an unhappy foreign government or even an al Qaida rival. But there was another unsettling possibility, too. None of us who sat through those murder boards could quite rule out sabotage by someone looking for a different ending.

Ultimately our Iraq unit never could conclude where the forgery came from. Simply establishing that the letter *was* a forgery was the most important part. Over the coming years, the question of the forgery would become the subject of a pair of official investigations from House and Senate oversight committees, though they accomplished little more than scoring political points. "The [Bush] administration figures who ordered and authored the apparent forgery—and their involvement in leaking it through foreign intelligence channels," John Conyers, Democrat of Michigan and chairman of the House judiciary committee, declared, "remain unidentified." For its part, the administration insisted, "the idea that the White House had anything to do with a forged letter purportedly from Habbush to Saddam is absurd."

CHAPTER 8

Special Friends

As emotionally draining as that summer in Iraq was, sporadic moments of silliness offered at least some sense of optimism about the country's future and our place in it. When I could step away from my plywood shack and SOF work, I enjoyed tagging along with Agency case officers on car rides away from BIAP. Sometimes those were sightseeing trips downtown — to the Victory Arches, for instance, the massive, crossed-swords monuments that form the entrance to Great Celebrations Square. Other times they were simple ice cream runs or trips into town for coffee, a luxury. At that point in my deployment I still couldn't wrap my mind around living off limited food when we could have been eating at restaurants in Baghdad, having authentic falafel. I had no supervision at all once my work was done for the day; if I wanted to eat at a restaurant, I chose someplace that wasn't full of Westerners — no need to tempt fate by dining in a target-rich environment — and went out to dinner. I think I always seemed more paranoid than most.

Tragically, soldiers were still dying. In general, whenever we left airport grounds I was more worried about the Glock 19 handgun on my own hip than about the weapons other people might be carrying. The Agency security officers I traveled with stressed that I shouldn't be unarmed, though after giving me a quick tutorial on handling and firing the 9mm weapon, they also determined that I should probably pull the trigger only if I was captured. There was little chance I'd actually hit the enemy with the handgun.

Back on base, meanwhile, I had a great coincidental reminder of home: one of my cousins, Commander Greg Erickson, was at the time a navy helicopter pilot flying missions for SOF. His Helicopter Combat Support Special Squadron 5, or HCS-5, was also based at the airport, so I saw him regularly. He and his squad mates were hard to miss. As many choppers as HCS-5 had, they didn't have much in the way of ground transportation, so Greg and his team commandeered one of the ancient orange Mercedes-Benz dump trucks abandoned on airport grounds. They scribbled a logo on the side of the rounded cab, and "the Great Pumpkin" became a staple for transporting pilots on BIAP.

Greg's squadron's mission in the summer of 2003 was primarily overwatch, and primarily with SOF. After the navy special operators selected a target, Greg would take an active part in planning the missions in order to provide overhead coverage — checking traffic, checking the site before they got there, and providing close air support or medevac service if necessary. In military words, his mission was to be ISTAR: intelligence, surveillance, target acquisition, and reconnaissance.

———

Greg told me about his very first mission, in which they were assigned to take down a house. They had a squirter — a guy running out the back door as the navy special operators' trucks came to the front. Greg followed him into a field, and the navy special operators were able to capture him. That's how close the helicopters could get to a target.

The Defense Department's General Order Number 1 kept things at the airport from getting too rowdy. The Pentagon mandate prohibited all military personnel from the "introduction, purchase, possession, sale, transfer, manufacture, or consumption" of alcohol, drugs, pornography, and most anything else that might offend Muslim sensibilities. The CIA, on the other hand, had quietly set up a bar within walking distance of our terminal.

Known as the HVT Bar, or the High-Value-Target Bar, the BIAP dive was set up in a nearby abandoned building—just the latest in a long line of Agency war-zone speakeasies. In 2001, as CIA personnel helped defeat the Taliban in Afghanistan, the "Talibar" appeared in the Agency's hotel headquarters, in downtown Kabul. Back at BIAP, the bar was only open late at night and featured naked light-bulbs that swung from the ceiling and cast long shadows across the sweaty patrons and captured artillery that decorated the walls. I really wasn't sure where the alcohol came from. The selection was sparse for the first few weeks, and I had enough arak to last me a lifetime. Over the years, a few different commemorative T-shirts were printed, displaying the sort of testosterone-fueled message likely designed by a guy. One shirt had HVT BAR: BAGHDAD printed on the sleeve and the words CHICKS DIG GUYS IN BODY ARMOR written across the chest. On the back, it read GUYS DIG CHICKS WITH GUNS. I don't own one.

That Fourth of July, the Agency set up a small celebration outside the bar, sharing its alcoholic bounty with a number of special operators and foreign intelligence service personnel we'd come to work with closely. After weeks of grinding away in Iraq, I was ready for a drink.

Around 3:00 p.m. that day, my cousin and his squadron motored over in the Great Pumpkin. Smoke wafted up from a nearby fire pit.

The meat—I heard it was antelope, though I was never quite sure—cooking over the pit was secured by a Navy SEAL who'd been spending his downtime on the grounds behind the airport, taking advantage of one of Hussein's former hunting preserves. A small sound system was rigged up for music. I wiped the dust off my sunglasses and cracked open a beer. As I settled into a lawn chair next to Greg, a smile crept across my face.

"Almost feels like home, huh?" he said, offering me a toast.

"Almost," I said, knocking my aluminum can against his.

That lucky family connection always provided a little respite from the daily drudgery in Iraq. If I didn't like the hot dogs and salad du jour at our palace, I would find Greg and we would frequent the air force mess, which always had better food.

Conversation inevitably returned to our day-to-day lives there, and I was struck by the differences in perception and understanding that could exist among those at the heart of the occupation.

"This isn't the war we should be fighting," I'd told Greg a few nights earlier. I'd invited him and other members of his squadron to our terminal to scavenge leftovers in its restaurant-style kitchen. "Al Qaida was our main threat after 9/11," I continued, picking through a plate of hot dogs with my hands. "Iraq wasn't even near the top of that list. And look around: you think the US government has any idea what it's doing when it comes to nation building?"

"How can you say that?" Greg shot back. He leaned back against an aluminum-plated countertop. "You want Hussein to nuke Israel? We're removing a corrupt and violent government to install a more stable one in its place. It's the right thing to do."

"But you can't replace every government you don't like," I told him. "Trust me, what you've been hearing is public spin; it's not actual intelligence." I pointed in the direction of Cropper. "Every single day, all those prisoners are telling me the same thing: there are no WMD, no terrorist connections, nothing." I could feel my blood pressure rising.

"If we want to find chemical weapons, we're in the wrong place," I proclaimed. "If we want to find al Qaida, we're in the wrong place." I sighed. "Why are we even here?"

That question had been looming ever larger over everything I experienced in Iraq that summer, from the terrible to the trivial. But as I sat there next to Greg and his squadron, watching the sun set on the Fourth of July, my preoccupations felt like a subject for another time.

As dusk settled, a few soldiers stumbled out of the makeshift CIA bar. General Order Number 1 had most people feeling pretty pent up, and because I was a woman and was breathing, one of the boys stopped to chat me up. He dropped down on one knee in the packed dirt right front of me, leaning on my leg so he could remain upright.

"You...are jush..." he said.

I was slightly taken by surprise at this Romeo's hard-to-resist expression of love. Even beyond the absurdity of the moment and my lack of interest, I couldn't imagine where this soldier expected we might explore his newly found feelings for me. It's not like there was much privacy on that base. My bed each night was surrounded by forty new "friends" in that Kremlinesque ballroom. No one had privacy—though that didn't stop some people. One evening I'd taken a shortcut through the palace and walked past a couple on a cot in the hallway in the midst of conscious coupling. "Any port in a storm" was clearly their rationale—maybe in more ways than one.

Regardless, I was happily unavailable. As I sat there smirking at Romeo, I had to consider things such as the gossip mill in those camps and the fact that the testosterone haze there creates damning double standards for the ways men and women are judged after those encounters. My fairly new relationship with Roger had weathered the distance remarkably well after a few months, even over e-mail and sporadic cell-phone calls. He'd just moved my belongings into our new house, and our wish list of renovations always gave us something to talk about. He'd acknowledged that with my being in Iraq, doing intense work, he'd begun to feel by comparison a bit like a muggle in our relationship—one of the laymen in the Harry Potter books who aren't blessed with the ability to perform magic. But he always made himself available to tell goofy stories or listen to me ramble even after the strangest of days and at the oddest of hours, and that was the best gift of all.

Following that Fourth of July party, I found a new benefit to being related to a pilot in Iraq: for a little adventure away from the base, nothing beats a helicopter.

As much as those Baghdad raids had given me a feel for the task force's ground transportation, I told Greg, I'd never been in a special operations chopper. I had no idea what that experience must be like. He and his squadron mates offered to rectify that situation. There was a reconnaissance mission in Ramadi, some sixty miles west of Baghdad, that was still in the planning stage. Given a little prep time, the task force teams used some of their free time to make practice runs.

"There's a source who's going to point out an insurgent safe house," Greg had said. "There's always room for one more on the chopper."

Soon afterward, when things quieted down at the plywood shack, my cousin found me an unused helmet and body armor and packed me into the back of a single-rotor SH-60 Seahawk.

The helmet was way too big; I was able to spin it 360 degrees around my head, but there didn't seem to be other options available so I kept quiet.

Greg wouldn't be joining us for the flight because he was in a mission-planning session, but he assured me I was in good hands. Outside the helicopter, the pilots finished their preflight check of the aircraft, then climbed into the cockpit. Greg stepped back from the starboard sliding cabin door and waved. As we lifted off, I watched BIAP slowly sink into a cloud of swirling sand. This is amazing, I thought. It'll be a perfect way to see more of the country.

What I hadn't been told was that sometime during the day, our flight plan had changed. Soon after takeoff, I could tell we weren't flying to Ramadi because the shadows weren't consistent with heading west, and I could see land I didn't recognize.

Looking out the window, I registered that there was a bar jutting out horizontally over the doorway on the outside of the helicopter. I'd casually noticed the thick, olive-drab rope pinned to it as I climbed into the Seahawk, but suddenly the fifty-foot coil of "fast rope" sitting by the cabin door took on vastly different meaning. These ropes are what tactical teams dangle outside a hovering helicopter, then slide down at just shy of breakneck speed when there is nowhere to land near their insertion point.

Moments later, I caught sight of tracer fire outside the helicopter. In front of me, the SEAL team leader pointed to the special operator on my right. "Do exactly what he says," the team leader mouthed over the noise of the rotors and air rushing through the cabin.

"My" SEAL offered me a quick crash course in key hand signals, among them the sweeping gesture that meant "move forward" and the clenched fist that meant "freeze." Then he added his new favorite as a nod to a movie that was frequently watched at BIAP, *Team America: World Police*: the upward arm sweep and the silent shriek that meant "panic."

I thought that signal might actually come in handy.

Soon the helicopter cleared a thicket of trees, hovering over the edge of a scrubby field that led to a little beige house in the distance.

The Seahawk began its descent. We'd clearly arrived at our destination. But the tension level inside the helicopter ratcheted up when we lost the advantage of altitude. As we set down in the field, urgency took over.

SEALs darted out of the helicopter, more than two hundred pounds of man and materiel apiece gliding in one effortless motion. My eyes narrowed; I felt like I was looking through a keyhole; was he really giving me that hand signal?

In retrospect, I don't know why I didn't grab the fast rope and strap myself to the helicopter like a three-year-old throwing a temper tantrum. I had no weapon, which was probably for the best. I could only see clearly for a few seconds at a time; the helmet didn't fit snugly on my head, so it slid down over my eyes if I wasn't holding it. Also, I'd just been taught a collection of hand signals, which suggested there might be any number of bad guys involved in whatever was about to happen. I'd seen enough of the aftermath of special operations raids to know that I wanted no part of the actual assault.

At the time, however, whining didn't seem appropriate. When my SEAL told me to follow him, I swung one leg out the door, then the other, and plopped down into a patch of grass. I crouched behind him and tried to focus on him. The helicopter lifted off right behind us.

"Careful," he mouthed, the whirring of the blades lifting off drowning out any sound. He was pointing off to our right.

Lying on its side in the packed dirt a few feet away was a matte-gray metal canister the shape of a soft-drink can. It had a white nylon ribbon attached to the top. I recognized it from pictures I'd seen not long before: it was a cluster bomblet — part of a frightful weapons system banned in war zones by more than one hundred nations but not by the United States.

Cluster bombs come in various shapes and sizes, but all incorporate dozens if not hundreds of individual "bomblets" packed inside a rocket. During the invasion, American forces had dropped cluster bombs from planes and launched them from the ground. In midair, bomblets, full of jagged metal shards, were ejected and rained down indiscriminately over an area as wide as several football fields.

The 1.5 million or so bomblets used during the invasion of Iraq were devastatingly effective at clearing out enemy strongholds. That's why the Pentagon refuses to discontinue their use. But I'd heard about their presence in Iraq for another reason: the munitions come with an infamously high dud rate. Anywhere from 5 to 15 percent of the bomblets, depending on the weapon, fail to detonate. Once at rest on the ground, the undetonated bombs effectively become land mines, making them equally devastating for civilians, children, and even coalition forces unlucky enough to stumble upon them. By the time of our landing in that field, US cluster bomblets had already killed a half dozen *American* troops in Iraq—and I immediately regretted not clinging to the helicopter.

"Watch your feet," my SEAL said.

"Oh, shit," I mumbled, even though I knew he couldn't hear me.

The cadence picked up as we advanced toward the mud-brick house. Grass and gravel crunched underfoot. I scampered along with my right hand holding the helmet back out of my eyes, fixating with each step on the few square feet of turf ahead.

Once we reached the side of the house, I crouched low and tugged at the neckline of my body armor. It was slick with sweat. Above me, exposed thatching from the roof hung listlessly, casting late-afternoon shadows along a pockmarked wall. I thought about the other raids I'd been on; I wondered who was inside the house and what it was going to take to get them out.

With that my chaperone waved his hand at me, then pointed at a line of SEALs swooping around the corner of the house toward the front door.

"Wait," I mouthed. "What's that mean? Should I go, too?"

I cast a glance over my shoulder just in time to see the last SEAL's boots sneak around the corner. When I turned back, still crouching low, my SEAL was already off, curling in the other direction around the back of the house.

And now I'm alone, I thought. This is not what I planned.

In that moment I had an out-of-body experience: I caught a glimpse of myself from above, standing there against the wall, alone and sweaty, completely out of place. Frankly, it was comical. If anyone was filming this, I looked like an asshole who was going to either be embarrassed or die. I wasn't sure which.

Improvising an action plan, I popped up and took a few steps toward the front of the house, clutching my helmet and watching for land mines. I moved as quietly as possible, then flattened myself against the wall. I sucked in my stomach for good measure.

I took stock of my surroundings; the only sound was a light southerly breeze rustling the grass nearby. No one's shooting, I thought. That's good. I exhaled.

I poked my head around the corner for a quick look at the front of the house. No one's outside, either, I thought. So they're inside the house, *and* they're not shooting. That's really good.

Suddenly the gravel crunched behind me. I spun around and faced straight down the barrel of a matte-black M4 carbine. My entire body seized. I couldn't have thrown my hands in the air if I'd wanted to.

With that, my SEAL, who'd looped back around the house to find me, lowered his weapon. "You all right?" he said with a grin. *"That,"* he said — re-creating the jabbing, pointing motion he made just before he and the others entered the house — "meant you should go with them." I was a tiny bit angry, but for the most part I was so relieved I just wanted to give him a giant kiss. I refrained. Clearly I was being hazed.

He led me around the front of the house, then inside. The other team members offered me a chair at the table in the run-down little kitchen, and we waited for the helicopter to return and pick us up while a few poked around the house.

Only there in the kitchen did I recognize something else. Among our group were two other women, who had obviously been with us the entire time. They were clad in the same gear as the men, so at a quick glance earlier I hadn't realized they weren't men. Roughly a decade before the Pentagon would end its official ban on women in combat, these two had barreled ahead of me into the house with carbines at the ready. When I asked about their presence, they told me quickly that some special operations teams were starting to include women in hopes of better interacting with the women and children found inside homes being raided. Then they turned away from our conversation and went back to picking up their gear. I suddenly was wishing I was fifteen years younger, envious of the experience these young women were able to have, and at the same time so ecstatic that women were finally allowed to be part of combat missions. I wanted to get their autographs.

As soon as I got back to BIAP, I called Roger at home for a slice of normalcy.

"Hey, the gym down the street is offering Pilates!" he said. "How cool is that?"

It was exactly what I needed to hear. Even if, to this day, he says he feels like Denis Thatcher to my Margaret whenever we tell that story.

The memory of those women clad in body armor stayed with me for the next few days. Those women were finally getting the recognition they deserved, which gave me a renewed energy for my job.

Beyond debriefing detainees, there was always a steady stream of other intelligence that I scoured. In particular, I enjoyed scrutinizing data from technical collection, piecing together networks much the same way I followed the money with the Agency's Office of Transnational Issues. This was big-picture research that extended far beyond narrowing the bull's-eye on the next individual to arrest.

I'd been up early one fateful July morning in 2003, preparing my notes for a SOF briefing. I'd felt a little light-headed that day, but that was hardly unusual in Baghdad. Whether it was because of the heat, the warmed-over hot dogs I'd eaten the night before, or the hasty bit of shut-eye I'd managed to catch in the "Thunderdome," I felt off somehow. But I took solace in the fact that people never felt fully like themselves at BIAP. Wars don't stop for wooziness, and I wasn't going to, either.

In the SOF conference room, I offered a quick hello to Charley and the various Pentagon commanders assembled. Some I recognized; others I didn't. I could never keep track of ranks or which close-cropped military planners were in the country at which time, much less which task force personnel might be in a briefing on any given day. If they were in that little conference room, I knew they were heavy hitters. That was good enough for me.

Charley took the early lead in the meeting, outlining the intelligence we'd been collecting. "With all that," he said, "I think—"

Suddenly I didn't feel so great.

Burgle, pppppppfffftt. That was my stomach, I thought, and that was not good.

I took a deep breath and tried to envision a happy place. Any happy place.

Burgle!

And like that I was gone. I bolted. I left Charley there in midsentence and hustled straight out the door.

I later read a report in the journal *Clinical Infectious Diseases* that said 76 percent of Americans in Iraq at the time battled diarrhea. After more than one million workdays were lost to the ailment by servicemen and servicewomen in Iraq and Afghanistan, the Pentagon put Defense Advanced Research Projects Agency — the same lab responsible for the underpinnings of the Internet, GPS, and cutting-edge fighter jets — on the case to find a quick cure. I didn't know that then, of course. All I knew was that the SOF commanders are not the kinds of guys you want to ditch in the middle of a meeting.

In the distance was my salvation: a row of blue porta-potties on the other side of the gravel lot. I tested a few long strides, then — "Nope, nope!" — went back to a clenched waddle to keep it all together.

I threw open the door on the first plastic throne. It smelled like a sewage sauna; the whole place sizzled in the Baghdad sunshine. I hopped in, spun around, and clawed at my pants. In that moment, I couldn't help but laugh at the memory of the SOF guys winking at me on the Fourth of July. "You're so pretty," I said out loud, in a mocking tone. I thanked every higher power I could think of that there was toilet paper in there.

Some fifteen minutes later, I stumbled out of the porta-potty and into my vehicle and drove to our terminal. Inside I found the CIA's staff medic, who took one look at me and said, "Oh, wow." He pointed at the nearest cot. "Why don't you lie down there for a second?"

The medic gave me enough Cipro for a small village. Still, walking back from the medic, I knew I was going to need to stay near some plumbing. The plumbing in our terminal was unstable at best, but it was the only plumbing we had.

I locked myself inside a bathroom in a less inhabited part of the terminal. There I lay down on the cool, dirty, and sandy tile floor. I looked at the ceiling and thought about home. Or movies.

Anything, really, except the wave of pain rolling through my torso every five minutes.

The next day I was able to escape the bathroom long enough to do a few hours of work; then I would collapse back there by the loo in a dehydrated heap. Ron and Percy even came to visit. "We just followed the crime scene tape," they said with a smirk.

They handed me a few coveted bottles of Gatorade.

"Thanks," I mumbled.

"Don't worry," they said. "Iraq isn't going anywhere."

By the following day, I was fully back at the grind again, taking my Cipro, working on a new stream of detainees at Cropper. Ron and Percy had been right, of course: those prisoners hadn't gone anywhere. It wasn't clear that any progress at all, even the incremental kind, was being made in our larger efforts in Iraq. As we entered the dog days of summer, I got the sense that a dark cloud was gathering on the horizon. There were still periodic silly moments to be found around BIAP, but the people with whom my work brought me into contact—those who knew Iraq best—didn't indulge in even a minute of optimism.

The first time I spoke with Tariq Aziz, I saw him in his underwear. I think he actually preferred it that way.

Nearly seventy years old at the time, Hussein's former deputy prime minister had negotiated his surrender shortly after the US invasion, reportedly waiting out the government overthrow in the comfort of his sister-in-law's home in an upscale Baghdad neighborhood. After giving US officials his location, Aziz was quietly detained by coalition forces in the middle of the night. There were no shots fired during the arrest, and neighbors said that when the military left, Aziz and a few others accompanied them in the backs of luxury cars. At the time I met him, the eight of spades in the

Bush administration's deck of wanted Iraqi fugitives was the highest-ranking detainee held at Cropper.

Aziz, I knew, always pegged himself as something of a showman. With thinning white hair swept straight back, he even looked the part. His looks made him well suited to act as Hussein's key spokesman during international trips, as Hussein rarely left Iraq because of security concerns. Aziz had even traveled to the Vatican a month before the US invasion to implore the Holy Father to intercede before conflict erupted. If anyone was in a position to have genuine insight into Hussein's thought processes, it was Aziz.

Early on in my time at BIAP, I'd sat in on a debriefing of the former deputy prime minister conducted by senior CIA officers in Baghdad. I was just part of the crew then, listening for disparities, but unlike Evil Hagrid, he was so cooperative that he wanted to tell his side of the story not only to us but also to *60 Minutes*. He had said Saddam did not trust al Qaida or any other radical Islamist group and didn't want to cooperate with them, even though he said Saddam viewed al Qaida as an effective terrorist organization for the way they attacked the United States.

I had planned on speaking with Aziz alone at some point, but when I got word one morning in late summer that he'd collapsed in his cell from heat stroke, I figured I'd better meet him sooner rather than later. I'd been told he had a history of heart attacks, which might have played a part in his decision to surrender, and that he'd been moved to the nearby infirmary. Either way, I thought, debriefing an official in his makeshift BIAP hospital room would be more interesting than staring at the listless gray hangar walls where I'd been working. The relatively relaxed security at the medical facility gave me an idea, too.

Aziz seemed to me a cantankerous cynic, and I was sure that prison life didn't appeal to his urbane sensibilities. The majority of photos I'd seen of Aziz showed him with a Davidoff Dom Perignon cigar clenched between his teeth, a bushy white mustache, and thick black glasses sitting high on his nose. On my way to the hospital I rounded up a few oranges and a pack of cigarettes.

As Percy and I entered Aziz's steamy hospital room, I set the fruit and Marlboros on the squat white end table next to his bed. His glasses rested there, too: a large indentation was visible on the bridge of his nose, where they normally sat. Aziz rolled his head toward us on his pillow and noted the nearby fruit. He watched as Percy and I found a seat on the cot right across from him. I was curious to see what Aziz might do next.

In Middle Eastern culture, the concept of personal space is very different from what it is in the Western world. Americans keep a comfortable two or three feet of distance between us and people we speak with. In Iraq, I'd quickly seen how that arm's length of space disappeared among men, who stood practically on top of one another as they talked. On the other hand, the opposite holds true when men interact with women. Even shaking hands can be an affront, as Islam generally prohibits men from having physical contact with a woman who is not a spouse or family member.

In that hospital room, Aziz sat up and swung his legs over the side of his bed until our knees nearly touched. He leaned toward me. It seemed like a casual show of dominance, but I didn't flinch. In a room with no air-conditioning, I could see the sweat beading on his brow and spotting his hospital gown. Aziz looked me directly in the eyes.

"What is your name?" he said in fluent English.

"Nada," I replied. "It's Czech."

"Then your parents should have named you Nadia."

He picked up the cigarettes and unwrapped the cellophane. He affected the air of a sophisticate.

"You know what Nada means in Arabic?" Aziz said.

"No," I replied.

"The dew on the morning grass."

Aziz lit the Marlboro and took a deep pull off it.

"What's your name?" I asked. "Your real name."

The sixty-seven-year-old gave a soft chuckle.

"Mikhail Yuhanna," he said.

"Michael John," I repeated.

Aziz acknowledged the translation with a quick flip of his eyebrows. "My family is Christian," he said and offered a little shrug.

In Hussein's regime, however, that Christianity warranted far more than a shrug. Born outside Mosul in 1936, according to my research, Yuhanna had earned his journalism degree at the precursor to the University of Baghdad, then joined the upstart Arab Socialist Baath Party movement there in the late 1950s. That's where he met a young Saddam Hussein and changed his name to Tariq Aziz in a show of solidarity with his fellow revolutionaries, most of whom were Muslim.

As Hussein began rising through the Iraqi government ranks after a coup in the late 1960s, Aziz was brought along, ultimately holding a number of different jobs. In 1991, as foreign minister, Aziz disagreed with — yet ultimately fell in line with — the dictator's decision to invade Kuwait. Hussein proceeded with the invasion even though, Aziz told me, he warned him that it likely would mean a disastrous war with the United States.

After that, partly because Aziz was right but mostly because he'd proved loyal, his prominence within the Iraqi government rose significantly. He told me proudly that "my friend Saddam" trusted him as a right-hand man, and, Aziz said, he knew more of the regime's secrets than anyone.

"There are no weapons, if that's what you want to know," he added, blowing cigarette smoke in my direction.

"What was it like with Saddam at the end?"

The old diplomat began spinning a tale about a final meeting of the dictator's inner circle hours before the war's start. "The invasion was imminent," he said. "Saddam said, 'I have an escape plan. I will not tell you what it is in case you are captured and tortured. But I would advise all of you to have your own.'

"I laughed," he continued. "I am the most recognized of Saddam's deputies. I would be found anywhere. I just stayed home and waited for the military to pick me up."

"Did you actually laugh at Saddam?" I asked. If so, I was surprised that Aziz hadn't been shot right then and there.

"Of course," he said. "What was he going to do to me?"

Aziz took another pull off the cigarette and sat back. He pulled his robe loose from around his waist, fanning himself in the sweltering heat. He was cheekily giving me an eyeful of his tighty whities. I didn't offer a reaction; I knew he was waiting for one.

Before I could get out my next question, however, Percy — who'd been silent this whole time — walked over to the bed, pointed at me, and riffed off a few stern lines in Arabic. It was as stern as I'd ever seen him. Aziz responded with a sheepish smirk and closed his robe. He reminded me of every belligerent nursing home patient I'd ever seen pass the time by coming up with new ways to shock the staff.

"Terrorists," I said to the former prime minister. "Sunni jihadists. Was Hussein inviting them into Iraq?"

"No, no," Aziz said. "Saddam didn't care about religion until the last few years, when he needed support. But there was no cooperation with jihadists — Saddam cared about maintaining a strong Iraq. He cared about standing up to Iran.

"I'm Christian," Aziz added. "Saddam didn't care. So just look at me."

Those final words hung there in the steamy hospital room. Aziz looked down at the cigarette in his hand.

"You hold me in these cells. Why?" he said. "I was a politician. I was not perfect. But I have not committed any crimes against civilians."

I could hear the agitation in his voice and wondered if he was having second thoughts about surrendering. Either way, I sensed our productive conversation was finished. As Percy and I got up to leave, I told Aziz that I might be back. We headed for the door, but I heard every word Aziz called after us.

"What will be left once America leaves?" he muttered. "There is no electricity. No food. There are no services for people."

CHAPTER 9

The Real CIA Must Be in the Basement — We're Just the Cover

By the end of July in 2003, my workdays were fully blurring together. I'd take note of a new name here, or some unexpected piece of information there, but many of those conversations with detainees felt like an utter waste of time. As a likely outgrowth of the US military response to an increase in attacks, Cropper was never in short supply of inmates, but ten minutes spent talking to most of them showed me how few deserved to be locked up in the first place.

This fact was further driven home to me one afternoon when Ron, Percy, and I sat down with an impossibly upbeat prisoner to talk about ties he might have to extremist groups.

"Can you tell us why you were with the group who was shooting at the US military outside the cell-phone store?" Percy translated the question.

"Me? No!" he said. "I've been in Baghdad all my life!" Even in a language I didn't speak, he had the delivery of a guy trying to buy me a beer.

"We're seeing more attacks here by the airport lately," Ron said. "Who's organizing them?"

"Attacks? How would I know?" the detainee said. "You can come to my house, yes? I'll show you a photo of me with a bottle of Jack Daniel's on my head! You think jihadists do that?"

That I could believe. He even gave us a rundown of all his

favorite hip-hop artists, and Ron gave him a few more names to look up when he got released. A year later, a scathing Red Cross report bore out what I knew: roughly 70 to 90 percent of Iraqis detained from April through December of 2003 were arrested by mistake. I had no doubt this whiskey-loving gentleman—who'd been brought in for thumbing his cell phone, theoretically a trigger mechanism for a roadside bomb, while he was near a military convoy—was one of them.

Ron planted his hands on the table and leaned over to look the inmate in the eyes. It wasn't particularly menacing, just probing. "Seriously," Ron said. "You don't speak any English at all?"

Percy translated the question. The detainee sat silent for a moment, then smiled. "Beer before liquor," he said. "I could not be sicker!"

I laughed. This guy was actually refreshing. He said he was a bit of a busybody who was calling his friend to talk about a raid happening next door when he was arrested. That's what the cell phone was for. He proceeded to tell us about the parties he liked to throw and the crazy things his friends did when they got drunk. For a moment, I was almost transported back to college.

"Come on," I finally said to Ron as we called for the guard. "I think we can tell them they can let this guy go."

Ron and I walked outside the hangar for some relatively fresh air. He didn't share my sense of amusement. "This is a waste of time," he muttered. "What do they expect us to learn from those guys?"

"What do you think the weapons team is hearing?" I said. "They've been out there talking to people in the city. That's got to offer more perspective than we're getting here."

With that the two of us changed our plan for the day and hunted down a Toyota parked near Cropper.

The pickup was one of a dozen or so the Agency had flown in for use by CIA personnel. Unlike the Pentagon, whose employees went around in armored carriers, and the State Department and USAID, whose diplomats were transported in caravans of fortified Chevy Suburbans, the CIA wanted its employees to operate anonymously. To blend in. So we drove this fleet of well-used trucks. Someone had hung trinkets from the rearview mirrors of the pickups, and from a distance, anyway, they looked like any other everyday truck we came across in Baghdad.

I always enjoyed the freedom of driving, ever since my childhood days on my grandparents' farm. In some ways, driving one of the CIA's Toyotas felt a little bit like being back home again. Just as important, those few minutes of motoring around provided a great opportunity to kvetch with coworkers about the food on base, about the overall mission, or simply about other coworkers.

The Agency's WMD-hunting team, for instance, had recently grown so large that they had moved from the western edge of the airport grounds to an annex on the far southeast. They were always the preeminent Agency team in Iraq. They would get the latest supplies and food and were the subject of some real jealousy and smack talk.

The centerpiece of the weapons team was a building coalition forces had mistaken for a structure protected under the Geneva Conventions and that had gone unscathed when the Americans overran the airport during the invasion. Life at the annex seemed good to anyone struggling to find a functioning toilet in the terminal.

In fact the annex was so secluded that neither Ron nor I had seen it up close. And soon enough, as we zipped across the airport grounds chatting about life in the States, the pressing question in the pickup became: How would we actually find the place? "Maybe that was the turn back there," Ron said, looking over his shoulder for some semblance of signage.

No sooner had he turned to face front than we arrived at an army checkpoint. A soldier peered into my rolled-down driver's-side window and gave the truck a quick once-over. He looked at Ron and me and waved us through.

Past the checkpoint, we rounded a corner, then hit an on-ramp. Out my window, a statue of Abbas Ibn Firnas — a Muslim inventor who sketched out gliders and other rudimentary flying machines some seven hundred years before Leonardo da Vinci — came into view. With its arms stretched wide and covered in a feathered flying contraption, the statue had become known to many troops as the Winged Man. I just knew it marked the eastern edge of the BIAP grounds — and that suddenly we were motoring out onto Baghdad Airport Road.

"Wait," I said. "This was not the plan."

That seven-mile highway was the main artery running from the airport into central Baghdad — in particular, the high-walled Green Zone, serving as the Coalition Provisional Authority's headquarters. Carved out around Hussein's former presidential palace, the Green Zone had a reputation as a fortified civilian town filled with yuppie DC office workers who wore combat boots for no reason. To get there, however, incoming workers who landed at BIAP had to take "Route Irish," as the airport highway was known to the military, skirting past Baghdad suburbs such as Amariya, Hamra, and Qaddisiya. That was originally done by design. Those neighborhoods were Sunni strongholds under Hussein's regime; even the despot had recognized how vulnerable a caravan was on that one main highway into town, and he didn't want to make the drive surrounded by enemies. Those former loyalists recognized that most any Westerner traveling into Baghdad from the airport must be someone worth taking a shot at.

The legendary anarchy that would ultimately envelope Route Irish and come to signify the wayward US mission in Iraq had not yet taken hold. But there were hints of the violence to come. Three days after Ambassador Bremer disbanded the Iraqi military, the first major attack occurred on the road. Others followed. No one kept statistics at the time to document the upswing in the number of roadside bombs planted at night or the unnerving machine-gun attacks on SUVs carrying aid workers, but the nascent signs of predation were unmistakable. Even if it hadn't yet become the most dangerous road in the world, it was already earning other nicknames from the people who traveled it regularly: Death Street. IED Alley. The Highway to Hell. As Ron and I joined the flow of speeding traffic, I was thinking we should probably have a plan if we were headed into Baghdad and maybe should have told someone where we were going.

"We should probably turn around," Ron said politely.

"Well, yeah," I replied, thinking maybe we should just get some ice cream and then head home, until I realized we only had one gun between us and, again, no one knew where we were. I scanned the stubby palm trees that flanked the six-lane highway all the way to the horizon. A deep, pitted median separated the three lanes of traffic heading in each direction. "But where should I turn around?"

Dusty blue-and-white traffic signs whizzed by overhead, pointing the way to Baghdad and Rutba and Fallujah beyond. It looked in many ways like a standard US highway, albeit one carrying many more armored vehicles. There were speed limits, technically speaking, but no one obeyed them. I hung in the middle lane, not blending in with local traffic or obvious coalition traffic. On my left, drivers in boxy white sedans slowed down to take long looks at me before roaring off into the distance.

Up ahead, a succession of red brake lights popped on, snaking off into a bottleneck at an Iraqi military checkpoint I could see in the distance. Ironically, the back end of a checkpoint line was one of the most dangerous places on the highway. A mile of stopped cars created a convenient setup for an ambush and made us sitting targets for insurgents, who could open fire from the other side of the endless median that divided the roadway.

"I'm going make a U-turn," I blurted out.

"A what?" Ron said. A maneuver that unorthodox in that location could attract the exact wrong kind of attention. "Look what we're driving!" he said. "You want to get shot by the military?"

"It's either that or possibly get shot by someone else. We only have one gun between us besides."

"Shit," Ron said, reaching over to get a firm grip on the handle inside his door.

I steered us into the left lane and glanced out my window. The median there opened into a makeshift turnaround point. There was no curb and, for the moment, no traffic coming from the other direction. Assuming no jihadist had planted a bomb among the scrubby brush, I figured this was about as good a spot as any.

"Hang on," I said, lifting my right foot off the gas and signaling, as if being polite and using traffic signals would be a clear sign we weren't a threat.

I cranked the steering wheel hard to the left to plow through the soft dirt.

We reached the inside shoulder of the westbound lanes and kicked a rooster tail of dirt across the road. I scanned the mirrors and spun my head around looking for angry soldiers. Happily, I didn't see any. Ron laughed at my cautious turn and last-minute decision.

Soon we were back at the statue of the Winged Man, and then we stopped at an entry checkpoint to BIAP. I waved my ID badge and stuck my head as far out the truck's window as possible, hoping to appear nonthreatening to the apprehensive young soldier at the gate. I have no doubt I just appeared crazy, but he let us through.

"Well, hey," Ron said once we finally spoke again. "We didn't get shot today!"

"It's still early," I said.

Once we found the WMD team that day, they hadn't been able to help much, either. My self-doubt began creeping back in.

When I volunteered for temporary assignment in Iraq, I had such grand hopes for what I might accomplish. At the time, the Agency official assessment, contained in its *Iraqi Support for Terrorism* report, said, "Our knowledge of Iraq's ties to terrorism is evolving," and "This paper's conclusions—especially regarding the difficult and elusive question of the exact nature of Iraq's relations with al Qaida—are based on currently available information that is at times contradictory and derived from sources with varying degrees of reliability." Naive and idealistic as it might have been, I wanted to crack the case and get to the bottom of those things. As my deployment began wrapping up in early August, I hadn't. Meanwhile, back in Langley, CIA higher-ups who faced continued historical questions from the White House might have been even more eager than I was to get clarity once and for all.

I decided to take one last run at a detainee I'll refer to here as Pettigrew. He was part of one of the Iraqi Intelligence Service directorates and was privy to the analysis of foreign military capabilities, particularly those of potential aggressors with political motivations. In April of 2003, the CIA had lured Pettigrew to a meeting by suggesting they wanted to recruit him as a double agent; in fact, they'd just wanted to arrest him. Subsequently, I'd come to know Pettigrew's wide-set eyes and bushy mustache well during my time in the high-value wing of the BIAP detention center. Evil Hagrid would have likely known if Hussein's government had been actively courting terrorist assistance, but Pettigrew would have been watching from a different angle. He would have known if jihadists such as Zarqawi had been trying to sneak into Iraq undetected.

The problem was that in the nearly dozen times I'd spoken to Pettigrew, nothing I asked ever seemed to penetrate his indignant sophistication. He never offered me anything useful. Mostly, the round man in his early forties just sat there with his hands folded in his lap, staring at the floor. Before my time in Iraq ended, I wanted answers that I thought he could provide.

Early the next morning, Percy and I walked to my shack. I fished a stack of paperwork from my backpack and set it on the table. A guard soon brought Pettigrew.

"Can you undo his shackles?" I said, and the guard agreed.

The former intelligence officer took his seat. He was clearly dispirited.

"Did you know that Zarqawi was in the country?" I said. Percy translated the questions.

"This again?" Pettigrew said softly in Arabic. "I told you I don't know where he is." He gave a dismissive wave of his hand. Pettigrew's body language made the translation unnecessary.

"How closely did the Mukhabarat watch him?" I asked.

"We didn't know anything about him," Pettigrew told me.

"I didn't believe you the last time you told me that, either."

It only made sense to me that Zarqawi was too much of a wild card for the IIS not to have kept tabs on. Even if there was no relationship between the sides prior to 9/11, it was possible that Hussein's regime might have forged one with Zarqawi and his newfound Ansar allies afterward, especially if Zarqawi's network could be a useful ally against US forces during the invasion. That sort of collaboration felt like a stretch, but faced with an impending invasion and inevitable defeat, who knows what lengths Hussein might have gone to?

"We would have made a deal on oil," Pettigrew had told me. "The

FBI could have searched for weapons wherever they pleased—we had no weapons of mass destruction. Saddam didn't want war," he'd said.

On February 19, Lebanese-American businessman Imad Hage had faxed his Defense Department contacts a list of five concessions Hussein offered through the intelligence service. The United States would be given "first priority" to Iraqi oil, according to the document; the Iraqi government would also offer its "full support" for the US negotiation of an Arab-Israeli peace process, assist the Bush administration in its counterterrorism efforts, help promote America's strategic interests in the Middle East, and allow "direct U.S. involvement on the ground in disarming Iraq."

The memo sparked a flurry of activity within the Pentagon, and subsequently at the CIA, to determine the offer's veracity. But after years of obfuscation and half-truths from Hussein, as well as uncertainty about the trustworthiness of the intelligence officers transmitting the information, the offer was deemed incredible. The United States soon invaded.

That all felt like ancient history now, Pettigrew told me. He was emotionally drained, he said. He just wanted to go home.

"Zarqawi," I repeated. "What did you know?"

Pettigrew slouched in his chair. He mumbled a few names—the Jordanian's possible Ansar contacts—and details about Zarqawi's initial path into Iraq. They weren't much, but they matched details I'd heard from Agency officers outside Khurmal and reports we'd gotten from a liaison intelligence service.

"Finally, the truth," I replied.

Pettigrew lifted his head and stared at me. Instantly he knew I knew more than I was letting on. That got his full attention.

"Is Zarqawi still here now?" I said. "Don't tell me you don't know—I'll think you've been lying about everything. You want to spend the rest of your life in here?" Up until this point I had fooled myself into pretending I was arguing with a belligerent acquaintance;

in this moment, however, I felt utterly sick of the situation we were both part of.

After four months in detention, Pettigrew's facade cracked. It started with a sniffle. Soon the tears were streaming down his face.

Frankly, I wasn't particularly impressed. Another thing I'd learned during debriefs is that many detainees presumed a woman would fall back on some innate motherly instinct and take pity on them. More than one manipulative sob session had been abruptly cut short when I'd remarked, "Let me know when you're done so we can continue."

At that moment, however, Pettigrew was not trying to be manipulative. He clutched his hands to his face and bawled, repeating the same phrase over and over. I glanced at Percy.

"He's saying he misses his son," Percy finally said. "Saddam had many enemies. He's afraid for his family's safety."

I tried to think quickly: Pettigrew was going to be of no help to me like this. I did feel empathy, though less so for him than for his children, who must have missed their father. So I improvised. "Look" I said, loudly enough to be heard over the sobbing. "Answer the question, and I'll let you make a phone call."

That impromptu strategy certainly hadn't been covered in the training I'd received. Years later, Cropper would institute a policy that allowed family visits once every two weeks and even permitted five minutes of physical contact for hugs. But during my time in Iraq, when many families didn't know where their relatives were being held, phone calls were the detainees' only form of connection with loved ones. For many, given a choice, staying indoors to make a call was worth far more than their few minutes of daily sunshine in the yard. Pettigrew immediately began to compose himself.

"Okay," I said. "When we meet tomorrow, I will arrange a call."

I spent that evening arranging the phone call. Only a few hours after striking the deal with Pettigrew did I think about the Pandora's box I might have opened. What if he'd established a code word ahead of time to pinpoint his location for supporters or identify a spot for an attack? My mind reeled with crazy possibilities.

True to my word, however, I summoned Pettigrew from his cell the next day. With an MP following close behind, Percy and I led the former intelligence officer outside the hangar onto the sidewalk. At just shy of noon on the sun-scarred landscape, everything seemed to glow white. The guard left Pettigrew with us and found a shady spot where he could perch in the distance.

"You have fifteen minutes," I said through the translator, handing Pettigrew a satellite phone. He raced to type in his home number.

I turned to Percy. "Make sure you hear every word," I said.

Moments later, I could hear a voice on the other end of the line pick up. It was a woman's; I presumed it was his wife. Pettigrew smiled.

"I'm okay, I'm okay," he told her. "Are you okay? How are my children?"

Soon I overheard another voice on the line. It was clearly a child's, and if the sound of his wife had softened Pettigrew's rough-hewn demeanor, the sound of his son melted it completely. Soon both were crying. "I'll be home very soon," Pettigrew said. "I love you."

I stared down at the sidewalk. In that moment I felt like a dirtbag, as if I'd somehow been responsible for breaking up this man's family. I had to walk away from the scene, just far enough away to no longer hear his sobs. "If he misses his family that much," I mumbled under my breath, "why won't he just tell me what he knows? That's the only shot he has."

When the fifteen minutes were up, Pettigrew handed the phone back without protest. The guard led him back to his cell. As I watched him go, the term "a broken man" was seared into my mind.

———

Saddam Hussein, the former Iraqi president, was found guilty of crimes against humanity for the 1982 killing of 148 Shias in the small city of Dujail, approximately forty miles north of Baghdad. Hussein was hanged for the crimes. I assume Pettigrew is still in custody to this day.

Toward the tail end of that summer in 2003, I wasn't the only one fixating on Zarqawi's simmering plans in Iraq. As the Jordanian rebuilt his network, al Qaida central decided it was time to send something more significant than fighters along those rat lines. Bin Ladin sent some of his top brain trust, including Sayf al-Adl, Zarqawi's main contact with the group, and a man I was about to learn far more about: Abd al-Hadi al-Iraqi.

As his nom de guerre indicates, Abd al-Hadi al-Iraqi is a local, born in Mosul, Iraq, in 1961. A skilled military tactician, the burly man speaks a half dozen languages and had risen to the rank of major in Hussein's Iraqi Army before defecting to Afghanistan to fight the Soviets in the 1980s. That battle may have been where he first met Sayf al-Adl, al Qaida's future military leader, but their initial introduction isn't nearly as important as what they would do together later. After being recruited to serve as an instructor at al Qaida training camps throughout Afghanistan, al-Iraqi had acted in the late 1990s as the organization's international operations chief. Then, like Adl, he'd been named a member of bin Ladin's ten-man personal shura council—an advisory group modeled after Islamic legislative bodies in the Middle East.

Given his heritage, it was not surprising al-Iraqi had interest in steering a strategy in Iraq; his influence had only risen among extremists. Sending 20 percent of al Qaida's most senior advisory board members on official business was no small feat, but the show of intellectual force was clearly important for bin Ladin. During his time in Afghanistan, Zarqawi and his lieutenants had canvassed the region, making loose connections with rebel groups in Jordan, Syria,

Saudi Arabia, Libya, Uzbekistan, Georgia, and elsewhere. Zarqawi's exact plans in Iraq were still fuzzy at the time, but his potential influence had become unmistakable. Together, bin Ladin hoped, Adl and al-Iraqi could counsel the feisty Jordanian on the best approach to the battles ahead.

It turned out, however, that Zarqawi hadn't been the only one busy over the previous few months—and that meeting ended up a bit smaller than bin Ladin had hoped.

As US forces toppled the Taliban in Afghanistan in late 2001, Adl and a few other prominent members of al Qaida had fled across the country's western border into Iran. There they were quickly detained by Iranian authorities and placed under "house arrest." What that term actually meant, however, was never clear to me—presumably, I always believed, because it was a house arrest of mutual convenience.

Al Qaida figures such as Adl found Iran a much safer landing spot than the mountains along the Afghanistan-Pakistan border, where the CIA was aggressively pursuing the Taliban and other militants. Al Qaida personnel in Iran were able to visit swimming pools and shopping complexes, and some were even permitted to travel relatively freely around the country.

At the same time, the Revolutionary Guard in Iran had found al Qaida useful to have nearby. Tehran, the country's capital, had been thrust into a harrowing position in American foreign policy when President Bush delivered his second State of the Union address, in January of 2002. In what is now widely remembered as the "Axis of Evil" speech, Bush had linked Iran to Iraq and North Korea as states that "pose a grave and growing danger" and "threaten the peace of the world." Bush pledged decisive action. "If we stopped now, leaving terror camps intact and terror states unchecked, our sense of security would be false and temporary," he'd said. "It is both our responsibility and our privilege to fight freedom's fight."

The implication was clear to everyone at the CIA and to those listening in Tehran. In the face of an American adversary keen to fight, it didn't matter that Iran's hard-line Shia government had deep ideological differences with the radical Sunnis of al Qaida. Keeping those refugees close made sense, the Iranian government knew, because the terrorist leaders could prove to be useful bargaining chips.

Then three explosions rocked the Middle East. Adl had made the most of his time under house arrest, plotting with other al Qaida leaders there in detention — and coordinating with foot soldiers abroad — to strike on the other side of the Persian Gulf. At around 11:15 p.m. on Monday, May 12, 2003, right as I was headed to the region, al Qaida members acting on Adl's orders drove a car full of explosives up to the front of each of three housing compounds in the Saudi Arabian capital of Riyadh. The ensuing bomb blasts sheared off huge sections of the apartment buildings, killing three dozen people, including ten Americans, and wounding more than two hundred.

Moreover, Iran tightened the reins on al Qaida leaders inside its borders — including Adl, right as he was heading off to meet Zarqawi and al-Iraqi. Adl never left the country, vanishing inside Iran until fairly recently. Now experts think he may be in Pakistan.

Al-Iraqi, on the other hand, made it safely to meet with Zarqawi. Exactly what the two discussed at that meeting was never entirely clear. It's possible that bin Ladin hoped al-Iraqi would take over Zarqawi's fledgling operation in full. That possibility was borne out in news reports, when al-Iraqi later told some of his Taliban contacts that Zarqawi bristled at the prospect of intervention. "I'm already here!" the Jordanian reportedly told al-Iraqi. "Why is the sheik sending someone else?" Had Adl been at his side, al-Iraqi may well have had too much clout for Zarqawi to oppose.

It was just as plausible, however, that al-Iraqi's trip was a fact-finding mission for al Qaida central. Given that he now found himself a coordinator among the region's disparate terror groups, Zarqawi's own stature had been amplified in the jihadist movement. Those groups all surely benefited from even a casual connection to al Qaida as well. But what al Qaida got in return was far less clear.

Like Adl before him, al-Iraqi seems to have found a connection with Zarqawi. The al Qaida lieutenant ultimately made a number of trips to northern Iraq throughout late 2003, alternately trying to persuade Zarqawi to officially join the organization and lecturing him for his perceived missteps in his approach to jihad. At the same time, al-Iraqi defended the brash Jordanian to bin Ladin and others in the al Qaida leadership. The connection Zarqawi and al-Iraqi forged during that initial meeting, and the ones that followed, proved pivotal to the future of al Qaida—and ultimately to the downfall of bin Ladin.

CHAPTER 10

It's All Sunshine and Rainbows Until...

It was a late afternoon in mid-August of 2003 when I stepped off an airplane at Dulles International Airport. After staying awake long enough to find my bag at baggage claim, I hailed a taxi and collapsed in the backseat until it pulled up to Roger's house. "Welcome home," he said as he hugged me. "You ready to see the new house?"

I was. I was also ready for a real shower, clothes that aren't made of 100 percent nylon, and a real bed. I slept most of that first day back.

At Langley the next day, the scene was surprisingly foreign. A number of the original analysts in the Iraq unit had already begun peeling off into other roles at the Agency—some in well-deserved promotions to advisory positions and others just getting as far away from burnout and the chaos of our unit as possible. I, too, was feeling the toll our work had taken, though at the time it never occurred to me to look for another position.

For the most part, my work as an analyst back at headquarters looked much the same as it did before I went to Iraq. Our shift work had ended and we resumed a "normal" schedule of working from 7:00 a.m. until 8:00 p.m. or later. Having made it through my trial by fire, however, I could see that there were a few key differences in my job. One of my new informal roles was to transfer our team's collective knowledge to the new branch members trickling in, helping to train them in the process. By then the data was significantly more in-depth than the stack of binders I'd been handed when I started. Also, I was no longer one of the most junior members of my team, so I wasn't inundated when I drank from the intel fire hose in the middle of the night. At home I joked with Roger that I'd found a more philosophical take on my work. "I basically get paid to think big thoughts, gather around whiteboards, and pontificate on my way to get coffee."

There was a grain of truth to that. As much as I was frustrated by our team fielding backward-looking questions about the evolution of various terror cells and their geographic and ideological connections throughout the Middle East in the days leading up to the attacks of September 11, 2001, I was becoming fixated on the puzzle of what Zarqawi and those foreign fighters were up to. Was he maintaining residency in Iraq or moving in and out? If the latter, how was he going to accomplish fighting the coalition forces?

As I gazed out the window at the green of the campus courtyard in the morning sunshine on my first day back, I tapped a finger against the cup of Starbucks coffee in my hand. *Puzzle* was a word I'd been rolling around in my head over the previous few days, ever since Cindy Storer, one of the original al Qaida analysts, had described her research to me. "It's not connecting dots; it's more like a jigsaw puzzle," she'd said. "Except there is no picture and there are no edge pieces. And not all the pieces fit the puzzle." I took another sip of my coffee and thought about how much we didn't know.

Days later, the first big piece of the puzzle that was Zarqawi fell into place.

As Paul Bremer and the Coalition Provisional Authority took control of postwar Iraq, I watched a second organization play a pivotal role in the attempted stabilization of the country: the United Nations.

Though the Bush administration had publicly feuded with the UN when it became clear that many members of the Security Council would not back American ambitions for military action in Iraq, once the war was over support from the international community in rebuilding the country was crucial. The UN mission in Iraq was headed by a fifty-five-year-old white-haired Brazilian envoy named Sergio Vieira de Mello, who had spent thirty-four years as a UN diplomat in war-torn countries, including Sudan, Lebanon, Cambodia, Bosnia, Kosovo, and East Timor. Named the UN's high commissioner for human rights in 2002, Vieira de Mello achieved something even more impressive soon afterward: he charmed President Bush.

During an Oval Office meeting with President Bush a few weeks prior to the invasion, I later heard, Vieira de Mello and the president had discussed the harsh treatment of detainees in Guantanamo Bay. Bush asserted that it could never be allowed to become a "country club," according to Jonathan Prentice, Vieira de Mello's special assistant, and that terrorists must be dealt with harshly. "I know," Vieira de Mello replied. "In East Timor I gave U.N. peacekeepers shoot-to-kill authority to go after the militia."

That President Bush and the UN's high commissioner for human rights would have a meeting of the minds over shoot-to-kill authority was unexpected, perhaps—but it was a key strategic gambit, Prentice later told colleagues. Bush immediately respected Vieira de Mello's authority and subsequently became enthusiastic about the UN's collaboration in rebuilding Iraq. "After cursing the U.N. or calling it irrelevant or comparing it to the League of Nations," Vieira de Mello told the *Wall Street Journal* at the time, "the United States very quickly came back, as it were, even though they will never admit it, in search for international legitimacy." He added,

"My guess is that the U.S. and the U.K. and those that have joined will realize... that this is too big, that building a democratic Iraq is not simple.... As a result they have every interest in encouraging others who are seen to be more impartial, independent, more palatable to join in and help create these new institutions."

That strategy, it soon became clear to me, was not lost on those determined to undermine the rebuilding efforts, either.

Vieira de Mello arrived in Baghdad not long after I did. I respected the fact that the UN had set up its offices at the Canal Hotel, in a relatively unfortified area three miles east of the Green Zone, across the Tigris River. Human rights work required interaction with the population, and Vieira de Mello embraced the mandate that then UN secretary general Kofi Annan had given him: the envoy to Iraq would "serve as a bridge to the Coalition," Annan had said, "but he will also have to distance himself from the Coalition." Vieira de Mello clearly was proud that his three-story headquarters, trimmed along the roof in the organization's signature azure blue and flying a massive UN flag out front, was approachable by everyday people.

At the hotel, the envoy's third-floor office looked out onto a gravel service road running along the western side of the building and, directly across from it, a hospital. At the end of the service road was a busy catering school. The US military had originally blocked off that gravel service road with armored vehicles to protect the hotel, but UN officials balked at the practice, not wanting to alienate people who might be trying to get to the hospital or the school. On one visit to the compound, I saw that the security around the Canal Hotel had been reduced to a group of unarmed Iraqi diplomatic police. Locals regularly met with UN humanitarian workers in the hotel cafeteria for tea and coffee—the UN certainly seemed to me more popular among Iraqis than the US forces were.

Sadly, that made the UN a key pressure point—and soon a terrible instance of a growing trend. Vieira de Mello knew a lot about helping rebuild societies after conflict and after dictators had been overthrown. He also pleaded with the CPA to slow down de-Baathification and make provisions for the needs of Iraqi Army veterans.

In May, the month I arrived in Baghdad—mere weeks after President Bush's dramatic "Mission Accomplished" speech—there were 117 attacks against coalition forces. That number rose to 307 in June and 451 in July. The bulk of them seemed indiscriminate or merely opportunistic.

Just before I left the country in August, a truck bomb detonated outside the Jordanian embassy in Baghdad, killing seventeen people, including two children, and wounding more than sixty. It was the deadliest attack in Iraq since President Bush had declared an end to combat operations, one I could instantly tell was far more elaborate than a simple roadside bomb erupting next to an armored personnel carrier. With it, the number of attacks against coalition forces that month crept toward 320, and I pushed myself to try to pick up on trends or operational tactics hidden within the rising tide of violence. One became clear to me after some thought.

Not long after the bombing at the Jordanian embassy, Turkey pledged to join the coalition, sending ten thousand troops to aid in stabilization and rebuilding efforts. Days later, a car bomb detonated outside the Turkish embassy in Baghdad—the first time a Turkish installation had been targeted by fundamentalists. Following that, Luay Muhammad Hajj Bakr al-Saqa, who by this time had become Zarqawi's trusted lieutenant, struck directly inside Turkey by plotting and financing truck bombings in Istanbul. Over the course of five days, fifty-seven people were killed and seven hundred wounded as the bombs exploded outside a pair of synagogues, the British consulate, and a British bank.

Those moves struck me as a clear attempt to disrupt any fledgling rebuilding the coalition had done up to that point. Taken together, they also made perfect sense as a necessary opening salvo for a group like Zarqawi's. As upheaval and chaos played out, an ominous internal threat assessment was distributed to UN employees. It read, "To date there have been no direct assaults on U.N. staff or facilities, but it is the consensus of the U.N.-Iraq Security Team that it is only a matter of time."

At approximately 4:30 p.m. Baghdad time on August 19, 2003, an orange truck with a brown cab carrying more than a ton of artillery shells, mortars, and other explosives turned down the service road beside the Canal Hotel. Rather than slow down along the small street, however, witnesses reported seeing the truck speed up, spraying the hotel's windows with gravel as it went. There was a screech of tires, the crunching sound of a metal impact — and then the sight of "one million flashbulbs going off all at once," a survivor said, as the truck exploded directly beneath Vieira de Mello's office.

Twenty-three people were killed in the blast, fifteen of them UN officials. Roughly 150 were injured. Vieira de Mello lay tangled in the rubble of his collapsed office for hours as rescue workers attempted to save him. By 7:30 p.m., he was drifting in and out of consciousness; by 8:00 p.m., he was dead. Within weeks, the UN pulled the majority of its remaining staffers out of Iraq. In that instance, at least, the plan to isolate the United States from some of its international collaborators worked almost instantly.

Having just returned from Baghdad, I scrambled to collect all the data I could from the attack. I knew the flow of foreign fighters into Iraq was only increasing, but if this represented Zarqawi's grand introduction to the international conflict, I needed solid information to work with. If the bread crumbs from the UN bombing led back to a different insurgent organization, the investigative work would be off my desk, shifting over to that organization's corresponding Agency unit. In my gut, though I sensed Zarqawi was behind Vieira de Mello's death, I just didn't have any idea how to prove it.

Sadly, however, the carnage of August wasn't yet done. Days later, all the data I gathered from the UN bombing began to pay off.

On August 29, 2003, an attack outside the Shia Imam Ali Mosque in Najaf killed ninety-five people, including Ayatollah Mohammed Baqir al-Hakim. Questions immediately swirled about who might be responsible.

It took a few hours to get any clarity at all about what had unfolded, but as soon as he could, my colleague and replacement in Baghdad, Neville, sent me instant messages containing the latest information he was seeing on technical collection—a database showing the latest signals intelligence the Agency collects from various sources. I really wanted his feedback: if I had a knack for spotting trends through a cloud of data, Neville had an uncanny ability to remember seemingly every detail from prior events. He was like a walking Google interface; together we could think through the various aspects of the attacks and try to figure out what they meant. Had it not been for him, I would not have known where to start looking.

Granted, it's frowned upon to have an instant-message conversation about intel collected before a cable is formally submitted. That chatter is known as back-channeling, and it can absolutely get you sent home. Then again, Agency personnel aren't known to be legendary rule followers. Bureaucracy is frustrating everywhere, but even more so when you feel like it might be keeping you from tracking a killer. My calculus in that moment following the Najaf bombing suggested that circumventing the rules—gently—wasn't likely to cause any additional harm. In a best-case scenario, we might really be on to something. I needed to know what Neville had found out.

I carefully probed him through IM; any sort of grand war plan from Zarqawi was still sketchy at best—but there was a clear connection between the style and sophistication of the attacks and at least some of the people associated with them. After analyzing raw data, we had been able to make a connection with the same person claiming to be at the UN bombing scene.

By 2:00 p.m. on the day of the mosque bombing, I was in Katherine's office suggesting that we include this information in an upcoming President's Daily Brief. "I'm certain this is Zarqawi's network," I told her. She instructed me to write up a draft of my analysis; then she and I met with Cornelius, our group chief, for his thoughts. I knew my analysis was in for some intense scrutiny, as it should be.

PDBs have been described by historians as the most exclusive newspapers in the world—ten-to-fifteen-page collections of articles written by CIA analysts and hand-delivered six days a week to the homes and offices of fewer than two dozen of the highest-ranking government officials in the United States. PDBs are so secret that they generally have to be read in the company of the delivering Agency officer, then given back, to be stored at Agency headquarters. Much of the written material in a PDB doesn't qualify as breaking news, if only because each article has to be scrutinized and rescrutinized by people in the Agency hierarchy, then ultimately chosen for inclusion by the CIA's deputy director of intelligence. What PDBs may sometimes lack in immediacy, however, they make up for in depth. They're intended to be unimpeachable assessments of some of the most nuanced and complicated global events. Coordinating all those approvals is never a quick process—and for my first article, on a topic as sensitive as Zarqawi, I knew I'd have to defend my analysis.

At the same time, if I was right, and a line could be drawn between the UN murders and the mosque bombing, I knew that time was of the essence. For the following four hours, Cornelius picked apart the conclusions in my drafts and sent me back to my cubicle to write new ones. I was able to come up with responses and assessments for every question he asked, however—and just as important, I managed to bite my tongue over the condescension I sensed in his tone. Best of all, once I sent my article out for coordination among other Agency analysts, many of the e-mails I received were supportive and complimentary, offering useful suggestions and raising additional insightful questions. Finally, after one last draft, the CIA "editors" above me finished fine-tuning the PDB in the middle of the night and said I could head home.

I don't remember the exact time I arrived at our house, but I do know I couldn't sleep. My mind raced not only because of the sheer scale of what I had accomplished that day but also because of Zarqawi's surging and disruptive influence in Iraq. In just the past ten days, he had been responsible for killing nearly 125 people. His tangential, trumped-up role prior to the invasion had been relevant for political reasons—but Zarqawi was now involved in murdering people on the ground. He was becoming the very threat the administration had suggested he'd been all along. That night, I truly began to appreciate what Zarqawi meant for the coalition's task ahead.

I lay in bed and thought back through the binders of background notes, the intelligence briefs, the PDBs written by other analysts—everything I'd read about Zarqawi—from an entirely new perspective. His history mattered to me only because it suggested what he might do next.

Soon the first beams of sunrise came streaking through the bedroom window. I climbed out of bed and headed back to the office.

———

A few days later, a bomb made from a familiar combination of explosives and leftover ammunition from Hussein's regime was detonated in central Baghdad, just a few blocks from the area where I used to occasionally grab ice cream. One person was killed. While the attack bore some similarities to the UN bombing, the target was different. This one exploded outside an Iraqi police academy.

Why a training center? I asked myself as I stared at the cable on my desk describing the grisly scene.

That was no accident, however: over the ensuing few weeks, Zarqawi's associates attacked a police station for the first time—in Sadr City, in the northeast corner of Baghdad, killing ten Iraqi officers. In late October, in a daylong series of assaults, five suicide bombers blew up vehicles at four Baghdad police stations and at the offices of the International Committee of the Red Cross, killing forty-three people, all Iraqis. Days later, a dozen more Iraqi officers and nineteen Italian police officers were killed during an attack at the Italian carabinieri training center in Nassiriyah, in the southeast part of the country.

He's terrorizing the Iraqis, I thought, picking up my pen. He wants to isolate the United States from local support.

In the following months, attacks on Iraqi police forces became tragically commonplace. Seventeen killed at a police station in Khalidiyah, in central Iraq; three Iraqis killed and twenty-nine wounded outside a police station in nearby Baquba; dozens killed—most of them Iraqis—outside the coalition headquarters in Baghdad; then another nine Iraqis perishing, many of them civilians, in an attack on a police station in Mosul.

My heart sank each time we got word of a new bombing. The country's existing security forces had been utterly disbanded after the invasion in an act of hubris; now new recruits were willing to fill the gaps and take on the most dangerous jobs in Iraq for roughly $140 a month. They were risking everything to feed their families. That realization was never more sobering for me than it was during a two-day stretch in early February of 2004.

First, on February 10, a bomb in the bed of a red Toyota pickup obliterated a waiting area outside the police station in Alexandria, in central Iraq. Fifty-six people were killed — most of them Iraqis applying for jobs with the police force.

The next day, a suicide bomber blew himself up at an Iraqi Army recruiting station in Baghdad, killing forty-seven people — most of them new recruits. Police officials, we were told, had asked the recruits not to gather in such large groups, as it could attract unwanted attention. However, the applicants, many of whom had driven hundreds of miles to be there, feared the ranks would be filled by others if they didn't force their way to the front of the line. They were clustered by the check-in tables when the bomb went off. Following that attack, the Bush administration was forced to divert nearly $2 billion in reconstruction funds away from infrastructure projects just to shore up devastated Iraqi security forces.

And then things somehow got worse, because a third prong of Zarqawi's strategy soon became clear: he was attempting to control his territory through fear. And to do that, he had to utterly shock and completely horrify us.

Many of the first responders, frontline operators, and analysts who study terror saw the depths of human depravity in unflinching detail on September 11, 2001. In a moment I won't forget — on May 11, 2004 — I experienced another up-close version of terrorism. That day, my deep thoughts about our latest cable were broken by a knock behind me on the cubicle wall. "You need to see something," my colleague Seth said.

"Okay," I said.

"No," he said. "It's not."

A video had been posted to a forum we'd been monitoring on a radical Islamist website. "It might be Zarqawi," Seth said. We walked into an office where there were three other analysts and a DVD player and sat down. I will never forget the moment Seth hit Play.

The image was grainy and digitally compressed, but the video began with a short scene of a bearded man sitting in a white plastic chair in front of a yellow wall. He wore an orange jumpsuit similar to those worn by detainees I'd seen in Iraq. His hands rested in his lap; it was unclear if they were shackled. "My name is Nick Berg," he said. "My father's name is Michael; my mother's name is Suzanne. I have a brother and a sister, David and Sara. I live in West Chester, Pennsylvania, near Philadelphia."

I'd later learn that Berg was a twenty-six-year-old telecommunications engineer who'd twice gone to Iraq in search of work rebuilding radio towers. His parents had last heard from him a few weeks prior to the video being posted.

Twenty seconds in, the video jumps to Berg, bound at the ankles and with his wrists clearly tied behind his back, sitting on the floor on a brown mat. Behind him, five hooded men in black clothing and olive-colored ammunition vests stand awkwardly against the yellow wall. The man in the center identifies himself as Zarqawi. It was one of the first times I'd heard his voice.

"For the mothers and wives of American soldiers, we tell you that we asked the US administration to exchange this hostage with some of the detainees in Abu Ghraib, and they refused," he says in a lengthy statement, read off what appears to be a stack of loose-leaf paper in his hands. "So we tell you that the dignity of the Muslim men and women in Abu Ghraib and others is not redeemed except by blood and souls. You will receive nothing from us but coffin after coffin slaughtered in this way."

I felt my body go numb as Zarqawi pulled a disgustingly small knife from a holster on his chest. Berg stared blankly at the camera; I sincerely hoped he'd been drugged. There was no doubt what was about to happen and no way to prepare myself to watch it.

It was possible that there would be clues in the video — a reference to an event, a location, or other hostages. Perhaps a voice pattern that matched that of other suspects we were monitoring; even something as simple as the intensity of sunlight in a room could prove valuable for forensic analysis. Furthermore, since writing my first PDB connecting Zarqawi to the violence in Iraq, I'd become something of our unit's de facto lead analyst on the Jordanian. If anyone needed to witness what came next, I did.

In the years that followed, as social media evolved and terror groups became ever more adept at harnessing the Internet to spread their hatred, I saw entire departments in the intelligence community created to parse through similarly awful footage in even more minute ways. The intel community had units specifically dedicated to reviewing jihadist footage; some of the footage included pornography with child victims.

Later the Agency would bring in a cadre of mental health professionals to counsel analysts and help them process the emotions associated with watching things like the tape of Nick Berg's assassination. Such a support infrastructure didn't exist on that Tuesday morning in May of 2004, however.

On the video, Zarqawi lunges at Berg, grabs a fistful of the American's red hair, and throws him onto his side. The other four men fall on Berg, pinning him down. Berg writhes on the ground as Zarqawi begins sawing through his neck. There were screams that haunted my dreams for days. It took an unholy amount of time for Zarqawi to lift the severed head and the camera to jerk back to the pool of blood on the ground.

In that moment, I was practically blinded by horror, the desire for vengeance, and utter despair. This, for me, was the feeling of true terror. I'd never witnessed anything like it before; I closed my eyes and tried not to vomit.

When I got home from work that night, Roger had dinner waiting. "How was your day?" he said.

I just shook my head. I sat down in the living room and scratched

Gus, our new Saint Bernard. I had no idea what to say. There was nothing I wanted to say. Virtually no one in my life, including Roger and my family, knew that watching videos like that was part of my workday — just that I was becoming increasingly angry and distant at home. And obsessed with my work.

Zarqawi's war plan had another prong, which was soon exposed in rare and explicit detail: joining forces with al Qaida.

In February 2004, Zarqawi sent a message from Iraq to al Qaida; he was clearly weighing the benefits of his group merging with the al Qaida network against the costs of sacrificing his autonomy in Iraq and having guidelines added to his approach to jihad. Those business negotiations seemed far from complete at the time, but the merger seemed logical, and when it happened, I knew the United States would find itself battling a much deeper and well-organized pipeline of fighters rushing into Iraq. I sat down with Cornelius's deputy, Lucius, and other department heads to discuss how we might frame this information for a PDB.

"I think we need to explain why this change will be significant, both strategically and tactically, when these groups unite," I said.

"No; that's too speculative," Lucius said. "You can't know that for sure. Be safe and stick to the facts: how they know each other, what they are doing now."

I grudgingly accepted the direction from above, and a few hours later Cornelius approved the PDB I wrote about the correspondence between Zarqawi and al Qaida central.

Unfortunately, that wasn't the end of the discussion. The next morning, the Agency's top briefers called us into an office to discuss the product. "We couldn't use this," they said. "We can see they are in discussions, but so what? We have questions about where this information is supposed to lead in the future. Our principals are going to ask us the same thing."

In that moment, I clearly didn't hide my amusement very well. As my newly minted branch chief began arguing his case with the briefers, I evidently displayed a look of clear exasperation—which was, I admit, unprofessional. One of the briefers, in fact, took it upon himself to mention it to the chief of the counterterrorism analysts—who then questioned me after the meeting. I think she was able to see why I was frustrated but wanted assurance I wasn't being disrespectful.

So I sat down and rewrote the PDB in accordance with the briefers' suggestions, as I believed it should have been done all along. I was quite proud of this second draft; the next morning, I even received an e-mail from President Bush's briefer commending me on the work: "The president wanted me to send his personal thank you," she e-mailed. The team that publishes the PDB even selected it as an exemplar brief that should be sent to each of the analysts as a model of excellence—one of the few times an analyst's name is ever attached to a specific product, a real badge of honor in the DI.

That final pat on the back, however, was overruled by Cornelius and Lucius, and using the PDB as an exemplar was shut down completely. "This one was a team effort here," he told the PDB editors. "It would be wrong to attach anyone's name to it."

Hearing Cornelius's decision from the PDB editors rather than Cornelius himself pissed me off. For me, an acknowledgment that I was contributing and working hard meant something. There's a real feeling of accomplishment that comes from having any lawmaker—much less the president—truly grasp the depth and nuance of the information analysts are trying to convey. For the branch, after years of having our analysis questioned, we finally had a piece that truly spoke to our assessment without layers of editing. After months of being questioned and looked down upon by management, I hoped the rest of the DI would feel a similar sort of victory: we'd finally gotten an important point across.

———

In late 2003 my phone rang at home just after 3:00 a.m. I rolled toward the nightstand and fumbled in the darkness for the handset. The caller ID read UNKNOWN NUMBER, which I knew meant the office.

"Hello?" I said, rubbing my eyes.

"I'm really sorry for calling at this hour," said Cornelius. He was great at being nice when he wanted something from me.

"It's okay," I said. "What happened?"

Over the previous six months, these calls had become far more common. They were never good news. Back at the office, my growing role on the team required me to be in such close contact with other intelligence agencies that the CIA's tech support personnel had installed a classified phone system at my desk. There'd been some discussion about whether one should be put in my house as well, but that proved to be a nonstarter for a standard analyst. But it also meant that our late-night calls were usually pretty cryptic.

———

Maybe it was the hour of Cornelius's call, or perhaps just the relentless slog of misery I'd pored over in the previous months, but the group chief clearly sensed my defeated tone. I knew what came next.

"I'm sorry," he said. "I'm going to need you to come to the office in case we need to write something."

By then I was often writing two briefings a week for President Bush about Zarqawi's terror connections and his potential plans. On some slower Agency accounts, analysts wrote two President's Daily Briefs a year. Yet even as my fortunes at the office steadily improved, my frustration with the work hardened. No matter how much ink was spilled over Zarqawi's motivations and aspirations, no bombs were dropped. No tactics shifted. Zarqawi kept on murdering people, I kept documenting it for the administration, and they kept seeking the answer to an entirely different question—where is the evidence of a connection between Hussein and al Qaida?

I do understand that part of this comes with the territory. Analysts don't make policy; that's a hallowed tenet in the intelligence community. We're programmed to scrutinize national interests, not domestic political motives.

I saw a dire and imminent threat ignored in the context of what was then happening in Iraq. I clearly had an interest in being more forward-looking with my PDBs, and I constantly felt like our work in the counterterrorism center was being treated as a separate entity from any sort of larger foreign policy strategy. Watching the rise of a threat like Zarqawi made clear to me that battling extremism is far more complicated than simply rounding up the right bad guys. Defeating Zarqawi's threat and influence required a cohesive strategy that incorporated the military as well as State Department diplomacy. The administration seemed to me so blindsided by almost everything unfolding in Iraq that they were constantly reacting to new developments instead of proactively implementing a strategy for stabilization.

Granted, if the line between highlighting opportunities for action and suggesting policy sounds like a fine one, well, it is. Fulton Armstrong, who spent his career in the Agency's Directorate of Intelligence before moving on to the National Intelligence Council in 2000, once described this type of analysis, known as opportunity analysis, as swimming without getting wet.

There, in the middle of the night, I sighed and walked out of the bedroom. Up to that point I had spent hours answering the continual historical questions about Iraq's possible support of terrorism, while the real intelligence story was the growing connection between

Zarqawi and Usama bin Ladin. Zarqawi was not only becoming more menacing for the United States; he was also inspiring disparate networks that had not necessarily trained directly with al Qaida. In exasperation, my colleagues and I kept wondering why we weren't paying more attention to the imminent, growing threat than to the effort to piece together a case for the invasion. I was starting to become a very angry person watching people die in Iraq and seemingly doing very little to stop it.

So I quit.

CHAPTER 11

We Asked Him Nicely

Cornelius stammered when he read my resignation e-mail and said he would secure me a promotion, which would come with a salary bump if I stayed. I don't think I believed him—and in my mindset at the time, I knew a few more dollars would make no difference anyway. I had never left a job, or any other type of relationship, so abruptly. But the Agency's Counterterrorism Center was certainly not going to collapse without me, and I had had enough.

There was no time for anyone in the Iraq unit to fret about my departure—there was too much work to be done. I knew that coming back as a contractor was frowned upon but still considered an acceptable practice by most of my colleagues because of the pay raise. I felt angst over giving up the central mission and walking back in the door as a contractor, feeling marginalized and not part of the team.

Days after I had quit, Scott, the group chief from CTC, invited me back into his office to discuss, in broad strokes, the ways the Agency was expanding to become a bigger part of the Global War on Terror and the new roles that were being created.

He mentioned the basic outlines for a new sort of staffer the Agency needed for its reimagined role in the hunt for al Qaida: a targeter. CTC was expanding again, he told me, and the Agency had a new approach in mind to counter terrorism. Finally the idea that we'd get them before they could hurt anyone else was gaining momentum.

The drone program employed by both Presidents Bush and Obama to kill high-value terrorist targets was the most visible and contentious but not the only tool used to extend the reach of the US government. Since its inception, the Agency has had a paramilitary wing that today is part of its Special Activities Division (SAD), for example. SAD personnel were inserted into Tibet in 1950 after the Chinese invaded to lead resistance fighters against the People's Liberation Army of China; during the Vietnam War, they ran the Agency's covert Air America program.

In the late 1970s, however, use of the Agency's paramilitary options began to wane under scrutiny from Congress following revelations in the *New York Times* that the CIA had, among other things, plotted the assassinations of Cuban president Fidel Castro as well as the leaders of Congo, the Dominican Republic, and other nations. Following 9/11, however, when the government searched for options to combat the new and nebulous threat represented by al Qaida, whatever resistance there was to giving CIA operations a wide berth crumbled. The Agency's special operators were the very first ones into Afghanistan following the 9/11 attacks, cooperating with the Pentagon to help decimate al Qaida and overthrow the Taliban. Their role only rose in scope and prominence during my time at the Agency.

Furthermore, the special operations missions in Iraq had showed how well interagency coordination could work for surgical strikes on terrorists.

"We can make kinetic operations happen and go get these guys," Scott told me, "but we need to locate them. You know Zarqawi's current network better than anyone else here."

And I desperately wanted to find him. The US invasion and its bungled postwar strategies had given Zarqawi the platform to grow into the very terrorist threat the administration had said he was all along. Switching over to the operations side of the Agency to run a team that could dismantle Zarqawi's organization piece by piece, I decided, was the way I could help change the world.

"You don't even have to change offices," Scott pointed out. "We'll just set you up on the other side of the room where you were."

"What is this job even called?" I asked.

"We're not sure about that yet," Scott said. "For now, it's just specialized skill officer." Within days, I was back on the third floor of the New Headquarters Building.

Because the Agency requires employees to sign stacks of secrecy and nondisclosure agreements, being processed out, as we call it, can take a week or more to work its way through the system. There were a few back-end administrative wrinkles to be sorted out when I was recruited, but since I hadn't signed any official paperwork signifying that my run at the Agency had come to an end, I could get a new ID card and reenter the building.

A funny e-mail name greeted me on my first morning. Each officer in the DO is given a bogus autogenerated name for his or her Lotus Notes account to protect the identity of those who are undercover. You don't get to choose it, and, no, I found out, they won't change it once it's in the system.

"That's mine? Seriously?" I asked the tech guy setting up my account. "Is that a stripper name or a shampoo brand?"

We often used those names in real life, too. A colleague would approach my desk and address me by my cover name. I would immediately chuckle, but eventually it became commonplace. We frequently didn't know the real names of people working in the DO.

For the first time in my career, I needed cover.

Agency employees at the time were, or had been at some point, undercover—their real names and jobs obscured beneath layers of props and lies. Analysts generally don't need it, but on the operations side there are multiple levels of cover assigned to officers depending upon their daily responsibilities. Run-of-the-mill case officers abroad might receive "official" cover—mostly just a false identity and a made-up job.

Even deeper is "nonofficial" cover, when the US government might even disavow any knowledge of an officer's existence.

Happily, I fell on the other end of the spectrum. Being based in Langley, I mostly just required a light, or "notional" cover—a fake job to talk about while overseas and a new identity. That identity I was allowed to choose—as long as it was utterly mundane. I was told, "Basically, make it so that once you start talking about yourself, no one wants to hear any more."

To sound authentic, and to be sure I wouldn't forget it, I spun aspects of my own past into an elaborate new story. I took my grandmother's maiden name. I concocted a story about working in the HR department of some faceless fictional corporation. I'd had enough experience in that field that I could credibly tell stories of performance assessments and budget allocations that would make people's eyes glaze over. If anyone asked, I said I was married. I even printed out a photo of a not-too-handsome guy I saw on the Internet to carry around in my wallet. My husband, I said, was a middle manager at an architectural firm—which I didn't know much about in real life, but I'd gone on a few online dates with architects. We had no kids yet, I said, but we were thinking about it. For now, the story went, we were content remodeling our new home. I was, of course, very happy with my life.

———

There was a surprisingly small number of us on the Zarqawi targeting team initially at Langley. They were mostly older analysts who'd been in CTC for a while, along with a smattering of career operations officers and one or two new hires. Directly above me in the team's hierarchy was a woman named Anne. She was one of the first targeting officers in CTC, and she was more experienced than the rest of us on the new team. Anne's knowledge of Zarqawi's group was rudimentary, but she didn't pretend otherwise. And she was excited to have me join the team: months earlier, she had been appreciative and complimentary of my PDB connecting the UN bombing to the attack in Najaf and Zarqawi.

The basic job, Anne explained to me, was to supply targeting information to the station—intense intelligence curation, similar to what I'd done during my months in Iraq. I realized quickly that we needed to use the cable traffic to date to set a baseline of information for the field so we had a record of current intelligence. We started developing the initial targeting packages, which offered detailed information about locations of high-value targets, giving US teams a far better shot at snatching those whose removal would have the most adverse impact on the group. There was no formal training for the work I was about to embark upon, but there was a methodology that I could understand, one that was gradually taking shape in my mind. Targeters were glad to share this methodology with one another over entirely informal conversations at lunch or on coffee runs.

I arranged as many of those meetings as I could, reaching out to other men and women who'd made the transition to this new role before I did. This group included Barbara Sude, a petite woman with a sly wit who was likely one of the preeminent al Qaida experts in the CIA's New Headquarters Building, if not the entire US government.

One of the original counterterrorism analysts looking at al Qaida, Barbara had a reserved academic air that did nothing to disguise her driving passion for the work. One of the first times we spoke, I'd seen that she kept cartoons tacked up over her desk, clipped from newspapers she'd read during her frequent trips overseas. I'd liked her immediately.

The other woman I reached out to was a forty-year-old mother of three, Jennifer Matthews, who had graduated from a small Christian college in Ohio nearly twenty years earlier with degrees in broadcast journalism and political science. She was clever and tenacious, and in the spring of 2002, Jennifer helped locate al Qaida middleman Abu Zubaydah. She'd personally flown to a black-site prison to witness Zubaydah's interrogations and waterboardings that summer.

The two women offered invaluable guidance for my new role—in particular, ways to apply my DI-side analytical skills and processes to the role of operational targeting. They told me about the new forward-looking focus in this job; about ways to digest new information and pull out salient details in a shift from creating broad evaluations to fine tactical assessments. All the while, they underscored, they were testing, corroborating, and trying to balance ways in which a new data point can fit into a larger picture. At times, they assured me, it could be a confounding endeavor—not because of how little information was available but rather because of how *much* there was.

As an analyst, I was often scraping for details to try to fill out some larger picture. By contrast, these targeters said, their job and my own was in many ways a subtractive art. Particularly within a nebulous organization such as a terror cell, one thread of intelligence could be miles long before it became clear whether it was useful in the moment. Or maybe at all. By the summer of 2004, details about insurgent groups were being vacuumed up like so many crumbs, thanks to the Agency's intelligence collection apparatus—and only once I truly understood the modus operandi of all the players involved could they be pieced together.

Digging into the work back at my desk, I created a database—which, at the time, was no more advanced than an ever-expanding Excel spreadsheet—containing all the miscellaneous facts I could cull from the Agency software that captured raw intelligence from overseas: names, dates, locations, tactics, leadership structures. I scoured interrogation reports, satellite images—anything that might help geolocate a vulnerable node in Zarqawi's network and make my analysis actionable. I threw myself into the work with a renewed sense of urgency.

Once I identified a pressure point, I met with other team members for an internal assessment of the target. Was the individual involved in what appeared to be an upcoming enemy operation, or was he in some other way an immediate threat to coalition forces? If so, we could coordinate with SOF, which would send a military team to capture or kill him. Even that raised questions, however: if the person is a threat, do we mitigate the risk with a kill operation? Or should we capture and interrogate him? SOF has responsibility over that call on the ground, but if we felt strongly about a capture operation we needed to make our case in advance.

On the other hand, someone always asked, if the person was merely an interlocutor, might the target be of more use to us in place so that we could monitor whom he talks to and where he goes? Or, by simple process of elimination, would going after a certain target automatically finger the source on the ground who'd provided us the information, thereby blowing an Agency asset? Sometimes days of work to identify a target led to the decision to do nothing at all.

———

Within weeks of my arrival on the operations side, the Zarqawi targeting team underwent new staffing changes. As another wave of analysts was brought on board, Anne transitioned to a different role in CTC—and I was promoted to the targeting team's branch chief. It was my first official management role at the Agency—and I promptly divvied up the team.

I took my top and most experienced officers and dedicated them

to picking apart Zarqawi's shura council, the group of senior mujahideen who helped guide the growth of his organization. Those
councillors were key figures themselves, but depending on their
roles we could be content not sending SOF after them immediately.
They were the most likely people to end up in the same room with
Zarqawi at some point.

Then I teamed up some of our younger officers and asked them to
focus on logistics — the web of miscellaneous couriers and middlemen who helped supply the terror cell and coordinate its movements.
I felt that dividing the team was the most logical use of the limited
manpower we had, and this approach matched the skill set of the
younger officers with somewhat less sophisticated targets. Couriers
don't have the same ability to hide as their elusive superiors do.
Those middlemen made easier targets for the less experienced staffers to identify.

I touched base with team members every morning to see if anything interesting had come across their radar screens; then I'd lose
myself in frontline cables from other departments that had filtered
into my branch's queue overnight. The branch was a mixture of
senior and new officers, and informal mentor and mentee roles
evolved as time went on. I removed as many potential interruptions
as possible: in my new role, I could ask someone who was already
heading out to pick me up some coffee. If a principal arrived at
headquarters looking for a briefing from a branch officer, I was glad
to assign someone else to it.

The chance to capture a courier, this time one of Zarqawi's low-
level gatekeepers, suddenly zoomed into view. We had been watching him for months and had decided that he was more useful outside
of our custody because of the intelligence we were collecting. He
had a few dating profiles in the various countries in which he was
working. The profiles alluded to some of the typical characteristics
you would find in anyone's profile, but he was clearly embellishing
the facts. He described himself as a wealthy businessman, taller

than he actually was, and to attract the ladies he posted a head shot that made him look much more sophisticated than his other pictures. He was a source of amusement.

I had a daily meeting in the late mornings with the Counterterrorism Center's senior management. Inevitably, the first question they asked and the last question they asked—and, really, every question in between—was about the whereabouts of Zarqawi and his organization's leadership and how I intended to find him.

Every day posed a challenge and an unending set of solutions to plow through. The difficulty lay in finding the right one. It was intense and exciting, finally being able to do something about terrorism rather than just write about it.

I saw quickly how much more competition and political maneuvering there was in the operations side of things, where everyone seemed to be "handling" one another at headquarters the same way they manipulated assets in the field. But even more than that, I was taken aback by the seemingly impenetrable patriarchal structure.

Periodically I'd hear people refer to the "girls" on my team and whether they were attractive. Casual mentions of a woman being overweight—which I never heard about men there—somehow morphed into speculation about her technical or leadership abilities.

There were glaring instances of harassment I was unable to do anything about. A young female officer spoke to me one afternoon about an invitation she had received for a party outside the office. She and a collection of other young women officers had been invited to a house party that included midlevel and senior-level male Agency officers. I was disgusted, but I knew I had no way to squash it. I told all the young women I knew on the list to take a boyfriend—a real boyfriend or a stand-in—and to leave early if they felt compelled to attend at all. I later heard that the evening had devolved into a session of drunken lap dances in the name of "networking," which, I'm sad to report, didn't especially surprise me.

In the daily meetings at the office, however, the low-level sexism was far more frustrating. At times I'd make a quick suggestion that was noticeably better received when one of the men in the room said the exact same thing a few minutes later. Initially I took that as a cue that I should be more assertive, but that had the potential to backfire, too. Pretending that I was predominantly a warm, deferential woman seemed to be a little too out of character for me, so I had to use my strengths as a DI analyst to get my points across. This was in addition to the fact that I was a targeting officer and not a certified operations officer.

To the CIA's credit, however, there was one thing I sincerely appreciated about the operations side, which was different from my time in other male-dominated work environments: no one micromanaged me. They demanded results, of course—but those higher-ups outlined my task and trusted that I'd find a way to accomplish it. In fact, the level of autonomy they gave me to run my team felt a little too forward-leaning at times. I continually weighed the decisions I was making against my steep learning curve, sometimes second-guessing myself.

Following those morning meetings, much of the rest of my day was spent talking to members of my team about various strategies for capturing a specific target and issues that came up from station. I also spent time approving cables our branch intended to send into the field and communicating with our embedded targeting officer in Iraq as well as with our liaison there from Special Operations Command. At some point each evening the sun would set, and a few hours later, around the time a sentence in a memo didn't make sense after the eighth time I read it, I knew it was time to call it a day.

My role came with standard managerial duties as well. I was directed to help rehabilitate the career of a young female staff officer who'd been asked to leave the Farm—the CIA's training facility for clandestine officers. She was polite, eager, and willing to do what it took to turn her career around. She ended up being one of our best desk officers.

Then there was Myrtle, the woman whose dogged—and bullheaded—personality most closely resembles the character moviegoers saw on the screen during *Zero Dark Thirty*; she was working in CTC's cyber division. We also had one of my Zarqawi team members sitting on the cyber desk—Ginny, a whip-smart woman who'd been intimately involved in tracking several big targets as they had traveled across Iraq. It's safe to say those weren't the easiest of days. The underlying tension between al Qaida and Zarqawi's network was mirrored within the walls of CTC. The AQ department still didn't see Zarqawi's organization as a serious threat, and, like most of us, they felt the Iraq invasion was distracting us from our initial task of going after al Qaida—those responsible for 9/11.

The work culture within the office was strained—get any group of hard-charging men and women in the same suite of rooms and you can expect tensions to reach the boiling point. Furthermore, in a compartmentalized bureaucracy like the CIA, it was common for two teams with similar overarching national security objectives to approach the same overlapping targeting scenario from very different angles—and subsequently stomp on each other's toes. We might have had a bead on a key member of Zarqawi's network—but what if taking out that target disrupted a larger mission the al Qaida team had in place? Then what?

Several times my team butted heads with other teams from the al Qaida department and Myrtle's unit over the best way to proceed. It was painfully clear in such situations how lone-wolf Hollywood protagonists make for lousy real-life coworkers. On those days, it was often all I could do to keep my team focused on dismantling Zarqawi's group and not their coworkers.

The Rosetta stone for our work was a six-foot-by-six-foot map of Iraq that formed the backdrop for an ever-growing link chart on the wall of our vault. On it, red and blue arrows sprung out from Zarqawi's known operations centers. From there we taped head shots to the wall to connect associates, timelines, and terrorist plots. We were focused predominantly on top-tier and second-tier players within Zarqawi's network, which was by then known as Jama'at al-Tawhid wa'l Jihad. I discovered early on that if I went too many levels deep with link analysis, I could've tied a bombing back to my dog. Link analysis in and of itself is a reasonable tool for trying to define a landscape, but the analysis behind the chart is what really matters.

In our less harried moments I found that wall philosophically fascinating. It represented the very height of the United States' modern intelligence-gathering capabilities and simultaneously reminded me of an elaborate Old West "Wanted" poster. I recognized that there was a definite hometown-cowboy ethos in the way I approached my job—a kind of deeply ingrained moral code that sprung from those childhood horseback rides I took with my grandfather when we went out to count head of cattle. To put it bluntly: if you've inflicted enough misery to warrant an entire targeting team at the CIA dissecting your every move, you've basically made the short list of folks who just need killing. Zarqawi had at least *claimed* that death—or martyrdom, in his eyes—was the ultimate honor in his war with the infidel. I looked forward to granting him that "honor."

The weeks leading up to the transfer of sovereignty in Iraq in June of 2004 unfolded in much the same grisly way as the war did. Another attack near a military base in Taji, north of Baghdad, killing at least nine. Then simultaneous assaults in five cities—Baghdad, Baquba, Fallujah, Ramadi, and Mosul—left one hundred dead.

Many of the gunmen who stormed a police station in Baquba wore yellow headbands, linking themselves to Zarqawi's group. Dutifully I went through everything we knew about the attacks—and wondered what more I could have done to stop them. The US civilian authority had handed the newly formed Iraqi government a quagmire.

I was upset over the constant violence and mayhem the Iraqis were having to live through—and I'd begun taking the violence increasingly personally. It felt like an indictment in some way. I always found myself thinking back in hindsight: "I should have seen that bombing coming"; "Why didn't I recognize what that miscellaneous data point meant?" It's impossible to believe that an analyst can identify every pattern as it unfolds or predict every incident. Doing so requires the necessary background intelligence intersecting with the understanding of what it means right now and the interpretation of what it leads to tomorrow. The job just hardly ever worked that way.

A significant critical moment for me occurred in early July. It didn't come at Langley or at home in the middle of the night. It came on Georgia Avenue in northwest Washington, DC, in the cavernous hallways of what was then the Walter Reed Army Medical Center. Errol, a DC-based livestock lobbyist from my hometown, and a staffer for a Montana senator joined me as I went to the hospital to visit twenty-one-year-old army specialist Patrick Wickens. I'd heard from my mother that he was there. In a phone call, I heard from Patrick's mother that he might like some visitors and probably a few of his favorite cookies to supplement the hospital food.

I didn't remember Patrick other than as a young kid; he was much younger than I. I knew his name, though—like me, he hails from Denton, and no one's *that* far removed from anybody else out there. Soon after leaving high school, his mother told me, Patrick enlisted in the army—and soon again the mechanic found himself based near Karbala, Iraq, some sixty miles southwest of Baghdad.

His unit — Maintenance Platoon, Service Battery, Fourth Battalion, Twenty-Seventh Field Artillery, First Armored Division — had been in country far longer than initially scheduled because its tour had been extended. And Forward Operating Base Saint Michael was a rough place to be stationed.

The soldier was sitting up in bed, wearing an olive-drab T-shirt and talking with two other people. A blue IV tube was taped to his right bicep; a blue plastic watch was strapped to his left wrist. His no-fuss military haircut had grown in a bit on top, but his black hair still sat high on his forehead. A white bedsheet covered the lower half of his body; I could tell from the doorway how much of it was no longer there.

"Hi," I said as he turned to see who was at the door. "I'm Nada. I'm from Denton. Your mom said we could come visit."

As we sat there at his bedside, Patrick told us that the base was under daily assault from mortar attacks. His unit had lost eight soldiers to a roadside bomb — and Patrick, whose duties included driving a ten-ton wrecker that doubled as a tow truck, was called upon to clean up after the incident. "It was a mess," he remembered. "We had so much contact with the enemy that everybody just figured it was a matter of when and where you would get it."

Fate arrived at 9:00 p.m. on May 14, 2004, Patrick said. He was pulling guard duty at the front gate. "I don't remember much about the attack," he said. "We were just standing around."

The first mortar round that night sailed overhead. But moments later, a second round knifed into the side of Patrick's thigh and blew his right leg off. He was thrown to the ground yards away from where he'd stood. "I tried to move," he later remembered, "but that wasn't happening."

It was then in the hospital room that the emotions began overtaking me. The details of the conversation all become fuzzy in my memory; I realize in retrospect how many feelings I was struggling to process as he talked.

In that hospital room, I mostly remember looking into his deep brown eyes as he spoke—and realizing so much of my own regret. I remember how *young* he looked and how shaken I was by simply walking the vast white halls of that hospital. Many of those hallways had been lined with pictures of Defense Secretary Donald Rumsfeld, actor Tom Hanks, talk-show host Regis Philbin, and other high-profile individuals who'd stopped by to visit the wounded.

Patrick told us that his fellow soldiers rushed to his side the night of the attack and soon flew him by helicopter to a hospital in Baghdad. Eventually he was flown on a C-130 to DC and transported to Walter Reed. But the specifics of his journey didn't sink in for me at the time.

I'd seen brutality in Iraq. And by then I'd heard so much about the 875 US troops who'd already been killed there. In Patrick's room I understood firsthand how the 5,300 wounded men and women were trying to pick up the pieces. Visiting him brought me face-to-face with the legacy of the violence I had failed to prevent. I couldn't help but think of the terrorists and insurgents out there, maiming other young men—and older women—even as we spoke. I hadn't been able to stop those terrorists, either.

We were about to learn more concerning Zarqawi's interest in joining forces with al Qaida, thanks to a shadowy and little-thought-of character in the war on terror: a courier named Hassan Ghul.

Virtually nothing is publicly known about the wiry Pakistani with the pencil-thin mustache—least of all his role in America's fight with al Qaida. I knew very little about Ghul before he became Zarqawi's interlocutor save that he was a target for the al Qaida department in CTC. Perhaps that's not surprising: the CIA initially had varying reports about him—even concerning his nationality. Much less was known about his full associations with various terror groups. Yet within months of the September 11, 2001, attacks, my predecessors in Alec Station recognized that Ghul had a peculiar knack for showing up during al Qaida's most dramatic moments.

Far from a *mujahid* warrior, Ghul was a facilitator—a man who moved money and personnel throughout terror cells.

Beyond al Qaida, CIA analysts had been able to trace Ghul's ties to another terrorist organization, Lashkar-e-Taiba. Those connections enabled him to operate inside Pakistan with impunity—and to know others who did the same.

As exasperating as that was, however, there proved to be a silver lining for the analysts in our unit and the al Qaida department: monitoring his movements as best we could helped underscore the value of couriers in the growing link chart on the wall of our Agency vault. We might not yet know exactly where high-value targets such as Zarqawi were hiding—but *someone* within the terrorist organization did. And a courier tasked with crisscrossing the Middle East to hand-deliver letters—the lowest-tech solution was the jihadists' most effective in terms of evading the ever-growing technological capabilities of the US government—was an obvious place to start.

Zarqawi's organization was beginning to assert itself in Iraq, Ghul would later tell us, and the Jordanian wanted to make a trade: missiles for manpower. Zarqawi had weapons, perhaps even chemical ones, that he was willing to give to al Qaida, Ghul said. In exchange, Zarqawi needed al Qaida personnel who could help whip his growing band of foreign fighters into better-trained shape. Al-Iraqi agreed to at least hear him out, sending Ghul to meet with Zarqawi in northern Iraq in January of 2004.

As soon as CTC picked up intelligence that Ghul had slipped across the border, we sprang into action. We arranged to casually spread word throughout the border villages that one particular mountainous stretch of highway would be only lightly patrolled in the coming days. That, of course, was not the case. Days later, a tall man in a light jacket and trousers was stopped in his vehicle outside the town of Kalar, along that exact route, as he neared the Iranian border. In Ghul's satchel they found a small blue notebook full of names and telephone numbers. In addition, they recovered two CDs full of documents as well as a flash drive.

———————

During the forty-eight hours after Ghul's capture, we received twenty-one different intelligence reports detailing information the courier revealed while in custody. The information included names of fighters al Qaida was considering sending to Iraq, four separate e-mail addresses Ghul had for Zarqawi, and even a point-by-point rundown of the ideological differences al Qaida central had requested that Ghul discuss with the fiery Jordanian. I held my breath every time a new cable arrived on my desk; Ghul was proving to be an even greater treasure trove of information than I'd anticipated.

At the end of those two days, Ghul had given them everything he knew. That was hardly the end of Ghul's story, however. Many of us, including some of the Agency's top al Qaida counterterrorism operations officers, targeters, and analysts, believed it could be possible that Ghul might know more than he'd been letting on.

At the time, I didn't have a good understanding of what was likely to happen to Ghul at the detention center. He wouldn't be treated with kid gloves — that was obvious. I'd never been to a black site and I didn't lie awake at night worrying about how members of al Qaida were being treated. The vague familiarity I had with the locations came from mere whispers overheard in the hallway as some Agency employee or another returned from one.

I, and the rest of the world, now have a fuller picture of what was actually happening. I know now that Ghul's trip — assuming it was similar to other rendition flights — likely began with his being prepped during a twenty-minute "security check." There, the black-clad men transporting Ghul would have stripped him, photographed him, and subjected him to a cavity search. He would have been wrapped in a diaper, then a jumpsuit, and blindfolded. Headphones would have been placed over his ears; then a loose hood would have been draped over his head. His hands and feet would have been shackled and likely secured to a stretcher, which then would have been loaded onto a small plane. There's no doubt it must have been a miserable flight.

Ghul spent two days at "Cobalt." After those forty-eight hours, he was rendered again to the CIA detention center code-named "Black," a basement prison complex located in a government building. Upon arrival, according to congressional documentation of CIA records, Ghul was "shaved and barbered, stripped, and placed in [a] standing position against the wall." His hands were suspended above his head for two hours at a time.

CIA interrogators requested permission for further enhanced techniques, writing back to headquarters, "[The] interrogation team believes, based on [Ghul's] reaction to the initial contact, that . . . [he thinks] there are limits to the physical contact interrogators can have with him. The interrogation team believes the approval and employment of enhanced measures should sufficiently shift [Ghul's] paradigm of what he expects to happen." I was not involved in the decision to approve those methods. To this day, for a man like Ghul, I'm not sure what I would have said if I had been.

Upon having the request approved by the Agency's legal department, interrogators subjected Ghul to fifty-nine straight hours of sleep deprivation, whereupon he began hallucinating. He was placed in a hanging stress position, after which he reported "abdominal and back muscle pain/spasm, 'heaviness' and mild paralysis of arms, legs and feet," according to the congressional documentation. Agency doctors reported his "notable physiological fatigue" and reassured Ghul that his symptoms would "subside when he decides to be truthful."

The Agency publicly states that "information derived from [Ghul] after the commencement of enhanced techniques provided new and unique insight into al-Qa'ida's presence and operations in... Pakistan." In particular, that refers to the crucial bit of information in the hunt for Usama bin Ladin: confirming the nom de guerre of bin Ladin's personal courier, Abu Ahmed al-Kuwaiti — the al Qaida leader's primary connection to the outside world.

After telling his interrogators everything he knew, Ghul remained shackled inside that dungeon for the next three years.

———

By October of 2004, however, it seemed clear that things were about to get much worse before they got better. The idea that Zarqawi would eventually align his network with al Qaida had by early 2004 struck me as almost a foregone conclusion. Official notice, such as it was, came in the form of a mission statement Ginny unearthed. Over the previous few months, it seemed, Jama'at al-Tawhid wal-Jihad had stepped back the bombings to orchestrate something of a business merger. Ginny called me over to her desk to have a look.

"It should bring great joy to the people of Islam, especially those on the front lines," the message began, "that Tawhid wal-Jihad's leader, Abu Musab al-Zarqawi (God protect him) and his followers announced their allegiance to the Sheikh al-Mujahideen of our time, Abu Abdullah Osama bin Laden."

"We knew it was only a matter of time," I said.

The letter acknowledged communications between the thirty-eight-year-old Zarqawi and al Qaida for the past eight months.

There was nothing funny about the posting's conclusion, however: "O sheikh of the mujahideen, if you bid us plunge into the ocean, we would follow you. If you ordered it so, we would obey. If you forbade us something, we would abide by your wishes.... Now then, people of Islam, come rally to the flag of the leader of the mujahideen, which we raise together, and let us...cleanse all Muslim lands of every infidel and wicked apostate until Islam enters the home of every city-dweller and nomad."

With that, Zarqawi's organization was reborn and renamed, and bin Ladin was fully connected to the insurgency that was battling coalition forces. From then on Zarqawi's network was to be known as Tanzim Qai'dat al-Jihad fi Bilad al-Rafidayn: Al Qaida in Iraq. Zarqawi himself had now ushered al Qaida into Iraq.

CHAPTER 12

A Bucket of Turtles

In the spring of 2004, a new player was brought on board to lead our team, and I would be his deputy. I'll call him Tom. He had been working in Afghanistan with the Northern Alliance military force prior to 9/11 and then in Pakistan after the attacks.

Around fifteen years my senior, with the equivalent Agency experience to match, Tom had been part of SOF before becoming a CIA case officer—a relatively rare career move. That kind of military background was practically de rigueur for someone joining an Agency paramilitary team but was much less common for someone interested in traditional fieldwork. Tom had become something of a legend on the operations side of the Agency after his role in the CIA's seven-man Jawbreaker mission, which inserted operatives and paramilitary officers into Afghanistan following the 9/11 attacks. There he'd helped coordinate with Northern Alliance commanders and US Special Operations Forces units, ushering in the swift destruction of the Taliban. Now, three years later, the Agency was sending him to our unit.

"Hi. I'm Tom," he said in a stone-faced introduction on the day he arrived.

"Yeah," I said, half trying not chuckle. "I know." I felt like I might as well have been talking to Clint Eastwood.

At the time, the Counterterrorism Center was still in its infancy—to say nothing of the targeting work we were helping pioneer. Because of the very nature of terrorism, CTC lacked the kind of specific geographic focus that defined long-standing Agency divisions such as the Office of Russian and European Analysis and the Office of Asian Pacific, Latin American, and African Analysis. The vast majority of my work revolved around Iraq, of course—territory inside Langley that was at the time also tightly held by the Office of Near Eastern and South Asian Analysis. The women and men in that division seemed to peg my team as a bunch of newfangled cowboys running around in their backyard killing people when we weren't meddling with their burgeoning relationships with local tribal leaders. They made it clear that they weren't especially happy about it. Coordinating with them always led to headaches.

Prior to Tom's joining the team, for instance, I had met with several of those Near East managers at headquarters to discuss our common interest in keeping Iraq from reaching a boiling point. My suggestion, prompted by a discussion I had with Ginny about Agency successes in Afghanistan, was to ask for their cooperation in establishing relationships with the tribal leaders in Iraq's Anbar region so they could help ferret out Zarqawi's network. In Afghanistan, I pointed out, CIA officials had quietly used everything from children's toys to Viagra to bribe rural chieftains into aiding American efforts against the Taliban. It had worked there, and I wondered if something similar might work in Iraq.

You would have thought I had asked them to blow up Baghdad given the reaction I received. I certainly understood that the Near East division's established relationships in Iraq were somewhat tenuous and needed to be treated delicately, but I considered the need to hunt down Zarqawi's men a good reason to ask. Establishing a relationship that encompasses a discussion of foreign terrorist threats with tribal leaders would provide an opportunity for us to work together. The Near East managers I spoke with clearly didn't want CTC playing in their sandbox, muddying the waters — they wanted primacy over those relationships, in my opinion. CTC was still considered the backwater of Agency work for many traditional officers. As soon as I mentioned the possibility of approaching the tribal leaders, the meeting ended abruptly.

With that in the back of my mind, I mentioned right away to Tom that I'd welcome any thoughts he had on how to grease the skids between various departments.

"Yeah," he said with a nod. "This place is like a bucket of turtles. Everyone's scrambling to get to the top."

"I—"

I paused, visualizing the turtles scrambling to get a foothold on the side of the bucket.

"I'll remember that," I said. Then I showed Tom to his office, around four feet away from mine. I was rolling out the red carpet, because after ten months of working as the de facto head of the team, I knew we needed someone with DO experience to join us. The Iraq Task Force had two other teams at the time, but we were the main focus.

I sensed that by joining my team, Tom was going to be a little bored. In his words, he had been on the SDS track — stupid dangerous stuff — too many times. Few well-traveled field agents welcome a rotation back at headquarters, but everyone has to do "their time" at the mother ship, and he was no different. But he appreciated the importance of the work we were doing, and having him on board brought me an immediate sense of relief. My analytical background had led me to this targeting team. I knew the subject matter cold — and I knew that I could pick up whatever intelligence-collection capabilities the DO demanded of me. But I'd never managed an asset in the field. I'd never run an operation. Putting analysts like me in charge of field agents is begging for trouble; it's possible one part of my rapid rise within CTC was that they simply didn't have enough staff at the time. I was honestly fearful that I might get somebody killed because I didn't know what I was doing. With Tom in place, I was able to take on the official title of deputy branch chief, focusing on our team's analysis and strategy, while he taught me how to coordinate with case officers in the field.

Technical and ISR (intelligence, surveillance, and reconnaissance) collection proved to be one of our biggest assets in Iraq. And on our team, the targeting side of things was really starting to hum. That was thanks in part to Ginny's work on the cyber desk, where she spent much of her days sifting through cyber collection. She was as much a code breaker as a cybersleuth.

Zarqawi and his men, of course, had been very aware of using operational security in order to not be traced or tracked. Everyone who uses a piece of technology leaves a digital trail; Al Qaida in Iraq was no exception.

All the data we collected got funneled into our growing data-base, which better informed our initial analysis. We could corrobo-rate hunches, and case officers on the ground could sometimes help confirm leads. When we had a target identified, we would send over a detailed package to our team member embedded with SOF in Iraq. The package included a summary of the target and any histor-ical data we had on him, why he was important, and what we thought might result from various approaches to dealing with him. What did we anticipate might be learned by interrogating him? Might his removal have serious consequences for the larger mission? Beneath that was a list of the data itself and various other details that led us to pinpoint the individual — similar to the notes stu-dents might include on their tests when a teacher asks them to show their work.

What happened next varied widely, both in the field and back at headquarters. Because often, it seemed, that's where cooperation ended. Our challenge being that whereas we needed to directly communicate with SOF, because of bureaucratic processes, the CIA personnel in Iraq would take the lead. It had proven a very inefficient process, so we decided to embed a targeting analyst with SOF from that point on.

General Stanley McChrystal is an imposing figure—taller than I am—and he's not one for small talk.

McChrystal arrived in Iraq with the elite responsibility of commander of the task force. By July 2004, General Michael Flynn was brought on board as the task force intelligence chief. As McChrystal outlined in his book, "Mike's impact was distinct. He arrived as it became clearer than ever that our fight against Zarqawi was, at its heart, a battle for intelligence."

It is not a secret now that Mike Flynn is not much of a fan of the CIA. From my perspective, things started to change between our team and his after his arrival. The pace became much more frantic and intel sharing slowed down dramatically. In retrospect, I should have gone to McChrystal to work out what they needed and what we could add instead of relying on interlocutors. There were plenty of people on board willing to work as a team.

I'd seen quite clearly how much door kicking, or raids, the operators did in 2003—but it was clear by the second half of 2004 that the raids had picked up momentum.

By the time I became a targeter, SOF had set up new headquarters at a central Iraq airbase.

When I first visited those headquarters a few weeks after taking over the branch chief position, it was immediately apparent to me just how different this incarnation of SOF was compared to the incarnation there in August when I departed.

Communication gaps were a large reason for my managerial site visit to Iraq soon after being named branch chief of the Zarqawi unit. I was almost relieved to be out of headquarters and back in Iraq. It was my first trip to the country since my stint there as an analyst in 2003, and I couldn't believe how much seemed to have changed. In Baghdad, the Green Zone felt like a polished little city unto itself. On the military bases I visited, all the toilets flushed. And at the airbase, of course, the nerve center for SOF was unlike anything I'd seen a year before.

There must have been a thousand people at the compound the day I arrived. Next to the hangar housing the command center was a building of similar size. That was the detainment facility, I was told, where night after night operators deposited the haul from their raids. Early on the units had conducted roughly one raid a day. By the time I visited, they were well on their way to ten times that.

As the insurgency, fueled in large part by Zarqawi's network, took hold in 2004, McChrystal bought into the idea that more doors needed to be kicked. Just as the CIA — the most hallowed intelligence agency in the world — responded to the attacks by stepping outside its established comfort zone and growing its paramilitary capabilities, McChrystal wanted SOF to expand its intelligence capabilities. To dismantle a terror network, he believed his teams needed to be more agile and could build a full intelligence component. SOF wanted more information about potential targets sooner so McChrystal could plan missions faster. This was echoing a long-standing, and not entirely unfair, criticism of the lack of collaboration among all government organizations.

Actionable, life-threatening intelligence collected by the CIA can be immediately shared with the military. But in order for the Agency to share strategic intelligence derived from human assets, CIA protocol dictates that the information has to be scrubbed clean of any detectable clues that might give away the source's identity.

Adhering to that standard is something the Agency takes very seriously—and unlike, say, supplementing official cables with a little back-channel communication to a teammate in the field, jeopardizing an asset's safety is a line you simply don't cross. It can get good people killed. All that scrubbing requires a methodical internal process to complete.

That's not to say we couldn't share intel collected in real time; we had to be discerning and careful of exposing sources. In addition, handing over raw intelligence from technical collection without context and detailed targeting research could prove an even bigger disaster. If SOF killed somebody simply because his or her name appeared in one of our records, it would have been on our collective shoulders, too, not just those at SOF. Context was important; the link chart on our wall was a reminder that not every rabbit in the hole is important or worth expending resources. Going after the wrong people can backfire tremendously, alienating the local population in addition to burning sources.

And then there were basic, frustrating, bureaucratic limitations to our sharing capabilities. Some government organizations, including the Pentagon and the State Department, use a separate database to hold and share classified information. The Agency has for years felt that SIPRNet, the Secret Internet Protocol Router Network, has unacceptable vulnerabilities and has instead used its own network for distributing classified material among CIA branches and personnel. The value of that separation was underscored by the WikiLeaks fiasco in 2010, when Private First Class Chelsea Manning illegally pulled 250,000 State Department cables—but not CIA documents—off the network and shared them with media outlets. Having government teams working off different computer networks was a factor in intelligence-sharing failures prior to the 9/11 attacks—and still, a few years later, the sheer clumsiness of the CIA workaround inhibited necessary communication between my team and SOF in Iraq. If SOF asked me for information about a specific person or location, the most efficient way to offer them details was to send them in an e-mail. But there was very little I was actually permitted to disclose in an e-mail.

SOF's effort to be its own intelligence agency immediately made me uneasy.

In real ways, SOF and the CIA were trying to cover the same ground by expanding in opposite directions. I believed both moves were equally misguided. In much the same way that a CIA analyst shouldn't try to do a case officer's job and vice versa, SOF shouldn't try to be an intelligence agency. And vice versa. Neither organization will ever be able to fully replicate, much less replace, the expertise of the other.

From where I sat, picking apart the enemy in Iraq required an intelligence approach SOF simply wasn't ready for or capable of. The military doesn't recruit and train its intelligence personnel the same way the CIA does. Furthermore, at the time I took over the Zarqawi targeting team in Langley, SOF didn't have the CIA's technological collection capabilities, or its human assets on the ground. They had terrific soldiers, and we were eager to use whatever information they could gather by kicking down doors, but they simply weren't seeing the same information we were. The bigger issue was that we both needed desperately to understand the scale of the problem Zarqawi represented.

Zarqawi's organization had started out as a loosely affiliated network. Now, inside of Iraq, a hierarchy and bureaucracy were taking shape within it similar to those of al Qaida central. I wanted to disrupt and degrade Zarqawi's group systematically in as few steps as possible. In most cases, I led my team to find shura council members, operations leaders, access players—bomb builders, mission planners, regional leaders, couriers, and perhaps some of Al Qaida in Iraq's recruiters. In 2003 we had already developed a good idea of *who* those people were using multiple sources, and it was only a matter of time before we pinpointed *where* they were as well. When we located one of those terrorists, we needed SOF to execute the mission because they had primacy in Iraq. I wasn't concerned about every low-level Iraqi foot soldier who once had contact with someone in Zarqawi's middle management.

SOF was taking a more horizontal approach, looking for insertion points where they could find them. *Boom-boom-boom*: they were daisy-chaining, grabbing a player and then going after the next viable target that guy knew.

We had a great relationship with SOF on a one-to-one basis; my team members and I could work very effectively with individual SOF operators. We could hold professional, productive videoconferences with our counterparts. I still think very highly of many of those men and women.

Burrowing through to an inner circle like Zarqawi's, I believed, required the insight that Agency teams achieve only after years of analysis, human intelligence gathering, technical collection, and assistance from foreign partners. We saw very quickly that the SOF military-style vision led to their misunderstanding individuals' roles within Zarqawi's network—if those individuals were part of the network at all. SOF commanders later told reporters that they were hitting the right individuals and raiding the right homes only around 50 percent of the time—and that they were satisfied with that. "Sometimes our actions were counterproductive," McChrystal acknowledged years later. "We would say, 'We need to go in and kill this guy,' but just the effects of our kinetic action did something negative and [the conventional army forces that occupied much of the country] were left to clean up the mess."

We had tunnel vision, too. Sometimes we were so focused on the network that we weren't asking the right questions about its activities this hour, this minute—from the station and from SOF. We needed to reinsert ourselves into the process.

Throughout late 2004, as SOF chased its target list, my team's packages of information increasingly began falling through the cracks. In one particularly memorable example from October of that year, we pinpointed a restaurant in Fallujah as the location where prominent mujahideen council members would be meeting on a specific day and at a particular time. But there was no movement from the military on the package. For reasons I was never clear about, the military simply didn't act on the information—until the day after the scheduled meeting. What became clear at that point, thanks to video taken from a warplane flying over Fallujah, was that just after midnight on October 12, US bombs reduced the restaurant—and buildings surrounding it—to rubble. But the council members were long gone by the time the bombs dropped; instead, according to reports, it was run-of-the-mill nighttime security guards who were killed in the blast. I was so disgusted that it marked one of the few occasions I instructed my team to send a follow-up cable to Baghdad underscoring the information we'd provided and the deadly results of their lousy follow-through. I wanted to make it clear that this was not our work.

By late 2004, we could see SOF approaches in Iraq becoming a quintessential example of how a tactical military operation can directly oppose a larger counterterrorism strategy. By necessity we had to allow some bad guys to continue to operate, because a slash-and-burn approach does not make trust and intelligence sharing possible. This meant keeping bad actors in place for the time being so they could inadvertently continue providing the CIA with valuable intelligence. I understand that highly trained operators find that approach disagreeable. But my team got equally tired of SOF complaining, "Why don't you have any new information for us?" and having to respond, "Well, the other day you killed the guy we were getting the information from."

Even as SOF units executed a growing number of raids throughout 2004, it was convenient for some in the government to downplay the threat that foreign extremists were posing to American interests in Iraq. Particularly as President Bush's reelection approached, the quest to justify the original invasion meant that the administration often discounted the enemy on the ground as insurgents — merely frustrated Baathists and "former regime elements," a phrase that seemed to pop up everywhere. A second category, that of the aggrieved, opportunistic local fighter, was acknowledged, but beyond that there was resistance to publicly attributing much of the violence to the third and most important faction: Sunni jihadists and other foreign elements tied to groups such as Zarqawi's.

That April, in the midst of the president's reelection campaign, I watched Bush defend his Iraq strategy in a prime-time news conference: "I feel strongly it's the course this administration is taking that will make America more secure and the world more free and, therefore, the world more peaceful. It's a conviction that's deep in my soul." Actual reports from the ground, however, left me no reason to be optimistic about the way the battle in Iraq was likely to evolve.

At the start of 2004, there were reports of some twenty-five attacks in Iraq per day; by late that year, there were approximately sixty per day. More than 160 US soldiers had been killed in the three months following the official handover of power — more than the entire number of soldiers killed during the war itself. By September, total US military fatalities in Iraq had passed one thousand. Those obviously weren't popular statistics, but they were accurate. Ginny was counting as many as one hundred disparate insurgent cells taking online credit for the violence. Many of those were fly-by-night groups that were little more than talk, vanishing as quickly as they appeared. But understanding which if any of them had to be taken seriously became an ongoing chore that illuminated a larger, dangerous point: Sunni strongholds showed — at least initially—broad popular support for destabilizing elements such as Zarqawi's network.

I could then see what Zarqawi did: Iraq was home to nearly 5.5 million Sunnis, more than a million of traditional military age. If Zarqawi could mobilize—by evoking grievances over wrongful detainment, perhaps, or the killing of a family member—even an infinitesimal percentage of them, he'd have at the ready a fighting force many thousands strong. It was true that Zarqawi's group was still maturing in its ability to foment violence in Iraq, but among enemy organizations, his prospects were clearly the brightest. He was the most public face of the killings that were disrupting the coalition occupation—only more so once bin Ladin acknowledged Zarqawi's oath of *bayat* in an audio recording that October. Describing the Jordanian as "the prince of Al Qaida in Iraq," bin Ladin called upon al Qaida sympathizers "to listen to him and obey him in his good deeds." It only made sense that aggrieved Sunni Iraqis would align themselves accordingly.

My team sensed that Zarqawi might be shifting his center of power south, away from the mountain ranges of Kurdistan and into a more central location: the so-called Sunni Triangle, northwest of Baghdad. In particular, by late 2004 we identified Fallujah, a city of three hundred thousand in the heart of the triangle, as a safe haven for extremists and their sympathizers. Our intelligence showed hundreds of non-Iraqi Arabs moving into the city during that year, bringing with them two Zarqawi trademarks: loads of cash and a militant vision of Islam. Our sources on the ground told us that the incoming Arabs compared themselves to the *muhajirun*— the earliest Muslims who followed Prophet Muhammad from Mecca to Medina. The locals in Fallujah, they said, played the part of the *ansar*, or the helpers in Medina who'd once taken in the *muhajirun*.

In April, Zarqawi's men had helped repel a coalition advance into the city after the highly publicized murders of four US contractors there. We'd received reports of residents in Fallujah spotting Zarqawi downtown, and many of the angry Sunnis in the city seemed happy to provide a new base for rebel fighters in Iraq. As the network of foreign fighters successfully recruited Iraqis to join their cause, Zarqawi's influence in Iraq became further entrenched, and his evil metastasized.

In a stroke of luck for my team, however, by late 2004 some of Zarqawi's men were beginning to wear out their welcome among nonmilitant Fallujans. Many longtime residents bristled at the extreme interpretation of religion, and the correspondingly heavy hand of punishment, being imposed upon them. Dissent among the ranks meant that we were able to recruit further assets to act as our eyes and ears on the streets—though we knew we had to be careful. In a few instances, those accused of spying for US intelligence agencies were murdered on the spot by Zarqawi's men. I felt much better knowing that Tom was overseeing that side of our work.

In late 2004, we caught a major break when Iraqi police arrested Umar Baziyani, a former head of Ansar al-Islam, with whom Zarqawi had originally allied in Iraq. Baziyani had split with Ansar and followed Zarqawi when the Jordanian pledged *bayat* to bin Ladin. At the time he was arrested, Baziyani was "emir" of Baghdad— one of the most prestigious roles in the newly formed Al Qaida in Iraq. That much we knew. But Zarqawi ran a very different organization from al Qaida. He wasn't as stringent about a hierarchy; his nodules of contact were more like concentric circles—hard for us to draw to their ends or discern their beginnings. Baziyani had the sort of organizational chart we needed—and days of interrogations by SOF yielded a wealth of information.

At this point, Baziyani confirmed to interrogators that Al Qaida in Iraq was in fact headquartered in Fallujah, though Zarqawi himself split his time largely between Baghdad and Ramadi—the two southern corners of the Sunni Triangle—farther west. Fallujah, positioned directly between the two, was a convenient location where Zarqawi could meet with his top deputy, a Syrian named Mahi Shami.

Like Shami, Baziyani was Syrian. None of those closest to Zarqawi, including his bodyguard and driver, was Iraqi. Purportedly following the example of Prophet Muhammad, who married his closest companions' daughters, Zarqawi had married the daughter of one longtime Palestinian associate. Following suit, Zarqawi's key deputies also married one another's daughters. The top of his network was very much a fanatical, interconnected family—and, according to Baziyani, they had given much thought not only to expanding their network's reach but also to succession plans in the event that high-ranking personnel were captured or killed.

To that end, Baziyani told his interrogators, they had established nine regional operations throughout Iraq, in locations such as western Anbar Province; the Kurdish northeast, along the border with Iran; and the Sunni stronghold of Mosul, near the border with Syria. Baziyani also told his interrogators that each region had an "emir," who organized food and shelter for the men under his charge with money that flowed down from the top. Those regional cells were allowed to operate largely autonomously.

With affiliates capable of striking virtually anyplace in Iraq, Zarqawi's constellation next needed a collection of military commanders to plan large-scale attacks and to help local Sunni sympathizers repel coalition advances. There were seven of those commanders, Baziyani said, in strongholds such as Fallujah, Mosul, Baghdad, and Anbar and Diyala Provinces, as well as in al-Qaim, a small town on the western border of Iraq that provides a gateway to—and from—Syria. In total, Baziyani estimated, Zarqawi had some fourteen hundred fighters at his disposal. By the time he formally aligned with al Qaida, the attacks Zarqawi claimed credit for had killed 675 Iraqis and forty US, British, and coalition soldiers and wounded more than two thousand people.

Finally, Baziyani detailed a component of Zarqawi's operation that would only grow in importance over the following years: that of media relations.

Days after President Bush's reelection in 2004, coalition forces mounted a massive campaign to pacify Fallujah once and for all. I got cables back at headquarters saying that military action was forthcoming, though we had no role in strategy for what became known as Operation Al Fajr (New Dawn). I felt sorry for the innocent residents about to be embroiled in misery; I wished there were some way that the United States could clarify that we were on the side of those residents who wanted Zarqawi gone.

On November 7, twelve thousand US troops stormed Fallujah, going from house to house to roust insurgents in the bloodiest stretch of urban warfare since Vietnam. When the shooting finally abated after more than six weeks of fighting, two thousand insurgent and foreign fighters were dead, and twelve hundred others were captured. More than eighty US troops had been killed. The destruction of the city had been nearly absolute; some 70 percent of the buildings in Fallujah were damaged or destroyed, including at least one hundred mosques. Zarqawi, unfortunately, was nowhere to be found. We later learned that he likely fled north from the city before the first shots had been fired. I read that he might have dressed as a woman so he could slip away undetected.

As news teams reentered what was left of the city, I watched as a CNN cameraman embedded with the Marines strolled through a decimated Al Qaida in Iraq, or AQI, concrete command center in Shuhada, a neighborhood in the south of the city. A black-and-white banner in Arabic was painted on the wall. It read AL QAIDA ORGANIZATION.

"You have to be kidding me," I said when I saw it. As absurd as the sign looked, it also announced a notable shift in operational tone for the organization. Bin Ladin operated from the caves and shadows. Core al Qaida was a clandestine network. Yet there in Fallujah, Zarqawi's group basically hung a sign on the side of the building announcing, "We've set up shop. Here's your caliphate government headquarters."

Along with computers and stacks of passports, soldiers found notebooks full of fighters' names, ammunition, medicine that had been stolen from USAID deliveries, and letters written by Zarqawi to his lieutenants. Practically infantile notes in the building such as "Go to the flour factory; there is something there for you" led coalition forces to nearby warehouses. In one of them they discovered a makeshift classroom where there were rudimentary drawings of US fighter jets and suggestions on how to shoot them down as well as a Ford Explorer that was being converted into a bomb. The SUV was registered in Texas; we never did figure out how it got there.

In the Jolan district, on the edge of the Euphrates River, in the northwestern corner of the city, Marines found something far more troubling. Inside a metal-sided warehouse, past the insurgent caches of rocket-propelled grenades and artillery rounds, the Marines discovered a crawl space barricaded with a safe. Pushing it aside, the troops saw an Iraqi man chained hand and foot, lying in his own waste. The virtual skeleton proved to be a still-living taxi driver who'd been abducted four months earlier along with a pair of French journalists — thankfully, he would survive.

Down the hall, Marines crashed through another door and found themselves in what appeared to be a ramshackle movie studio. On the table was a glass with ice in it; whoever had left had just done so in a hurry. Nearby, Marines found two video cameras, klieg lights, and instructions on how to get footage to the Baghdad offices of some of the regional news networks. On the back wall of the room hung the black-and-green flag of Ansar al-Islam. The floor was caked in dried blood. The moment I read that last detail in the intelligence report I received, I knew it was the room where Nick Berg had been murdered.

———————

By early 2005, as SOF daisy-chained its way through the Sunni Triangle, a few notable members of Zarqawi's network ended up either dead or in US custody—and back at headquarters, we could "X" them off our link chart.

In November of 2004, a Saudi national known as Abu Waleed Saudi, a military aide of Zarqawi's, was killed outside Fallujah. The next month, a tip from a fed-up local Iraqi led SOF to Fadil Hussain Ahmed al-Kurdi, a courier who helped Al Qaida in Iraq communicate back to al Qaida central in Afghanistan, and to Abu Marwan, who commanded AQI's terrorist operations in Mosul. Then, in a move I was satisfied to see, SOF killed Hassan Ibrahim, who had lorded over the execution studio in Fallujah.

Our grim game of cat and mouse was officially on. Even as Zarqawi's network sustained losses, others within it rose up to continue the brutality. In mid-December, AQI responded with a pair of simultaneous car bombings in two Shia holy cities, blowing up a funeral procession in Karbala and Najaf's main bus terminal. Sixty people, mostly Iraqi civilians, were killed.

A host of AQI characters—as well as a list of people detained erroneously—whom the Pentagon invariably described as Zarqawi's "lieutenants," were arrested in mid-January 2005. Abu Omar al-Kurdi, a pudgy thirty-six-year-old veteran of various jihadist camps across Afghanistan, was one key score I was particularly pleased to see captured. His specialty was rigging old artillery shells into massive explosive devices. He was Zarqawi's headline bomb maker—the man whose signature devices, we'd been able to prove, had been used in both the UN and Najaf bombings in August of 2003 and in nearly three dozen other attacks in the capital since then. Kurdi's bombs had killed hundreds. He was eventually hanged by the Iraqi government.

Zarqawi would make his thoughts on current events known in the form of audio recordings and official AQI statements. Iraqis voted to select a 275-seat national assembly that would draft the country's new constitution. Zarqawi raged against "this lie that is called democracy" and insisted that "whoever helps promote this and all those candidates, as well as the voters . . . are considered enemies of God." His written statement concluded, "Having warned you, we are relieved from any responsibility."

More than a dozen small-scale attacks were carried out by insurgent groups at or near the thirty thousand polling stations across Iraq on election day — we were holding our breath that an attack on a polling station would not be successful. In the face of the extraordinary military security at those centers, most attacks killed only one or two people — tragic, but not as bad as it could have been. On the whole, it was a momentous day for the 14.2 million registered Iraqi voters — many of whom loudly decried the senseless ongoing violence perpetrated by jihadist groups. The line was becoming ever clearer between dangerous elements who wanted bloodshed and those Iraqis who simply wanted to go home and rebuild their lives. There was a growing overlap between the two groups — both wanted America out of their country. And on one dramatic February day in 2005, SOF got a tip from an Iraqi citizen who decided to help fight back against terror.

On February 20, midafternoon Langley time, I yelled into Tom's office: "C'mon!" He looked up quizzically, and I started to explain as we headed to another US facility; then the two of us crowded behind the monitor in the live feed room.

A local gave a tip to an Arab-American soldier in the task force. He said that within a given late-night window, Zarqawi could be found in a white truck driving down a stretch of highway north of Baghdad. The task force was busy establishing an ambush.

I stared into the monitor, looking over the trees and roadways in the black-and-white feed, waiting for something to happen. For an agonizingly long time, nothing did.

I turned to Tom and shrugged. "Where is he?" I asked. "Are we even sure it's him?"

I wasn't the only one frustrated. Based on the tipster's guidance, Zarqawi was so late to the location that the members of the task force figured the mission was a bust and made preparations to leave the scene altogether.

Almost at that very moment, however, a white truck appeared on the horizon, trailing another vehicle in a small convoy.

"That's him," Tom said quietly.

Suddenly I could see the pickup zigging and zagging around army special operators' roadblocks—and then the driver laid on the gas. The truck flew across our monitor, barreling toward a secondary checkpoint. One of the SOF operators leveled his mounted M240B machine gun at the vehicle.

This is it, I thought.

An operator requested the okay to fire.

Yet that didn't happen. Without a positive ID of the vehicle's occupants, the lieutenant in charge acted responsibly and refused the order to shoot, opting instead not to shred the truck with machine-gun fire. As the white pickup truck screamed past, Zarqawi, now visible through the window, wearing a Blackhawk tactical vest and holding an assault rifle, was screaming at his driver. "He was shitting his pants," one special operations source later told the *Army Times*. "He knew he was caught."

"Where is he going?" I muttered, almost to myself.

Army SOF personnel raced after the truck. A few miles past the blown checkpoint, Zarqawi's truck sliced hard to the right off the highway, roaring down a small gravel road. Dust from the tires clouded the feed, but I could see that every time they hit a bump, the truck went airborne.

As the truck entered a heavily wooded area, the vehicle screeched to a stop. Zarqawi grabbed his rifle, an ammunition clip, and a fistful of the cash he was carrying and bolted off into the trees. He was smart enough to know we couldn't get a positive signature on him through the foliage. "Zarqawi became hysterical," his driver, Abu Usama, told interrogators after the army special operators caught up to him. "Zarqawi did not know where he was because he demanded repeatedly, 'Who lives in this area? What sub-tribe is here?'"

On the monitor, we watched the flashes of Zarqawi racing through the trees. Then he lucked out for the second time that night: the feed cut out at that moment. Inevitably, even the cleverest of technologies doesn't operate as seamlessly as we'd like. By the time we had eyes on the area, Zarqawi was gone.

Tom and I looked at each other, and a storm of expletives swirled between us. Yet we soon realized there were reasons for optimism. Zarqawi had left behind in the vehicle other weapons and roughly the equivalent of $100,000 in euros — which hinted at a deeper potential connection with al Qaida's European affiliates than we'd previously understood. What's more, his driver was captured by American forces. And Zarqawi left a laptop computer.

Unfortunately, even that silver lining began to erode. For nearly two weeks, SOF sat on the computer despite our repeated entreaties for them to deliver it to our technologists, who could crack it faster. "Give it to someone else," we pleaded in our cables to SOF. "Intelligence agencies are equipped to break the encryption quickly."

Days later, Tom and I argued my case on-screen, in a secure videoconference call with McChrystal and one of his top aides. After a forty-five-minute round of PowerPoints and status updates, Tom said, "Any updates on that computer? We're ready to move on that intel."

The general looked to his aide, who responded, "We have confirmed that it's foreign-made and that it's encrypted and we've been unable to open it."

I tried not to kick Tom under the table—and not to say anything that might accidentally alienate our counterparts. But to McChrystal's credit, the computer was sent to another facility shortly afterward; it's possible that he hadn't understood the inability of his staff to deal with the encryption. All I could think of at the end of that meeting was a quotation Tom used periodically: "We are getting sucked into the vortex of stupidity."

On Zarqawi's seized computer, there were e-mails and contact information, along with a collection of photographs on the hard drive. I spread them out on a table in front of the other analysts and targeting officers.

Beyond that, Zarqawi had a giant stash of porn, which by then I knew was de rigueur on jihadist computers, seventh-century interpretation of Islam be damned. What was most memorable was the bizarre collection of animal pictures he'd downloaded—including one creepy snapshot of a snake swallowing a giant crocodile or alligator whole. They weren't funny or even interesting. They were just...weird, and they fed the impression we were forming of Zarqawi's incongruous persona as I understood it—a fanatical, hypocritical, murderous dropout who was capable of masterminding a terror network that for years confounded the most powerful military and intelligence agencies in the history of creation yet who had the general maturity of a nineteen-year-old.

Whatever he may have been, however, Zarqawi was not the type to be cowed. Days after he came face-to-face with SOF, I got another call in the middle of the night. One of Zarqawi's men had detonated a car bomb outside a health clinic in the predominantly Shia city of Hillah, sixty miles south of Baghdad. The attack was aimed at police and Iraqi Army recruits, yet dozens of women, children, and other civilians also fell victim to the bloodshed. More than 125 people were killed; it was the single deadliest act of the entire Iraqi insurgency.

As I lay there clutching the phone to my ear in our bedroom, Roger rolled over to look at me. He could clearly sense my anxiety rising. "I think you oughta dump your other boyfriend," he said with a sleepy smile. He closed his eyes again.

I turned back to the phone. "I'll be in soon," I said.

CHAPTER 13

Shift in Momentum

I checked my watch, my foot tapping urgently beneath my desk. At nearly 4:30 p.m. on Groundhog Day in 2005, I was racing to finish yet another cable containing the latest intelligence collected by my team. Tom and I were the only two people on our team with the release authority to send cables out to our stations in the field, and I wanted to get this one off my desk before leaving. It was the last remaining file in my internal network "queue"—a term so old-fashioned it pretty well mirrored the World War II–era, all-capital-letter font we still used for the actual cables—but by then I was running late, and Tom knew it. He stuck his head into my office.

"You know, I have sent a cable or two before," Tom said. "I can take care of that."

"I know, I know," I said. "I'm just trying to clear out my queue."

"All right," he said with a shrug and walked away.

As our team had found a groove and as our areas of expertise began complementing each other's, Tom and I had become good friends. There was real camaraderie to be found in feeling like we were on a misfit island of targeters within a larger Agency that didn't understand how to embrace our work. Meanwhile, Tom intrinsically understood the impact that a CIA career has on people who can't talk about it beyond office walls. Given his experience, he could probably see the toll it was taking on me better than I could.

"But seriously," Tom said, coming back a minute later, "you don't want to be late."

He was right. A few months earlier, Roger had proposed. Truth be told, it was more of a conversation than a YouTube-able moment on bended knee. After we attended a friend's wedding together, I asked him, "Is that going to happen for us? Because, you know, I'm busy, and we shouldn't waste each other's time." After a heated discussion, he said, "Okay," and asked me to marry him. It was actually a fine way for it all to unfold; I've never been much of a romantic. I'm emotive, but rarely *emotional*. I roll my eyes at that silly gender stereotype.

On that chilly day in early February of 2005, as I scrambled to finish the cable, Roger and I were scheduled to be officially wed by Judge Thomas Fortkort at the Alexandria Circuit Court in Alexandria, Virginia. Judge Fortkort is Roger's uncle, and he'd agreed to perform the civil ceremony in advance of our larger wedding celebration, which would be held out in Montana later in the month. I'd dressed up a bit, wearing a black skirt to work that day—some of the women on my team joked that they didn't think I owned anything but pantsuits—and a green cashmere sweater. I'd scheduled our special court date as late in the afternoon as I could so that I wouldn't have to miss much work, but clearly it wasn't late enough. I looked up to see Tom still standing in my office doorway.

"I'm not leaving until you do," he said.

"*Fine,*" I huffed. With that, I sent the cable to Tom, shut down the computer, and raced over to Alexandria.

I grabbed the first parking spot I found and surely pumped way too many quarters into the meter. I ran under the grand brick archways outside the courthouse and up the stairs through the front door. Roger was inside waiting.

"Sorry—am I late?" I said as I caught my breath.

He smiled. Just then, at the other end of the hall, Roger's aunt Diana and cousin Mike—our witnesses for the ceremony—emerged from a stairwell and waved excitedly.

"See?" Roger said. "You weren't late at all."

The judge breezed through the legal aspects of the ceremony and performed a little reading. Diana, his wife, shed a few tears. It was lovely. A few weeks later, we were all together again out in Montana, at our ceremony and raucous reception at the 320 Guest Ranch, just north of Yellowstone National Park. More than seventy-five friends and family were there to celebrate with us. All my hesitation had disappeared by that time.

Back at home, Tom also got to know Roger well, and we had regular dinner dates with Tom and his wife. One evening we sat in a northwest DC restaurant telling them about our misadventures when we were adding a room onto our house.

"We were ripping up the kitchen floor to put in a new one," Roger said. "Gus [our recently adopted Saint Bernard] is nearby, just passed out. He's basically an area rug. But when I hammered on a board, a rat ran under my leg past Gus's nose. Gus totally lost it! He was flying around the house after that thing."

"Bear in mind, he's one hundred and forty pounds," I added. "He can rest his chin on the kitchen table."

"So the rat runs out of the kitchen and into the living room toward Nada — and when she sees it, she loses her mind. She's screaming like mad and climbs up the back of the couch," Roger said. "Gus is tearing through the living room, *destroying* things. He flips a chair, almost knocks over the bookcase, then he slams into the couch Nada's on and practically dumps her on the ground."

"The rat's running for his life," I said, "and Rog figures he'll pin the thing by flipping over an end table to block the door. I started to say, 'C'mon, city kid, what's that going to do?' but I didn't have time. The rat hurdles the end table, goes flying through Roger's legs — and he's half bent over, looking up to see this one-hundred-and-forty-pound dog with his ears pinned back, about to hit him like a freight train."

"It was like it happened in slow motion," Roger said.

"Gus leaps over the end table, and Roger *dives* out of the way," I said. "The rat goes running down a plumbing column into the basement. Gus turns the corner at breakneck speed and goes racing down the stairs after him."

"We cornered the rat behind the washing machine," Roger said, "and I finally killed it. But even after I took it away, Gus could still smell it. He spent forever down there, just turning in circles and sniffing at the washer.

"Nada finally said to me, 'Did you show Gus the dead rat?' And I said, 'Um, no.' She said, 'You have to make sure he knows.'

"I thought, 'Well, okay,'" Roger said. "So I took him out to the garage and showed him the rat in the trash. I guess he was satisfied. He went right back to sleep."

We all had a good laugh at the memory. "Sounds like quite an adventure over there," Tom said. "Just let us know if you need any help."

Truth is, we did. And sure enough, the very next weekend Tom showed up at our house with tools, and he, Roger, and I spent a fuzzy Saturday drinking perfectly bottom-shelf bourbon and finally—more than a year after we'd moved in—ripping up the cruddy ceramic tile on that kitchen floor once and for all. I didn't think about work at all that day.

I smile at those memories now, because those are some of the few relaxed moments I remember from that period in my life. The pressure I felt throughout 2005 was simultaneously suffocating and deflating. At the office, ongoing interdepartmental squabbles and external communications breakdowns with SOF began eating away at what little optimism I had left about my team's ability to effect change. I bounced between wanting to throw up my hands and quit again and trying to invest myself even more fully in the job, as if to somehow conjure up a breakthrough. One fourteen-hour plane flight blurred into another as I spent increasingly long stretches with our team members in Iraq and our intelligence counterparts in other Middle Eastern nations, hoping that being in country might illuminate some fact I'd been missing. Outside the office, I found myself checking the news constantly, perpetually awaiting the next phone call asking me to come in because AQI had set off another car bomb. I still felt responsible for the murders Zarqawi committed, and my growing frustration mixed with that disappointment into an ugly cocktail of guilt and helplessness.

Anxiety manifested itself in various ways. At home I was testy and easily provoked by things going awry. And with the loosely compartmentalized chaos of our ongoing remodeling, there was always something going wrong. Because I had so little control at work, my lack of ability to control chaos at home often felt like more than I could bear. When Roger caught me clenching my jaw and asked me what was the matter, I never could articulate it.

Outside our house, whether at work or on the street, I became oddly numb to almost anything remotely threatening. In one episode I've never seen reported anywhere, we received an internal security e-mail at the office saying that a Middle Eastern man in slacks and a button-down shirt had walked around the edge of the perimeter fence on the Agency's Langley property. He stumbled a bit, apparently, then keeled over onto the ground. Eventually security went out to check on him, and the man was declared dead right there on the grass. I remember thinking, "That's weird," and then not a word was ever spoken about him again. I didn't ask for details, nor did I follow up on it in any way. In retrospect, *that's* weird. I hadn't thought about that incident again until Roger brought it up many years later.

As taxing as intelligence work was, the rewards were piling up that spring for the CIA in particular, thanks in no small part to an ingenious program crafted by the CIA's agency-wide cyber team and executed with great skill in our Zarqawi branch by Ginny.

In the years before smartphones, insurgents and other fighters wanting to send e-mails did so without awareness that they could be tracked. Tom and I devised an operation using authorities under Foreign Intelligence Surveillance Act section 702 utilizing some of our operators on the ground in Iraq to provide feedback on specific targets. With Ginny's help we had two types of collection feeding our targeting packages and providing validation of targets. This was the kind of analysis targeters specialized in.

In some ways, the most notable part of the process was how straightforward it seemed. Zarqawi and his top men were clever about the basics of avoiding detection, but particularly in the era before Edward Snowden's leaks about US intelligence programs, I can't imagine that those fanatical fighters had any understanding of the true technological capabilities the CIA and the National Security Agency possessed. Soon we were in receipt of the kind of information that made it possible to strike back at a few key players in Zarqawi's growing operation.

The team specialized in sending actionable targeting packages forward on individuals and nodes within the network.

One individual, Rawi, had been instrumental in coordinating the movements of foreign fighters, vehicles, and weaponry into Iraq along that rat line. The full scope of Zarqawi's network was coming into clearer focus by the day.

Soon after, a gunrunner named Abu Abbas was captured in Baghdad. Abbas had been responsible for stealing as many as four hundred rockets and 720 cases of plastic explosives from a weapons facility in the nearby township of Yusufiya in early 2003. It was Abbas who had provided the raw materials Abu Omar al-Kurdi used to make his catastrophic bombs. He pointed the military to his remaining stockpiles of weapons, which he'd buried in multiple locations on and around a farm in Yusufiya.

Then we landed an even bigger score, in the northern city of Mosul, the capture of Abu Talha, AQI's emir of that city and a key member of Zarqawi's inner circle. Talha, too, had split with Ansar al-Islam a few months earlier and, according to detainee reports, met

with Zarqawi as often as once a month in various locations throughout western Iraq. We considered him a logical successor for the top
spot in AQI if and when Zarqawi was eliminated. The CIA had
been analyzing and identifying key players inside of Ansar al-Islam
since at least 2001.

In Mosul, Talha oversaw a few hundred fighters, executing
approximately fifty car bombings. Within Zarqawi's ranks, Talha
stood out. As opposed to being a Sunni ideologue, Talha was a former Republican Guard with close ties to Hussein's former government. His focus was on disrupting the implementation of democracy
by means of attacks on politicians and polling places. That was particularly true in light of the successful parliamentary elections in
January, which led to a Shia, Ibrahim al-Jaafari, being named prime
minister in April. The lion's share of Jaafari's cabinet posts were
filled by Shias.

Former Sunni Baathists such as Talha had been livid at the
appointments and the marginalization of their religious sect. According to a DOD press release, Talha began wearing a suicide vest
nearly twenty-four hours a day and had pledged never to surrender.
Yet in the midst of a whirlwind afternoon during a SOF raid on a
safe house in a quiet corner of western Mosul, Talha did just that.
He offered even more details about Zarqawi's communication and
travel patterns. He languished in a cell for a few years, then was executed by the Iraqi government.

Into Talha's place as the emir of Mosul stepped a man whose true
menace would only be realized years later: Abd al-Rahman Mustafa
al-Qaduli. Having joined AQI only months earlier, Qaduli had little
paper trail to speak of. He, too, would be arrested a few years later,
though he fared better in confinement than Talha did. Qaduli was
released from an Iraqi prison in 2012, at which point he joined the
leading extremist group in the region — and the world — at the
time, the Islamic State of Iraq and Syria, or ISIS. There he worked
his way up to second-in-command, becoming the group's top finance

official and a general planner for ISIS's international attacks. Ultimately, in March of 2016, three days after ISIS fighters killed thirty-one people at the Brussels airport departure area and four months after ISIS fighters murdered 130 people in attacks across Paris, US Special Operations Forces units killed Qaduli as well.

Our successes in dismantling Zarqawi's network added up. In May of 2005, the Defense Department published a slide that counted seven of his lieutenants dead, thirteen others captured, and only one other remaining at large. Zarqawi was clearly on the run. But threatened animals tend to be the most dangerous animals, and Zarqawi and his men began striking out in all directions.

Weeks after that slide was shown, Zarqawi's men abducted three dozen Iraqi soldiers riding in a pair of minibuses southwest of al-Qaim, saying in a message-board posting that they were taken for crimes "against Sunnis and their loyalty to crusaders." That was followed by the killing of eighty-seven-year-old Dhari Ali al-Fayadh, the oldest member of the parliament that had been elected in January. A car loaded with explosives detonated next to Fayadh's white van as he was being driven to parliament from his farm outside Baghdad. Fayadh's son and two bodyguards were also killed in the blast. The run of scattershot attacks, whose death tolls almost invariably included Iraqi civilians, sent a message not just to us but also to al Qaida central: Zarqawi is a menace.

I had long understood the strategic and ideological chasm that existed between Zarqawi and the group to which he had shortly before sworn allegiance. Yet never was that laid out more clearly than in a 6,300-word letter Ginny brought to my attention in the summer of 2005, which was quickly spread among intelligence agencies. The missive, written by Ayman al-Zawahiri, al Qaida's second-in-command, bullet-pointed the organization's larger plans for the future of Iraq and offered a stinging rebuke to Zarqawi for his strategic mismanagement of jihad there. In the letter, Zawahiri reflects upon Zarqawi's attacks on the Shia population and the grisly beheading videos AQI had been delivering to Al Jazeera. It was immediately apparent to me how much damage Zawahiri feared the upstart Jordanian might be doing to the larger group's reputation, causing them to lose what he described as a "media battle" for the "hearts and minds" of the Muslim world.

"Many of your Muslim admirers amongst the common folk are wondering about your attacks on the Shia," Zawahiri wrote. "The sharpness of this questioning increases when the attacks are on one of their mosques, and it increases more when the attacks are on the mausoleum of Imam Ali Bin Abi Talib [in Najaf]."

Zawahiri continued, "Can [your] mujahedeen kill all of the Shia in Iraq? Has any Islamic state in history ever tried that?"

I was struck by how much the pages seemed to ooze condescension. Why Zawahiri was risking exposing himself by communicating raised real questions for me about how apoplectic he — and, by extension, bin Ladin — must have been. It was enough to make me hope they might just send an al Qaida henchman to northern Iraq and snuff out Zarqawi themselves.

In the letter, Zawahiri continued: "Among the things which... the Muslim populace... will never find palatable... are the scenes of slaughtering the hostages. You shouldn't be deceived by the praise of some of the zealous young men and their description of you as the shaykh of the slaughterers, etc. They do not express the general view of the admirer and the supporter of the resistance in Iraq."

In the letter, Zawahiri beseeched Zarqawi to follow a four-part playbook created by al Qaida central: focus first on expelling the Americans from Iraq; second, establish clear authority over whatever amount of Sunni territory in Iraq can be controlled; third, gradually extend the reach of that new Islamic "state" into neighboring countries; and fourth, at some point bring terror to Israel. The strategy bore profoundly little resemblance to what Zarqawi was doing in Iraq at the time.

I estimated that a key shift in momentum was upon us, thanks to Zarqawi's murderous overreach, which appeared to alienate even his newly cemented allies. If the Jordanian felt a growing threat from the administration above him, I was determined to keep him looking over both shoulders at once.

An AQI operative named Sulayman Khalid Darwish was Zarqawi's paternal uncle and fourth-in-command. Years earlier, Darwish had trained with firearms and explosives at Zarqawi's camp in Afghanistan; Sayf al-Adl, Zarqawi's original champion within al Qaida, told our liaison colleagues that the two had connected in Herat. But by the time we came to understand Darwish's importance, he was far less a fighter and more of an executive officer in logistics.

When I took over the targeting team, Darwish's major influence was coming from his activities on the literal outskirts of the group. The former dentist spent much of his time in his native Syria, perfecting document fraud. Darwish's crucial contribution to AQI was a steady supply of fake passports that could get Zarqawi's jihadists into any country—most easily Iraq. Further, Darwish had become AQI's chief waypoint for the funds Zarqawi's network collected abroad. Every few weeks, Zarqawi dispersed the funds among his regional emirs and put new recruits to work. At that point, an estimated 90 percent of the suicide attacks in Iraq were carried out by terrorist forces AQI recruited and trained.

Darwish's role was so vital to the ongoing operations of the organization that the US Department of the Treasury froze his assets—meaning that any accounts found belonging to him in the United States could immediately be confiscated. Treasury then appealed to the United Nations to add Darwish to the consolidated list of terrorists tied to al Qaida, a designation that would result in member nations freezing his assets in their countries as well. "This terrorist financier is helping support al-Zarqawi, who has launched violent acts against our troops, coalition partners and the Iraqi people," then treasury secretary John W. Snow said in a statement announcing the action. "Identifying financial operatives and choking off the flow of blood money moves us closer to our ultimate goal of fracturing the financial backbone of the Iraqi insurgency and Al Qaida." In June, it was reported that Darwish was thought to have come across the border from Syria into Iraq near al Qaim and to have been killed through Operation Spear.

The Iraq department had grown substantially; a counterpart team had been built to focus on Zarqawi's external network, in addition to some of the fighters moving across the border.

By the end of 2005, seven Tier I leaders, as we labeled them — regional emirs with direct access to Zarqawi — had been killed or captured. Nearly forty Tier II leaders, who oversaw local areas beneath them, had been killed or detained. We were cutting off AQI's funding and rat lines and taking out logistics facilitators, bomb makers, and military planners. Had things kept on that course, I'm convinced Zarqawi's influence was poised to flame out. I even found moments of cautious optimism in my work.

Then everything went completely to hell.

At 8:00 p.m. on February 21, 2006, four men dressed in the signature camouflage commando uniforms of the Iraqi police crept up to the door of the al-Askari mosque in the ancient Iraqi town of Samarra, roughly sixty miles north of Baghdad.

Samarra had in late 2004 been the scene of heavy fighting between US forces and insurgent groups as the coalition sought control of the city of two hundred thousand in the run-up to Iraq's national elections. That military operation was successful at the time, but throughout 2005 and beyond Samarra became a micro-cosm of the dysfunctional American mission in Iraq as the United States fought for temporary calm there only to watch insurgents return once the shooting stopped. The violence in Samarra was rarely as high-profile as that in nearby Fallujah or Ramadi, but by February of 2006, unrest in Samarra was still a thorn in the side of military planners.

Across the street from the al-Askari shrine that night, an Iraqi police unit kept surveillance over the mosque, which was topped with a bulbous dome covered in seventy-two thousand pieces of gold that reached more than two hundred feet into the sky. In the daylight, it shimmered throughout the flat beige city. The four intruders, in black masks, quietly carried an array of weaponry.

Outside the complex, an Iraqi Army battalion was based some one hundred yards down the road. A few hundred yards beyond that, a few platoons of US troops were stationed at a small civil-military operations center. But under the cover of darkness, the four terrorists made their way across the complex, then slipped through a gate in a nine-foot-high wall that surrounds one of the holiest shrines in the Shia Muslim world. It was supposed to have been locked at 5:00 p.m. — leading us to suspect that at least one of the nine security guards hired by Sunni authorities in Samarra knew to expect company.

Originally built in 944, the shrine at al-Askari marks the final resting place of two ninth-century Shia imams, the holy descendants of Prophet Muhammad. What truly gives the shrine its radical devotion, however, is a third imam, Muhammad al-Mahdi — Islam's so-called Hidden Imam, who is believed by many Shias to have disappeared from that building into a supernatural realm, much the same way Christians believe in the resurrection of Jesus Christ. At some point, Madhi's followers believe, he will reappear for the Day of Judgment. Zarqawi intended to hasten events.

Inside the shrine, the four members of AQI overpowered the nine guards, then tied them up and took their weapons and keys. None of the guards was killed. Throughout the night, the intruders set to work wiring explosives inside the dome and along the supporting walls beneath it. Then, sometime before dawn, they slipped out the same way they'd come in and vanished. Soon after, the guards managed to free themselves and broke through a locked door leading out to the safety of the courtyard.

Moments later, just before 7:00 a.m. on February 22, a massive explosion rocked the mosque's golden dome. Six seconds later, a second explosion fully sheared off the top half of the iconic landmark and left in its place an ominous nest of twisted rebar and a cascade of rubble that spilled over the building's blue tile wall into the courtyard below. Everything around it was covered in gray dust. The security guards fled, never to be heard from again. No one else was hurt—a trend that, sadly, would not continue.

The moment I heard about it, there was no doubt in my mind who was responsible; I knew the bombing was just the sort of audacious strike al Qaida central would have deplored. The attack was straight from Zarqawi's playbook—an escalation of small-scale sectarian attacks that had already created a kind of cultural powder keg in Iraq. Blowing apart one of the world's holiest Shia sites was such a deliberately provocative religious attack that I wondered if the Quds Force, the notorious special operations forces unit from Iran, Iraq's predominantly Shia neighbor, might even come after Zarqawi.

They did not. However, calling the mosque bombing "our 9/11," the aggrieved Shia population finally went in search of its pound of flesh—and far more. Thousands of armed Shias flooded into Baghdad on flatbed trucks, joining up with simmering militias there, creating an energy that soon boiled over. The largest of those militias—the self-proclaimed Mahdi Army—began carrying out the gruesome torture, often involving power drills, of Sunni insurgents they managed to capture. Meanwhile, in one similar incident in the southeastern corner of the country, gunmen wearing Iraqi police uniforms seized a dozen Sunni men from a jail in Basra, dragged them from detention, and promptly executed them. Over the following two days, my team got reports from the ground about more than 150 Sunni mosques being torched or strafed with bullets and ten imams being killed. By the end of the week, we estimated that roughly one thousand Iraqis were dead from the violence sparked by the al-Askari bombing.

Conditions continued to deteriorate when the largest Iraqi sects fully turned on each other. In what history now recognizes as a pivotal moment in postwar Iraq, Sunni-Shia violence overshadowed the damage previously done by the Sunni insurgency. Some 2.7 million people would be displaced inside Iraq by the end of the year, and two million more would flee for refuge in neighboring countries. Farmers and shopkeepers were driven to join militias and take up arms in the fleeting hope of securing their own safety. US forces found themselves in the position of being a kind of third armed faction in Iraq, never quite sure when to intervene and completely befuddled by their new role in a conflict that had properly descended into malevolent chaos. Against the fiercest urging by al Qaida's top command to avoid killing other Muslims, by early 2006 Zarqawi had his civil war.

As newlyweds, Roger and I had already moved into a comfortable rhythm of daily mundane routines, coupled with long hours at work for both of us. The frenetic pace of my job seemed normal.

As conflict raged in the streets of Iraq that February, something equally important was unfolding inside the command center at the central Iraq air base.

A new crop of interrogators — officially air force criminal investigators, though they simply referred to themselves as gators — had arrived after a condensed six-week training program at Fort Huachuca, in Sierra Vista, Arizona. The new team was joining a small team of hold-over gators and was greeted by two valuable detainees waiting for them inside the "gator pit."

The detainees were different from others awaiting interrogation, however. They hadn't fought with firearms. They carried holy books.

Along with its visible military presence, AQI's functioning in Iraq required a quieter but still necessary religious presence in the country. As civil society there crumbled soon after the US invasion, clerics held increased sway over a population searching for order and stability. Much as Zarqawi found comfort and direction in radical Islam while in prison years earlier, the same could be said of impressionable young Iraqis in 2006. AQI's influence in mosques in Iraq was a modest one, but given that there was a fraying pipeline to foreign fighters, those houses of worship became an ever-more-important recruiting ground. By 2006, imams who agreed to preach in favor of Sunni extremism were increasingly valuable to the terror network.

Early that year, a pair of imams — Abu Zaydan and Abu Ali — were grabbed during SOF raids of AQI meetings near Yusufiya. Over a few weeks of interrogations, it became clear that they had only recently, and even reluctantly, joined AQI in hopes the Sunni network would protect their families from roving Shia militias.

They confessed that their contributions were mostly limited to encouraging new recruits to join Zarqawi's cause. Of more interest to interrogators, however, was their task of granting final blessings to the AQI bombers suiting up for suicide missions. That meant the imams held a loftier rank within the organization than those base-level killers, even if they didn't directly oversee the foot soldiers. We'd spent years picking apart AQI's operations-side hierarchy; now there was hope that combing the religious side of the network might offer us a straighter shot to the top.

Even if that didn't pan out, their task of offering final blessings meant that these imams in custody knew of meeting spots frequented by key players within the organization. Soon enough, both Abu Zaydan and Abu Ali pinpointed a handful of farmhouses and safe houses in Yusufiya as locations of weapons stockpiles and video studios where bombers filmed their final testimonials.

That information was immediately passed along to special operators. For weeks, no activity was detected at those safe houses — until just after 1:00 a.m. one night in mid-April, when a blue truck and a white sedan pulled up outside one of the farmhouses. Within minutes, SOF launched into what we came to know as Operation Larchwood 4. Cross-referencing known individuals at the farmhouse, we understood their target to be a local commander known as Abu Sayyif, a media specialist in the nearby Abu Ghraib regional cell who mostly spent his days posting recruitment videos on the Internet.

The task force boarded the helicopters for the quick flight from Baghdad. Some of the personnel carried chemical lights to mark the landing zones; others packed explosives to breach locked doors. A smaller helicopter flew behind in support, as did a giant AC-130 Spectre gunship high above. In addition, they were joined by a small support group that would supply extra firepower if necessary.

Soon the four SOF assault teams arrived at the target and hopped off their helicopters at the end of a wide orchard that stretched north from the farmhouse. The teams quickly made their way through the darkness southwest along the grove of date palms and around the back of the farmhouse. There they split into two units, to simultaneously prosecute the assault from the southern and eastern sides. Two team members, sent ahead as spotters, spied a carport on the southeast corner of the building. An open door there led into the house. At just after 2:00 a.m., everything seemed quiet.

The spotters hurried back to their teams to report the good news. Little did they realize how much their luck was about to change.

One team swept silently back to the carport, past a parked automobile there, and into the darkened hallway.

Pop-pop-pop: a sudden volley of shots came from inside the house.

Three soldiers were hit and scrambled to retreat back out through the carport. The wounded collapsed behind a sand berm at the end of the driveway, their teammates ripping open medical kits to treat them. From the second floor, a new shooter strafed the sand berm with gunfire. Then an explosion rang out nearby as another militant hurled grenades from the roof.

From high above, the AC-130 had eyes on the action and could have sprayed the entire house with a storm of 20mm rounds from its Gatling-style cannons. But the mission was to capture whoever was inside the farmhouse, not bury them inside it. Instead the men of the task force threw their own grenades back and maneuvered themselves to reenter the house.

Moving through the carport a second time, two more coalition soldiers were hit — one shot, another wounded by a grenade fragment. But this time they shot back, killing an enemy gunman in the corridor. Back at the air base's command center, explosions from the firefight temporarily blinded the pixelated video feeds from the orbiting surveillance aircraft.

One of those platforms proved its worth, however, catching sight of a man running from the rear of the house, then taking cover behind a nearby parked car. The soldiers were alerted to his position and cut him down before he could detonate his suicide vest.

Inside the darkened farmhouse, the bloodied coalition soldiers began clearing rooms. In one they happened upon another militant and shot him dead. In another room, they found women and children cowering in fear and guided them to a corner for their safety. More shots were fired as the task force secured the rest of the house — and then it was time to deal with the extremist who'd been hurling grenades.

One soldier crept up the darkened stairway toward the roof, rifle at the ready. Just as he approached the doorway to the outside, the combatant unleashed one final attack and detonated a suicide vest he was wearing, packed with C-4. The shock waves blasted the soldier back down the stairs, though he was able to get to his feet and hobble away to shelter. The militant, on the other hand, was completely dismembered by the explosion; his head was later discovered among debris on the other side of the roof. With the shooting finally done, five jihadists were dead. Five coalition soldiers had been wounded.

Downstairs, task force members were collecting videocassettes, computers, and anything they could find of intelligence value. My team would get our hands on those soon enough. The task force cuffed five people, including Abu Sayyif, a doughy English speaker who appeared to be in his midthirties, and four others whose identities weren't yet known. They were led out to the waiting helicopters. Before leaving, soldiers gathered up four AK-47 assault rifles — along with a weapon they never expected to find at that farmhouse: a rifle generally carried by members of the coalition units within the United Kingdom Special Forces.

As soon as the task force arrived back at the air base, the task force's forensic teams dug into the computers gathered from the bloody raid. There they found videos of Zarqawi proselytizing and one of him, dressed in all black, wielding a hulking machine gun during scattershot target practice in the desert.

Beyond the updated images of Zarqawi we could add to our wall, those computers held footage of something even more curious. In one video, Zarqawi was seen casually sitting cross-legged on a mat, next to a rifle leaning against the wall to his right. Far from the AK-47s I'd become accustomed to seeing in mujahideen clips, this black assault rifle appeared to be a Diemaco C8 carbine with a massive optical sight, a matte-green thirty-round magazine plugged into the system, and even a 40mm grenade launcher mounted beneath the barrel. I recognized it as a United Kingdom Special Forces weapon—the exact same gun that had been recovered in Yusufiya. I couldn't believe what I was seeing.

Was Zarqawi supposed to be at the farmhouse? I wondered. Could he have left before the task force arrived? Did we really just miss him again?

CHAPTER 14

Perpetual End of the Road

Back at the air base, the gators immediately began taking runs at Abu Sayyif, the known detainee from Yusufiya. All five of the men captured at the farmhouse were insisting that they were gathered there for a wedding, yet there was no sign of a bride, and for what was supposedly a celebration, there were a conspicuous number of men wearing suicide vests.

Obviously, the story was bogus — but what exactly were they doing there? Were they filming final testimonials for an upcoming attack? If so, the number of vests packed with C-4 augured a massive plot. What was their target?

Or, approaching the question from a different angle, what if those men weren't bombers at all but rather a security team? Who were these other detainees to warrant that kind of protection? How did that square with finding Zarqawi's gun in the farmhouse with them?

It took a few days, but Abu Sayyif finally broke. The balding Iraqi required no interpreter, mostly mumbling answers to the questions posed by his gators in a soft English accent. He was not, he admitted, the videographer for some make-believe nuptials. He was a pediatrician by trade. Desperation — for his own safety and for his mother's in the face of Shia brigades — drove him to Zarqawi's network. Handling local media operations was also a chance to make money at a time when civil unrest had made working at his medical practice unsafe. He had no true allegiance to al Qaida, and the few days he spent in custody at Balad—much less the prospect of years of incarceration at Abu Ghraib or, worse, a death sentence from the Iraqi government—loosened him up enough to make him say that one of the other detainees, identified as Mubassir, was his boss. At which point all eyes focused on Mubassir—who was even more certainly not the simple cameraman he claimed to be. And time was of the essence.

Ten days after the arrests in Yusufiya, Al Qaida in Iraq did something I puzzled over at the time: they released what became an infamous video of Zarqawi wearing a black bandana, his trademark ammunition vest atop a black shirt, and black pants. It was an edited-down version of the video footage I'd watched after it was captured in the Yusufiya farmhouse.

In the video, Zarqawi is seen standing in a landscape barren and beige except for a few hearty patches of scrubby brush. His arms are wrapped around a massive M249 squad automatic weapon, a machine gun that comes with a foldout bipod at the front and fires more than a dozen rounds per second. In the video, Zarqawi levels the weapon at an unseen target off to the right of the frame and sprays a barrage of bullets. He appears stocky but sturdy; it was the first time I could ever remember him daring to show his face.

When the video was released, I was unsure if Zarqawi had simply gotten sloppy. Perhaps it was bravado that led to this public display of machismo, or maybe he felt that a public demonstration was necessary to reassert his alpha status among Sunni insurgents feeling the heat of the coalition crackdown. Even more irksome to intelligence officers was the possibility that Zarqawi knew exactly what had been found at the farmhouse and decided to release the material before we could. Some in the intelligence community saw it as Zarqawi taunting us, bragging about slipping through our fingers again in Yusufiya. I worried more about the hunt ahead. If Zarqawi really knew what we knew and was recalibrating accordingly, acting on whatever intelligence could be gleaned from the men in the farmhouse became that much more urgent.

The interrogators got back to work. They sensed that Mubassir held the key.

As all this unfolded behind the scenes, the Pentagon publicly responded to Zarqawi's latest video in an unprecedented way. It released outtakes from the filming recovered in Yusufiya, played for reporters at a weekly press briefing in the Green Zone in early May. I thought it a bizarre and even somewhat petty move on the part of the Defense Department—but I couldn't blame them for having the primal urge to prick holes in Zarqawi's mystique. I laughed, too, the first time I saw the outtakes.

"What you saw on the Internet was what he wanted the world to see," Major General Rick Lynch, the American military spokesman, said at the briefing. " 'Look at me, I'm a capable leader of a capable organization—and we are indeed declaring war against democracy inside of Iraq, and we're going to establish an Islamic caliphate.' " Lynch was openly mocking Zarqawi.

In the version of the video shown at the press briefing, Zarqawi is seen striding purposefully across the barren landscape from left to right. The zoom jerks in, going from a full-body shot of the Jordanian to an image of just his torso, in the center of the frame, with his forearms bulging around the machine gun.

Thump-thump! the weapon barks.

Thump! Thump! Thump! Thump!

Click.

Zarqawi cocks his head like a confused puppy and stares down at the trigger, which has stopped responding. Off camera, someone shouts in Arabic, "Go help the sheikh," and another man dressed entirely in black scampers in from the left side of the frame and sheepishly fiddles with the machine gun for his boss.

Thump-thump! the weapon barks again; then Zarqawi unleashes the fully automatic hail of bullets he publicized to the world.

The follies didn't end there. Later in the video shown at the briefing, Zarqawi hands the machine gun to a subordinate and begins marching back to a white pickup truck with a feathery red swoop painted on the side. Zarqawi's white New Balance sneakers are prominently visible below his tribal-chic jihadist wardrobe. The first subordinate hands the machine gun to another—who unwittingly grabs the weapon by its scalding-hot barrel and drops it.

Zarqawi and his men looked amateurish—as indeed they could be. I knew Zarqawi had an ego and was practically obsessed with his stature in the insurgent community. Poking the bear was clearly the latest tactic in the Pentagon's unfolding "information operations" campaign in Iraq, the friendlier-sounding modern incarnation of age-old psychological warfare. If those outtakes truly did cast doubt on Zarqawi's ability to lead, or make it seem like his jihad was a lost cause, perhaps a few Iraqis would choose to avoid his group and some good could come from releasing the unedited video. Still, if the goal was to prick holes in Zarqawi's overinflated aura, I cringed a bit at the military's word choice.

"Why he's their leader, I don't know," Lynch concluded at the press conference. "It's just a matter of time before we take him out."

The military was convinced that the endgame had begun. Interrogators had begun tightening the noose on Zarqawi's network. Meanwhile, my team at the Agency was tracking a new lead of its own, this one a product of the collaborative groundwork I'd helped lay with other governments' intelligence units.

In late May of 2006, liaison units made a crucial capture of their own along a border with Iraq: an Iraqi government customs officer who'd worked the main highway from Amman, Jordan, to Baghdad. In that role, a twiggy young man named Ziad Khalaf al-Karbouly had helped AQI smuggle money and materiel between the two countries, and he had provided safe passage for the suicide bombers who'd detonated themselves outside three Amman hotels six months earlier.

In a confession Jordanian authorities aired on prime-time TV, Karbouly said that Zarqawi personally knew of the customs worker's plans to abduct a pair of Moroccan diplomats and that Zarqawi had instructed him to murder a Jordanian truck driver in September of 2005. "I told [the truck driver], 'I have to kill you' and he started pleading and said, 'Don't kill me,'" Karbouly said in his broadcast confession. "Then I told him 'I have to kill you,' and so I pulled my personal gun and shot him twice in the head."

That incident, followed by the hotel attacks, resulted in Karbouly confirming the identity of, and contacts for, a shadowy AQI spiritual figure named Abu Abdul-Rahman al-Iraqi.

Rahman's existence wasn't news to our team back at the Agency — the first time we'd uncovered a photo of him, a number of months before, his wide face and close-cropped black hair and beard left me thinking he could have passed for seventeen years old. We suspected he might have been the ghostwriter for many of Zarqawi's religious screeds and letters to al Qaida central. Rahman was higher up in Zarqawi's network than we'd understood, having shortly before been granted the lofty status of Zarqawi's newest spiritual adviser. Rahman was the central religious scholar helping craft Zarqawi's tenuous public theological case for murdering Shias; he was also acting as AQI's liaison to radical clerics all across Iraq.

Around the same time, back at the air base after a few more weeks in detention—reportedly spent reading Harry Potter books—Mubassir broke. Mubassir added that Rahman never drove himself and that there was always trickery involved in the important trips. Only when Rahman got into a small blue vehicle would he be taken to see Zarqawi.

Instantly Rahman became the key. Coalition forces set out to locate the adviser, focusing on the Sunni Triangle. There, a growing network of locals in and around Fallujah and Ramadi were chafing at the extremists' heavy-handed pseudo-governance and might be swayed to help. Soon guidance from human assets on the ground helped pinpoint a series of houses to monitor.

The chase was on. The Agency team I helped build felt certain: Rahman would lead American forces to Zarqawi.

———

Much of what I know about Karbouly's arrest and the final endgame that followed comes from secondhand information.

By the spring of 2006, our Agency team was receiving few daily reports from the task force about the missions they were running in the hunt for Zarqawi. We heard even less about what they'd collected on those missions. The task force's intelligence wing had grown to a point where they were not pursuing our assistance any longer but were operating without it. The professional relationship remained cordial but forced. Without any true sense of what was happening on the ground, all of us on my team struggled to figure out exactly how we were supposed to contribute in a meaningful way to the hunt we'd once identified, defined, and spearheaded.

As conditions in Iraq tumbled further out of control, the targeting of a single individual, and with it the hoped-for dismantling of a single extremist organization, became far less urgent. Some military planners and administration officials continued to suggest that if Zarqawi were taken out, the head would be lopped off the Sunni insurgency and the civil war would dissipate. Many of us didn't believe it would be so simple to contain: there were political pressures adding to the sectarian strife that went beyond Zarqawi's impact on the insurgency. The administration's self-serving implication was that Iraq wasn't spiraling out of control — it could be and would be stabilized once we eliminated key bad guys they had been talking about for years. I knew, of course, that was profoundly simplistic.

But this didn't mean that we should abandon the search for Zarqawi. By the spring of 2006, the insurgency inside Iraq had sprawled to encompass dozens of loosely affiliated groups. Zarqawi's own network had entrenched itself by recruiting local former Baathists and militant young Iraqis, which suggested that AQI had staying power even if the flow of foreign fighters to the country diminished. In addition, as much as eliminating the most prominent terrorist in Iraq was a crucial step in the quest for peace, the al Qaida backing that enhanced Zarqawi's profile also made him that much easier to replace. In the event of his death, if Zarqawi's internal ranks couldn't produce a strong enough successor, al Qaida central would simply insert one.

———————

Zarqawi's death did not signal an immediate downturn in violence. Abu Ayyub al-Masri, the Egyptian who had been Zarqawi's deputy, was quickly promoted to replace his late boss, and the civilian death toll kept climbing.

———————

Ground conditions, unfortunately, were things that multiple divisions at the Agency rarely seemed to agree upon — and our team suffered bureaucratically for it. Once the chaos in Iraq had fully achieved systemic status, it was hard to find an overarching, articulable end goal for Iraq that could be brought about by the US government—other than removing the foreign terrorists. An endless game of whack-a-mole was unnerving for all of us. And one by one throughout early 2006, as part of cyclical transitions on the operations side that naturally occur when agents return from overseas postings, my team members stopped spinning their wheels in our branch and left for other assignments.

Then Tom, too, who'd shared my growing frustration with the bureaucratic shift, followed suit. He took another department-level position.

———

I understood why everyone was moving on; that same thought process had been sneaking into my own mind over the previous couple of months. I was exhausted by the work, mentally and physically, and growing more agitated by the day. I'd dedicated years of my life to trying to stop the rising tide of violence in Iraq, and what did I actually have to show for it?

Even as the Pentagon had amused itself by releasing Zarqawi's video outtakes, another nine Iraqis were killed and forty-four wounded when a suicide bomber blew himself up that same day outside a courthouse in Baghdad. Across the country, a ghastly civil war led to the tortured remains of civilians being dumped in the streets. SOF was moving at a frenetic pace, assaulting house after house—and it was only as the seeming futility of it all really began to set in that I realized these raids would not have an impact on the overall effort against terrorism in Iraq; rather, I thought they would deter a long-term strategy. On the first raid I'd been on—years earlier, during my time as an analyst in Baghdad—my nerves were steeled as I awaited word of the task force's results that night. How many bad guys did we catch? But in the spring of 2006, it occurred to me that I had no way of knowing how many people had been killed based on targeting packages I'd put together. Even the successful strikes gnawed at me: that raid got our guy, I'd think about a mission, but in the process, we killed four other people. Who were they?

My sleepless nights began to be haunted less by things I'd seen overseas than by a hollow realization that one person really might not be able to solve a problem like this. Maybe I couldn't change the world—and maybe it was time to do something else.

"What if I tried for a job overseas?" I asked Roger over yet another reheated late-night dinner. "How do you feel about the Levant? We might end up fat because we love the food, but maybe that's not a downside?"

I tried to sound upbeat. He just looked at me for a while.

"Can the Agency help me find a job over there?" he said.

I said. "Well, no. Probably not."

We sat silent again.

"I just turned forty-five," he said. "It doesn't seem like a good time to pull myself out of the workforce."

He wasn't being dismissive or resistant—he was just acknowledging reality.

"No, of course not," I said. "You're right."

I thought quietly about something else: I'd recently turned thirty-seven. I remembered conversations I'd had with Gina Bennett, one of my original mentors in the Iraq unit, about family and the realities of motherhood for Agency employees. "One of the best Mother's Days I ever had was when my kids had our traditional chocolate-chip pancakes for Mother's Day breakfast," she once said in an interview, "and I attended via a laptop in the dining room. I could almost smell those pancakes." There was something lovely and sad in that all at once.

In 2008, Bennett's picture was shown in a photomontage that formed the backdrop for Alicia Keys's performance of "Superwoman" on *The Oprah Winfrey Show*. Bennett is shown with her husband and children, all sitting atop that CIA seal in the lobby of the New Headquarters Building. The photo caption simply read, "Gina: CIA Counterterrorism Analyst. Mother of five." It was fitting recognition. I never forgot her telling me that if I had children, there would be days when it felt like I could only give 50 percent to work or 50 percent to my kids. "It doesn't mean you're failing," she told me. "But it does mean you're always juggling."

I'd searched for women at the Agency who proved that the feminist aspiration of "having it all" was an actual option. But at least at the CIA, they didn't seem to exist. In 2013, the CIA declassified a trove of documents that included a 1953 report entitled "Career Employment of Women in the Central Intelligence Agency." It was produced by a team unofficially known as the petticoat panel. Male senior staffers blamed women's lack of professional advancement on the women themselves, because of "this business about people getting married and pregnant at your operational inconvenience." At the time, chief of operations Richard Helms, who later became director of the CIA, said that supervisors had to make a simple calculation when it came to promoting women. "You just get them to a point where they are about to blossom out to a [high pay grade], and they get married, go somewhere else, or something over which nobody has any control, and they are out of the running."

What would having children mean for my own career? I wondered. Sitting there at the kitchen table with Roger that night, I sensed that staying close to home to raise a family limited my potential career progression at almost any government institution or business — but that transferring overseas was nearly impossible if it meant persuading my husband to interrupt his career in the technology field for a few years of hanging out in the desert.

Eventually, in April of 2006, we made a choice together: I took a deep breath and transitioned away from the Zarqawi team and accepted a position listed on the Agency's internal jobs database with the National Resources Division (NR) out west. That division fills an interesting niche in the Agency's portfolio: it's staffed by operators, based domestically. Further, NR officers entice foreign nationals on American soil to spy for us when they return to their homelands. The work is often pooh-poohed by CIA operatives living with the inherent threats and anxieties that come with overseas postings — but if that work wasn't feasible for me at that point, at least this undercover work got me out of headquarters and kept me doing something similar to the counterterrorism work I'd loved at Langley.

"It's the right move," Roger assured me. "You've done everything you could do in DC for the moment." Roger found a job and followed me west.

With that, my role leading the Zarqawi team was filled by a targeter who transferred in from another branch, and I focused on new targets. As a CIA detailee, I worked with a JTTF, or joint terrorism task force, a multiagency partnership made up of investigators, analysts, linguists, and other experts from across the intelligence and law enforcement spectrum. Those task forces are overseen by the FBI, which generally has jurisdiction over counterterrorism operations inside the United States. I reported to the regional FBI office every day as a targeting officer, analyzing whatever foreign angles or connections could be valuable to a given investigation. The work moved slowly, as counterterrorism operations tend to do, which was clearly a frustration for many of the FBI agents I interacted with on a daily basis. They would have preferred more traditional criminal work. Never did our work involve the headline-grabbing takedown of a pedophile or mobster or the satisfaction of stopping a serial killer.

I was glad to have begun a new chapter in my life, but before long, I began realizing how much I missed the thrill of a high-profile hunt. I often found my mind wandering, wondering what was happening back on my old team at Langley. To this day, part of me wonders if I left too soon.

June 7, 2006, dawned bright as always in Baghdad. I, meanwhile, was someplace off in the Alaskan wilderness, having joined my new JTTF team there only weeks earlier. Back in Langley, none of my old teammates could have known how much the day held in store.

Many of the details I've collected about that late-spring day come from video footage I've since seen, insider accounts I've read, and firsthand stories shared with me from former associates involved in the events. Some of it, however, I had been keeping a casual eye on from afar. At the time, it was still hard not to.

On June 2, for example, Zarqawi had again made headlines after his latest violent video rant. "Oh Sunni people, wake up, pay attention and prepare to confront the poisons of the Shiite snakes who are afflicting you with all agonies since the invasion of Iraq until our day," he said. "Forget about those advocating the end of sectarianism and calling for national unity." It was piercing rhetoric, but by then it was so familiar that I paid it almost no mind. I was mostly pushing myself to focus on the new job. Little did I realize that it would be the last time any of us would ever hear from him.

Midmorning Baghdad time on June 7, Zarqawi's spiritual adviser, Rahman, was spotted climbing into a silver sedan outside his home by an unmanned surveillance aircraft. He headed off into Baghdad, as he usually did at that hour. On this particular day, however, the sedan wound its way through various neighborhoods, then turned back to its starting point and drove home. To those monitoring the action, that maneuver seemed immediately odd. Then, as McChrystal recounted in his book *My Share of the Task,* after pausing at Rahman's home for a bit, the sedan bolted east across Baghdad and merged onto a six-lane highway running north from the sparse eastern fringe of the city into the heart of Diyala Province. At Balad, that was enough to get people scrambling.

On the outskirts of Baghdad, Rahman's car slowed to a stop along what there was of the highway's shoulder, and the cleric exited the vehicle. The sedan sped away.

Rahman could be seen from above walking back along the shoulder, against the flow of traffic. Seconds later, a stubby blue Kia Bongo pulled up beside him. I'd seen those 2.7-liter trucks all over Baghdad during my time there; they are to minivans what Chevy's El Camino was to American sedans — ugly but efficient. They were also ubiquitous enough in Iraq to blend in on a crowded motorway. Rahman climbed into the passenger side, and the truck merged into traffic.

Outside Baghdad, the Bongo drove a few hours northeast, finally reaching Baquba, a city of four hundred thousand and the capital of Diyala Province. In that city's commercial district, the truck pulled up outside a building that appeared to be a restaurant. Rahman exited the vehicle and entered the building, walking past a man who appeared to be standing guard.

Soon a new vehicle pulled into the parking area next to the Bongo truck — this one a white pickup with a red stripe on the side. It looked exactly like the one from Zarqawi's video outtakes. Rahman emerged from the building and got in the white pickup; it left the parking lot and drove out of town. By then no fewer than nine surveillance aircraft were orbiting the area, including one tracking the silver sedan back near Baghdad, one on the Bongo truck in the

Baquba parking lot, one on the transfer-point restaurant itself, and one on the white pickup with a red stripe carrying Rahman, now merging onto Route 5 and heading west.

SOF's destination soon came into view a few miles outside Baquba, as the pickup merged onto Route 3 heading north and entered the small town of Hibhib.

The pickup drove to the end of the main street in Hibhib, then turned right onto a dirt road that led north along the edge of an irrigation canal through a thicket of palm trees. Approximately a mile later, the pickup turned right again into the driveway of a two-story beige house and came to a stop outside the gate. A man appeared from under the house's carport and walked down the driveway to meet them. A few words were exchanged; then the gate was opened and the pickup pulled forward, stopping under the carport. Rahman exited the vehicle and walked into the home. The pickup reversed out of the driveway and drove away. It was just shy of 5:00 p.m., and the palm trees ringing the home cast long shadows across the house.

It remained unclear who besides Rahman was actually inside the building. Was it Zarqawi? If so, was he alone? "I'm not going to promise you that's Zarqawi," one SOF team member said, according to McChrystal. "But whoever we kill is going to be much higher than anybody we've killed before. So I'm saying absolutely — whack it." Yet if Zarqawi wasn't inside, killing Rahman would eliminate the best lead on Zarqawi.

Just then, however, the surveillance drones caught sight of a man emerging from the shadows outside the home, walking to the end of the driveway. He was clearly heavyset and dressed entirely in black. At the gate, he glanced both ways along the dirt road and, seemingly satisfied that no one was coming, returned to the house.

It was decided that SOF would send a team to the house to

control the area and scour it for information once the dust had settled. But if they wanted Zarqawi once and for all, bombs were the way to go.

By mid-2006, the United States flew more than twenty types of aircraft to support coalition objectives on any given day, from massive troop carriers to unmanned surveillance platforms. In the early evening of June 7, two American F-16s were overhead on routine six-hour operations to hunt for improvised explosive devices along the major highways crisscrossing Iraq. But they were armed in case of contingencies—and just after 6:00 p.m., they had one. On urgent request from SOF, the fighter jets were instructed by ground control to immediately engage the safe house in Hibhib.

Because the men on board weren't expecting the mission update, one of those planes was caught in the midst of midair refueling when the call came. The other F-16—flying as a "single ship," in air force parlance—was ordered, in view of the exceptional circumstances, to leave his wingman and destroy the target with a single five-hundred-pound GBU-12 bomb.

At 6:11 p.m., the pilot of the lone Fighting Falcon came screaming down over Zarqawi's safe house on a dive—and then *pulled up* without releasing a bomb. As was clear on the live video feed, the house still stood. Surely everyone inside it heard the fighter jet's roar and had begun scrambling.

Amid what must have been a storm of expletives, joint terminal attack controllers realized that their heat-of-the-moment orders were incomplete. The pilot had been told he was "cleared to engage"—but he not was not given the "cleared hot" designator to release his ordnance. As the jet knifed back into the blue sky, the task force knew it had to hit the home before anyone inside went running into the woods. Zarqawi had managed that trick before.

The F-16 circled back. The new code was relayed to the pilot; he locked onto the target and dropped the laser-guided weapon. Endless seconds seemed to tick by as the GBU-12 hurtled toward the earth. The video from the surveillance drone rotated around the target, but the home just sat there.

Then, just after 6:12 p.m., the bomb tore through the roof of Zarqawi's safe house. Monitors at the air base flickered white as the eruption blasted plumes of debris in four directions at once — one down the driveway, as the front of the house was blown apart; both north and south along the dirt road, as the home's side walls vanished; and straight up in the air, through what was left of the roof. Around the house, dust billowed up through the orderly lines of palm trees like smoke through a vent. Inside the house, the second floor collapsed down onto what was left of the ground floor — and those upon it.

Then the F-16 was ordered to double back and drop a second five-hundred-pound bomb — this one a GPS-enabled GBU-38 — on the wreckage. SOF wanted "to ensure the target set was serviced appropriately," as one air force general later put it.

Within minutes, Iraqi police stationed nearby arrived on the scene. They were followed by SOF, who arrived to surround the property at approximately 6:40 p.m.. The unit found an ambulance parked in the driveway, which by then led to nothing but a yawning crater in the countryside. Police officers were struggling to hoist a stretcher into the back of the vehicle. After a few tense moments of guns-drawn uncertainty — were these actual police or al Qaida operatives in stolen uniforms? — they secured the officers' weapons and closed in on the ambulance. The gurney hung halfway out its back doors. They pulled it from the vehicle and set it on the ground.

On the gurney was a large man dressed in black, struggling for air. It was Zarqawi. The Jordanian had actually survived the bombing — though barely. The shock waves from the bombs had burst the blood vessels in his lungs and ears, to say nothing of the broken right leg and massive internal injuries he'd suffered. One of the SOF medics knelt over Zarqawi and cleared his airway. In the crater, team members found the remains of two women, including a young girl, as well as those of Rahman and another man. Zarqawi himself lasted almost half an hour before succumbing to his injuries. At 7:04 p.m., at the feet of US SOF operators in a dirt driveway outside an obliterated safe house, the most wanted terrorist leader in Iraq died.

———

I walked through the lobby of our hotel just after seven the next morning. I was reviewing my latest assignment with the JTTF and was deep in thought about the day ahead. Or, at that hour, perhaps I was simply concentrating on the coffee in my hand.

"Nada."

One of my coworkers was whispering in my direction from halfway across the lobby.

"*Nada.*"

I heard her before I saw her; when I finally located my coworker, she pointed to the TV on the wall.

"Death of Abu Musab al-Zarqawi," said the words on the bottom of the screen.

I ran over to the TV, half in disbelief. Could it possibly be true? The news bounced over to footage of President Bush speaking earlier that morning, Washington time, in the White House Rose Garden. "Zarqawi's death is a severe blow to al Qaeda," he said. "It's a victory in the global war on terror, and it is an opportunity for Iraq's new government to turn the tide of this struggle."

I was speechless. I felt like jumping for joy. I felt like hugging someone. Mostly, I *really* wanted to hear more details — we were twelve hours behind Baghdad, and information was already trickling out.

I rummaged around in my purse for my cell phone, but there was no service.

"Is there a US government facility nearby?" I asked my coworker. "Anyplace at all with a classified phone system?"

"Sorry," she said, "there's not."

So I stood there just holding my phone for what seemed like hours, glued to the replays of the same sound bites and the same green-and-white surveillance video of the bomb blasts at the safe house. Even when the military proudly displayed photos of Zarqawi's dead body—his puffy face bruised, his left eye swollen shut, a small gouge across his left cheek—I could still barely believe it had happened.

The forty-eight hours after that are still something of a blur in my mind. When the SOF operators returned to the air base, they reportedly laid Zarqawi's body on the floor of the compound next to Rahman's.

Soon public statements were issued. The US ambassador to Iraq at the time, Zalmay Khalilzad, publicly cheered the death of the "godfather" of sectarian violence in Iraq. *Time* magazine featured Zarqawi's head shot on the cover with a giant red X over it—their designation for "America's most hated enemies," a treatment the magazine had used only three times before in its history: once for Adolf Hitler, once for Japan during World War II, and once for Saddam Hussein in 2003. But perhaps the moment it became most real for me was when AQI itself confirmed Zarqawi's death, noting in a statement online, "We herald the martyrdom of our mujahid Sheik Abu Musab al-Zarqawi, and we stress that this is an honor for our nation."

"The martyrdom of Abu Musab al-Zarqawi," I kept repeating to myself. "He's actually dead."

Over the next two days, I went through every emotion I could imagine—excitement, envy of my colleagues, pride at what we'd accomplished together. And then I even felt a twinge of sadness or frustration or maybe both: I never actually met him. As odd as that might have been to reflect upon, I spent years of my life trained on his next move. I never questioned him, and I never looked him in the eye. To this day, I wonder what that moment would have been like.

There was something else. In addition to providing updates about the Zarqawi mission, the news was telling us that within twenty-four hours of taking him out, SOF teams across Iraq hit fourteen new targets. Our military machine in Iraq rolled on. Yet the day after Zarqawi was killed, suicide bombers struck three separate locations in Baghdad, murdering at least two dozen people. Dozens more were wounded. The jihad machine rolled on as well.

The AQI statement announcing Zarqawi's death had concluded, "The death of our leaders is life for us. It will only increase our persistence in continuing the holy war so that the word of God will be supreme." I knew that someone new would soon fill Zarqawi's role in Iraq, and it was difficult to know what approach the insurgency would take under that leadership. The long road ahead was underscored by the somber and measured response Nick Berg's father, Michael, offered CNN when asked about Zarqawi's death. "He is a human being. He has a family who are reacting just as my family reacted when Nick was killed, and I feel bad for that," Michael Berg said. "His death will re-ignite yet another wave of revenge."

He was right. In the year after Zarqawi's death, from mid-2006 to mid-2007, roughly thirty-five thousand civilians were murdered in Iraq, the deadliest stretch to that point in a war that would continue for another four years, until December of 2011. In the year after Zarqawi's death, more than one thousand American troops were killed in Iraq, the bloodiest twelve-month stretch of the entire war for them as well.

As difficult as statistics like those were for me to process, I knew they didn't mean that Zarqawi's importance at the end was overstated, and they didn't mean that his death was insignificant, either. If Zarqawi's power may have owed something to mythmaking in early 2003, the destruction his network wrought over the ensuing years—at places of worship, at places of aid, and upon all manner of political processes and security initiatives intended to stabilize Iraq—was profound. One comparison I always held on to: from 1998, when bin Ladin had issued a fatwa declaring Americans legitimate targets, then bombed US embassies in Kenya and Tanzania, through 2006, al Qaida central was responsible for some four thousand deaths around the world. That included the attacks on 9/11. Zarqawi's network alone might have more than doubled that.

It is true that by 2006, AQI was only one of many groups that together constituted the insurgency bedeviling American troops. A new leader would rise up to claim Zarqawi's throne—and as then Iraqi prime minister Nouri al-Maliki said at the press conference announcing his death, "Whenever there is a new al-Zarqawi, we will kill him." Yet Zarqawi's leadership ability—a combination of magnetism, fanatical vision, and strategic cunning, as unexpected as it might have been—was distinctly his own legacy, albeit one that is easily adoptable by others. I have no doubt that by the spring of 2006, Zarqawi's ideology represented a more immediate threat to American interests than bin Ladin did. The June 7 air strike blew a hole in his legacy. But perhaps just as important, his aura did not die with him.

Zarqawi's death brought only a temporary lull in activities from Al Qaida in Iraq. At the time, many observers filled the brief void with debates about the appropriateness of the Pentagon's release of images of Zarqawi's battered cadaver. It reminded me of another of Tom's sayings from the targeting team: "Success is all sunshine and rainbows until you show them the dead-guy photos."

The reprieve from AQI's predations lasted a mere six days.

———

Many of the American players in that fateful strike were recognized accordingly. The F-16 pilot who bombed Zarqawi's safe house didn't know until sometime the next day who was actually inside it. He received the Distinguished Flying Cross for his performance. Two members of the interrogation team at SOF received the Bronze Star Medal from McChrystal, given for heroic or meritorious achievement.

Within the CIA, Zarqawi's death didn't occasion any awards—though I recognized that the final feeling I came away with was even more valuable: relief. The mission I'd eagerly sought, since almost the moment I transitioned into the Agency's Iraq unit, was to help the United States take out that madman. It was done.

I've realized in the time since then that it's possible that no professional job I'll hold in the future will mean as much as one I've already had. The colleagues I worked with who embraced the magnitude and responsibility of the sort of work we did—who sacrificed as much as I did, and far more, for the larger mission and still maintained a passion for making the world a safer place—make corporate America pale in comparison. I remember Roger telling me once about the bureaucracy at his technology firm and the stacks of paperwork he had to file before signing a nondisclosure agreement with a client. "Really?" I said. "I had to get through less red tape to target somebody."

I left the JTTF and retired from the Agency for good in 2007. But even now, whenever I read an article about conditions in Iraq, I think, "I hope someone is following this aspect of things and paying attention to that nuance."

The feeling persists to this day, in part because even as time marches on, there are steady reminders of my former work and the unrest I left behind. Al Qaida, of course, still exists. After a few years of relative stability, Iraq, unfortunately, has once again been plunged into bloody chaos at the hands of Islamist extremists. And in good ways and bad, the CIA is still hard at work trying to figure out how to combat it.

Epilogue

I was moving around my house in a daze when the phone rang on December 9, 2014, years after I'd left the Agency. It was just after 7:00 a.m. Pacific time.

Although I didn't know it then, earlier that morning, the findings of a years-long Senate intelligence committee investigation into CIA interrogation techniques during the Global War on Terror finally became public. The findings in the officially titled "Committee Study of the Central Intelligence Agency's Detention and Interrogation Program" were at times ghastly, suggesting that interrogators, who were often poorly screened during the hiring process, had used enhanced methods far more often than had ever been publicly revealed; that those techniques—including extensive waterboarding, mock executions, and something described as "rectal feeding"—veered toward the barbaric; and that ultimately there was no clear actionable intelligence gained from torture. By the time the phone rang, the East Coast media were already in high dudgeon: "Senate Report on CIA Program Details Brutality, Dishonesty," declared the *Washington Post.* "Panel Faults C.I.A. Over Brutality and Deceit in Terrorism Interrogations," read the *New York Times.*

At that point, I hadn't read any of it. The night before, a little after midnight, I had experienced the very personal tragedy of losing my mom, Eloise Whisenhunt, to cancer. She was seventy-one.

Even its inevitability at the end hadn't managed to prepare me for the moment of her death.

Of course the caller didn't know that; there's no way he would have. The voice on the line was from the Agency's central Office of Security, which provides comprehensive and worldwide security programs and protection for CIA personnel. He got right down to business.

"You were named in the report," he said.

"I what?"

I racked my brain to figure out what he was talking about.

"In the Senate torture report," he said. "It's just a footnote, but it appears a few times. It's from a talk you gave at the Council on Foreign Relations."

"Are you kidding me? I just lost my mom — I don't need this right now," I snapped. "What does the report say?"

"It says, basically, 'Nada Bakos...states...that Hassan Ghul provided...critical information on Abu Ahmed al-Kuwaiti [and his connection to bin Ladin] to Kurdish officials prior to entering CIA custody. When asked about the interrogation techniques used by the Kurds, Bakos stated: "...honestly, Hassan Ghul...when he was being debriefed by the Kurdish government, he literally was sitting there having tea.... He wasn't handcuffed to anything. He was — he was having a free flowing conversation. And there's — you know, there's articles in Kurdish papers about sort of their interpretation of the story and how forthcoming he was."'"

Unfortunately, I knew exactly what he was talking about. In April of 2013, I had joined a panel discussion at the Council on Foreign Relations for the screening of an HBO documentary about the CIA's pursuit of al Qaida called *Manhunt*. At one point, conversation had turned to Ghul, and I made those comments based on my recollection of events and a story I'd read on Rudaw, a highly regarded Kurdish news outlet. That story was entirely true, as far as I knew, and seemed harmless to mention.

I made similar comments in the film, but after my interview, I wondered if I shouldn't have said what I said. Subsequently, I took the initiative to reach out to the Agency with a copy of my remarks and to apologize in advance if I'd crossed any lines. I was panicking, sending a note to every former CIA friend I could think of. I took my security agreement very seriously, even after leaving, which is why I proactively notified the Agency of my comments.

Thankfully, I was not in legal jeopardy. At the time, the CIA and the Senate committee had very different views of Ghul's responses, a difference of which I was unaware. The CIA contends that Ghul divulged more useful information at a black site. Therefore the story on Rudaw, which I'd repeated, didn't provide the same level of detail as the Agency testimony—a fact I suspected the Senate was highlighting. It was the only reason I could imagine the report would mention it. Suddenly, there on the phone, the pieces fell into place in my mind, and my frustration boiled over.

"They used my fucking name?" I said.

There was silence on the line for a moment.

"I'm sorry," the caller said.

I took a deep breath.

"No—I'm sorry," I said. "That wasn't about you."

"Of course. We're reaching out to everyone who was named in the report, and we want a team to come visit your home sometime this week. Is that possible?"

"Sure," I said. "We'll be here. And thanks: I appreciate the call."

"Absolutely," he said. "Please accept my condolences on your loss. I lost my mom a few years ago, and I can tell you that the pain will subside but you will always miss her."

Three days later, a four-person Agency support team flew in from Washington and drove to our house. My stepfather was there with Roger and me when the doorbell rang. The three of us were working on arranging my mother's cremation and other logistics of her death.

I met the visitors at the door—the distinctive business-casual look of Washington, DC, had a jarring government vibe to it. I immediately found myself wondering what the neighbors must think of the crowd on my doorstep.

I almost started to cry when I recognized one of the men. We'd met years earlier when he was a member of the Agency's staff—on a team created as a protection force in high-risk overseas posts. That CIA unit is largely made up of former military—the man at my door was certainly built like a member of the military—and seeing him there made everything feel a little safer. He was someone who understood the kind of work we had done and the kind of enemy we'd faced.

"It's good to see you again, Nada," he said. "Can we come in for a bit?"

For the first hour or so, the security team flipped through a binder about risk assessments, detailing any threatening online chatter the Agency had collected in the wake of the report's release. There wasn't much. Nonetheless, together we talked about our potential vulnerabilities, and the team from DC suggested a raft of ways to maximize our home's protection. From there, we walked the team around our house and property, taking additional notes for fortifying our security setup. "We'll be keeping an eye on you, too," they said, "but there are things you might want to consider." As luck would have it, our past trials in DIY installation would later come in handy as we followed up on their suggestions.

Eventually, after a few hours, we all thanked each other, and I showed our visitors to the door.

"You've got everything covered," my former colleague said, "and you've got our cards if anything comes up. There's nothing to worry about."

I forced a weak smile.

"Thanks," I said. "We appreciate it."

As I closed the door behind me, my body sagged. The previous forty-eight hours had felt longer than any I could remember. It had been nearly a decade since I'd left the Agency's Zarqawi-hunting team. I'd spent a handful of years—*just a fraction of my life*—helping battle Al Qaida in Iraq. Yet I remembered some of it as though it had been yesterday. And a team had just flown in from across the country to talk about what could happen tomorrow. I leaned my back against the door and sighed.

Roger walked over to me.

"Does this ever end?" I asked him. "Ever?"

"I don't know," he said, "but we'll make it work." He wrapped his arms around me, and I closed my eyes.

The larger perspective, of course, always comes later. These days it comes during unwelcome moments, when the brutality of war and counterterrorism fill my mind and I'm left with the shame of war and the emptiness of my own moral dissonance. What could I have done better in my own work? Why didn't I stand up and try to stop what was happening there?

Two years prior to the visit to our house, as I was flying home after working as a producer on a documentary about the Boston Marathon bombing, I had my first genuine panic attack. My grandmother was literally dying as I boarded the plane, and the passenger sitting next to me, an elderly gentleman, was almost exactly her age, a fact I had determined through small talk. During the flight, I turned to ask him a question about his grandchildren, but I couldn't speak, let alone breathe. I went to the back of the plane and told the flight attendant I was either having an asthma attack or a panic attack, I wasn't sure which. She said I was pale and should sit down. Then she quickly flung down the latch holding the jump seat against the wall and steered me toward it. After placing an oxygen mask over my nose and mouth, she announced over the intercom, "Is there a doctor on this flight? If so, please come to the back of the plane." After only a few seconds, a man knelt down next to me and introduced himself as an oncologist from

Boston. He took my pulse and then asked the flight attendant to help me lie down on the floor before I passed out. I remember fading in and out, listening to the murmurings between the doctor and the flight attendant. Eventually the flight attendant was on the phone with a doctor on the ground, describing my symptoms. I immediately lifted my mask and said, "Please do not land this plane." I was horrified and embarrassed—and besides, I was fairly sure I wasn't dying. Turns out there were two reasons for my lack of oxygen, a newly diagnosed tree nut allergy and a panic attack on top of it.

My mom's husband, a Vietnam veteran, noticed the lingering aftereffects of my job at the CIA before I did. I was gradually becoming disconnected from my family and friends; my recurring anxiety and panic attacks rendered me unable to function normally. I began speaking to a therapist and was diagnosed with post-traumatic stress disorder. I've learned since then that many people who were at the CIA share a similar struggle.

A landmark study conducted by the RAND Corporation in 2008 found that nearly one in five Iraq War veterans suffers from PTSD. In 2012, the Department of Veterans Affairs quietly released a more damning figure: nearly 30 percent of the 834,463 Iraq and Afghanistan veterans it had treated at VA hospitals since 2001 have been diagnosed with PTSD. I was also hardly alone in fearing that it represented some kind of weakness and trying to dismiss it. That same year, the nonprofit organization Blue Star Families found that only 35 percent of service members displaying symptoms of PTSD have sought treatment.

But I wasn't a soldier, so why I would experience PTSD? Shame began to make me feel that I was mentally weak and lacking the ability to cope with traumatic events. Turns out shame and guilt can be PTSD's best friends. While I was employed at the CIA, PTSD was not discussed as part of our jobs; we assumed it was never going to affect us. Later, after talking to some of my colleagues, I realized that the war on terror has affected many of us.

Within a two-year time period, I lost my grandmother, I lost my mother, and I was diagnosed with PTSD. Coping would be the only word to describe how I lived through the initial stages of hitting rock bottom. I stayed home, didn't want to leave the house—and sometimes I *couldn't* leave the house. I felt claustrophobic everywhere—outside, in a car; the feeling had no connection to the size of the space I was in. I have always loved to fly, everywhere, anytime, but at that point I could hardly stand the thought of being trapped in a metal tube. I wasn't afraid of dying in an airplane crash: in fact the only solace I had was knowing that I could get out of an airplane after it eventually ran out of fuel and crashed.

It has taken years of therapy and hard work to move through the anxiety, panic, and new way of living. PTSD has given me a different vision of what I want and a renewed sense of what I feel is important.

It's only recently that I've come to appreciate how serious a misnomer the word *disorder* is: we were all exposed to horrific things in Iraq and in the larger battle against terrorism. If we take into account the millions of refugees and those left behind who have had to experience the trauma of war, it's a sobering reminder that war should *only* be a last resort.

———

I know all too well that stories about counterterrorism rarely have a clean beginning or a well-defined end. Counterterrorism has had and will always have multiple fronts: extremist cells grow and divide—multiply, even—and can seemingly emerge continuously.

Amid reports the Agency collected of a power struggle for Zarqawi's vacant position, one shadowy figure soon emerged: Abu Ayyub al-Masri, an Egyptian cohort of Zarqawi's who had trained in al Qaida terrorist camps in Afghanistan. His brief dossier—a bit of bomb-making experience; an ability to shuttle foreign fighters across the Syrian border; a familiarity with the various extremist groups in the region — checked all the boxes required of someone leading part of a jihadist network. But the full al Qaida offshoot in Iraq? When I heard about his promotion, I scratched my head.

In another of the remarkable twists that only become legible in hindsight, there's likely a reason for that. I have come to believe strongly that Usama bin Ladin never intended for Masri to get the job.

In the summer of 2006, with Zarqawi recently deceased and a restless Iraq seeming ripe for conquest, bin Ladin, I've long suspected, was finally in a position to handpick the leader of the then most visible al Qaida franchise in the world. For that vaunted role, I'm convinced, bin Ladin chose Abd al-Hadi al-Iraqi, the al Qaida senior adviser who had met Zarqawi in 2003, right around the time I first set foot in Baghdad.

Soon after Zarqawi's death, it became clear that the Agency had done so much damage to the rat lines bringing foreign fighters into Iraq that al Qaida central started directing international recruits toward countries such as Algeria, Somalia, and Yemen. As a result, bin Ladin surely believed that al-Iraqi, who was born in northern Iraq and at one time served in the Iraqi Army, could be a galvanizing figure in an Iraq-based terror group that was becoming ever more dependent on local manpower. It made sense to appoint a native son to lead AQI and the aggrieved Sunnis in the midst of their civil war. Al-Iraqi was familiar with Zarqawi's theater of war, thanks to his regular visits to Iraq; furthermore, his travels throughout the Middle East on behalf of al Qaida would have given him the connections and fund-raising acumen to steady the group. Al-Iraqi had even proved his ruthless mettle a year earlier, masterminding the July 7, 2005, attacks on London's public transportation system, which killed fifty-two people. I'm convinced he was exactly the sort of well-connected killer bin Ladin would have chosen to officially succeed Zarqawi.

But these were exactly the credentials that made al-Iraqi a

well-known figure among targeting teams at Langley—first to the branches specifically devoted to al Qaida figures and then, once al-Iraqi made contact with Zarqawi, to my team. Al-Iraqi was arrested in the fall of 2006 as he passed through Turkey on his way to Iraq. For the second time, I'm convinced, bin Ladin's handpicked emir for the most important wing of his global terror group had been stymied. And that moment marks the start of a thought experiment I've long toyed with.

Soon after his arrest, al-Iraqi was put on a plane and began an odyssey that lasted until he was ultimately delivered to the Guantanamo Bay detention camp in April of 2007. He's still there today. Now in his midfifties, al-Iraqi faces life imprisonment for war crimes while his case winds through the military court system.

Meanwhile, with no representative from al Qaida central to challenge him, Masri, the Egyptian, took hold of Zarqawi's former network. Lingering bad blood remained, however, and connections between Masri's group and bin Ladin's network rapidly frayed. To improve its local appeal, Masri changed AQI's name to the Islamic State of Iraq. He appointed Abu Omar al-Baghdadi, a like-minded local jihadist who shared the wanton lust for destruction that Zarqawi had championed, as his fellow leader of the Iraq-based organization. Together they masterminded the hell that was wrought throughout Iraq from late 2006 through 2007, including the massacres and annihilation I'm convinced bin Ladin would have fervently rejected.

What would have happened had the United States simply not pinched al-Iraqi on his way across that Turkish border in 2006? What if al-Iraqi, bin Ladin's handpicked successor, had assumed control of Al Qaida in Iraq? I often wonder. Would a quieter, relatively "gentler" version of AQI—as contradictory as the concept may seem—have enabled the coalition to more quickly and successfully stabilize the country? Would the existence of that devil have been preferable to what took its place?

Of course I will never know the answer to that question. What we do know is that Masri and Omar led the organization until October of 2010, when a joint Iraqi and US SOF assault upon their meeting place west of Baghdad killed them both.

In the greater counterterrorism arc, the thread of extremism in Iraq hardly ends there. But for a moment, soon after Masri was meeting the same fate as Zarqawi, global focus instead turned to a shabby bedroom more than one thousand miles to the east, on the outskirts of Abbottabad, Pakistan—the culmination of a hunt that truly gained steam once the CIA picked up Hassan Ghul.

Back in 2004, Ghul, the al Qaida courier snatched en route to meet with Zarqawi, spent a few days in foreign custody before being turned over to the CIA. According to public records, during casual conversations referenced in the Senate torture report, Ghul told debriefers that bin Ladin "was likely living in [the] Peshawar area" of Pakistan. He further speculated that bin Ladin's "security apparatus would be minimal"—perhaps only one or two bodyguards—"and that the group likely lived in a house with a family somewhere in Pakistan." Lastly, he added, "It was well known that [bin Ladin] was always with Abu Ahmed [al-Kuwaiti]."

That last line got everyone's attention.

Now, January of 2004 was not the first time the intelligence community had come across Kuwaiti's name. A phone number for the Pakistani courier had been collected by the CIA two years earlier. An e-mail address was added six months after that. Those details appeared on the contact lists and in the address books of other high-level al Qaida operatives who were arrested. Kuwaiti was obviously someone worth knowing about within that organization, but investigators were deeply uncertain about his importance. Also, predictably, when Kuwaiti's al Qaida contacts got arrested, the courier discontinued using the contact information the Agency monitored. Ultimately those data points, the Agency has said, were "insufficient to distinguish Kuwaiti from many other bin Laden associates until additional information from detainees put it into context and allowed CIA to better understand his true role and potential in the hunt for bin Laden."

That's where Ghul came in, offering some of the most accurate detainee-related intelligence yet on Kuwaiti and his relationship to bin Ladin. In conversations with debriefers overseas, Ghul tabbed Kuwaiti as one of three individuals most likely to be found with bin Ladin, describing him as the al Qaida head's "closest assistant," who "likely handled all of [bin Ladin's] needs"—including shepherding messages to and from other al Qaida contacts. That's also when the conversations with Ghul became far less casual.

After he was rendered and subjected to enhanced interrogations, the Agency has said that Ghul described specific instances of Kuwaiti passing along letters from bin Ladin. Ghul also refuted the accounts of other high-value detainees who'd scoffed at Kuwaiti's importance and insisted that the courier had "retired" from al Qaida—stonewalling from the detainees that seemed, after Ghul's admissions, to indicate they were deliberately obscuring Kuwaiti's importance. That was a clear signal: by 2007, a CIA targeting study concluded, "these denials, combined with reporting from other detainees...add to our belief that Abu Ahmad [al-Kuwaiti] is [a high-value target] courier or facilitator." That sort of "detailed tactical intelligence," the Agency has said, was a "milestone in the long analytic targeting trek that led to Bin Ladin."

With his crucial role within al Qaida clarified, Kuwaiti became far too important to stop. His arrest might net the Agency new information or it might not—but if he could simply be monitored, an internal Agency memo from 2008 suggested, Kuwaiti might lead investigators directly to bin Ladin. The truth was that the CIA was short on any other real leads to the emir of al Qaida at the time. "Although we want to refrain from addressing endgame strategies," the memo said, "detaining [Kuwaiti] should be a last resort, since we have had no success in eliciting actionable intelligence on bin Ladin's location from any detainees [besides Ghul]." In 2010, a team of targeters led by Myrtle, the woman I'd worked with years earlier, built upon analysts' efforts and made that Kuwaiti intelligence actionable.

Kuwaiti's location was soon traced to an unexpectedly upscale enclave in Abbottabad's northeastern suburb, Bilal Town. Kuwaiti and his family lived in a compound worth an estimated $1 million, along with his brother and his brother's wife and children. The compound was surrounded by walls as high as fifteen feet and topped with multiple tiers of barbed wire.

The children only left the walled complex for school. The home had no Internet connection or phone line, and any cell-phone calls were taken well away from the property. Kuwaiti and the other residents could be seen burning their trash in the yard as opposed to simply setting it outside for community pickup.

There were indications that a mysterious third family lived on the compound's top floors — except those family members, it seemed, never left the house at all. That is, with one exception. Overhead surveillance routinely caught sight of an unidentified man strolling the compound's inner courtyards. Based on shadow patterns, they estimated that he was reasonably tall and thin. Agency analysts referred to him simply as "the pacer."

The intelligence community kept its ears on Kuwaiti's phone, and when the courier cryptically told an old friend during a call, "I'm with the same ones as before," word went straight up the chain of command. On April 29, 2011, President Obama determined there was a probability that the unknown pacer was bin Ladin and that the United States had to act. "Look, guys, this is a flip of the coin," he told his advisers. "I can't base this decision on the notion that we have any greater certainty than that." What became known as Operation Neptune Spear was a go.

Shortly after midnight Abbottabad time on Monday morning, May 2, 2011, members of a SEAL team arrived at bin Ladin's compound and executed those orders. The emir of al Qaida and four others were killed during the raid. When the president addressed the nation soon after, I let out a sigh of relief.

Bin Ladin's death didn't cripple al Qaida, of course. The organization continues to grow and divide and reemerge in countries such as Yemen, at the southern tip of the Arabian Peninsula. And sometimes, unfortunately, I see it returning to the very same places where I once helped root it out.

———————

I've never bought the idea that the "surge" of US troops in early 2007 — when President Bush authorized the deployment of thirty thousand additional forces to Iraq — was a success. Iraqi civilian casualties indeed fell throughout that year, but the exact reasons why are far more nuanced than the idea that those additional US troops saved the day — a backward-looking myth that persists to this day, as Arizona's Republican Senator John McCain told CNN on September 11, 2014: "We had it won, thanks to the surge," he said of the Iraq conflict. "It was won. The victory was there."

In reality, the nuances of what unfolded with the surge should be important to anyone trying to understand ground conditions in Iraq now, because they were not all good. Thousands of new twenty-something American soldiers were sent into neighborhoods with very little language training or cultural understanding. To help stanch the blood flow, coalition forces arrested some five thousand people during the summer of 2007. That brought the total number of detainees at the time to roughly twenty-three thousand, the highest number since the US invasion in 2003. It was a quintessential example of the way a superficial tactical advance could lead to larger strategic failure: many of the US-run facilities have had the same effect on those inmates as prison did upon Zarqawi. We know now, for instance, that as my team at Langley hunted the Jordanian, a separate key extremist was washing through US facilities in Iraq.

In 2003, when the United States invaded Iraq, Abu Bakr al-Baghdadi had been busy finishing a doctoral degree in Quranic studies at Saddam University, in Baghdad. A year later, Baghdadi was being held by US forces at Camp Bucca, the main American-run prison camp in Iraq at the time. It appears he had been arrested in Fallujah while visiting a friend whose name showed up on a coalition "Wanted" list. Over the coming years, many more such incidental arrests would fill US detention centers.

The reason for holding Baghdadi for ten months has never fully been ascertained. He may have held fanatical ideologies, or he may have been one of the 90 percent of inmates who, according to Red Cross reporting, were arrested "by mistake." Whatever Baghdadi's mind-set going into that prison was, there's no doubt about his state of mind when he emerged. The same is true of any number of the inmates at US-run Iraqi prisons I visited. "Many of us at Camp Bucca were concerned that instead of just holding detainees, we had created a pressure cooker for extremism," said former air force security officer James Skylar Gerrond, who was Bucca's compound commander from 2006 to 2007. "When some of Baghdadi's personal history started to come out," Gerrond told *Mother Jones,* "I started to reflect on my deployment and what the conditions were at the facility during that time."

Quietly, inmates began referring to Camp Bucca as "the Academy." One of Baghdadi's fellow detainees told *Al-Monitor,* "New recruits were prepared so that when they were freed they were ticking time bombs." Longtime prisoners would take a new arrival under their wings to "teach him, indoctrinate him, and give him direction so he leaves a burning flame." That approach lingered at Bucca long after Baghdadi was released, in December of 2004—just after al Qaida had made Zarqawi's Iraq offshoot an official franchise.

Following his time in detention, Baghdadi reportedly connected with a relative who had joined al Qaida and was put in contact with a representative of Zarqawi's group in Iraq. AQI sent him to Syria, and from Damascus Baghdadi helped oversee the network's online propaganda mill. He continued on in a similar role once Zarqawi was killed and, like AQI's founder, soon climbed the ranks of the newly named Islamic State of Iraq under Masri and Abu Omar al-Baghdadi through sheer force of will and demonstrated brutality. In the spring of 2010, he was selected by the group's senior consultative council to take over after Masri and Abu Omar al-Baghdadi were killed. That succession—another step in the thought experiment I occasionally ponder—may have been enabled by al-Iraqi's capture in 2006 and exacerbated by the surge. And if so, it set the stage for everything Baghdadi has since unleashed.

As Baghdadi began putting his imprint on the organization throughout 2010, he filled its upper ranks with fellow radicalized inmates who'd been detained at Camp Bucca—many of whom were captured during the surge. The following year, Baghdadi capitalized on regional instability by expanding his group's influence and capturing territory in neighboring Syria; by 2013, Baghdadi had enough of a foothold there to rename his network the Islamic State of Iraq and Syria, or ISIS (sometimes known as the Islamic State of Iraq and the Levant, or ISIL). ISIS established a de facto capital for their caliphate in Raqqa, Syria; then Baghdadi set his sights on expanding across western Iraq.

Baghdadi systemically dismantled border security between the two countries, creating a pipeline through which radical foreign fighters were once again funneled into northern Iraq. ISIS recruits in Iraq and Syria have unleashed waves of barbaric violence, beheading policemen, chopping the hands off of thieves, selling women and children into sex slavery, and mass-executing Iraqi soldiers who opposed them. Much of it has been filmed and posted online and disseminated widely through social media channels that didn't exist in the days when I hunted Zarqawi. Yet as his organization rose in global recognition, what has been most startling to me are the haunting echoes of the past.

———

There were reportedly more than 275 suicide bombings in Iraq in 2013, nearly all of which US officials attributed to Baghdadi's network. I didn't have to read past the headlines to know that the group's main targets were mosques, playgrounds, and markets within Iraq's Shia community. I recognized all that from Zarqawi's old playbook: "If we succeed in dragging [Shias] into the arena of sectarian war," Zarqawi wrote to the al Qaida leadership nearly a decade earlier, "it will become possible to awaken the inattentive Sunnis as they feel imminent danger." Baghdadi advanced that message further than even Zarqawi did, so much so that in the summer of 2014, the Grand Ayatollah Ali Sistani—Iraq's highest-ranking Shia cleric, who traditionally shunned any sort of political vocation—summoned civilian Shias to take up arms in defense of their homeland. In a scene reminiscent of early 2006, Sistani's call was promptly answered by "thousands of gun-toting men, who emerged in Baghdad, Basra and other Iraqi cities to declare their readiness to join a holy war," said the *Wall Street Journal*. What was old was new again.

In another unsettling parallel to Zarqawi's reign of terror, Baghdadi's indiscriminate thirst for blood has made al Qaida central squeamish. Videos of ISIS militants drowning and immolating prisoners, including journalists and aid workers, have led the most notorious of all terror groups to once again dissociate itself from ISIS and from what was happening on the ground in Iraq. Baghdadi's network "is not a branch of the al Qaida group," al Qaida's general command said in a 2014 statement. "[Al Qaida] does not have an organizational relationship with [ISIS] and [al Qaida] is not the group responsible for their actions."

Regardless of its decrease in territory and evolving media strategy, ISIS remains the most prominent extremist network in the world. Many of Baghdadi's followers are young enough to have only faint memories of the September 11, 2001, attacks that thrust al Qaida into international infamy; others had not yet been born at the time. In fact, one of ISIS's most shocking tactics has been to have school-age children gun down its prisoners.

Regardless, some of today's mujahideen see al Qaida as out of touch. Bolstered by a surprisingly savvy public relations wing—which even publishes annual reports for its financial backers, accounting for the numbers of assassinations, car bombings, and cities occupied that year—ISIS appeals to the social-networking generation of extremists. Al Qaida continues on as a covert terrorist organization, thrives through affiliates, and inspires radicalization of individuals.

I had been hoping the next president of the United States would engage in a political collaboration with the entire region and put pressure on the governments that are part of the proxy war inside Syria. A zero-sum solution would fail—and has failed—miserably. During any major humanitarian crisis, focusing on a perfect political solution instantaneously is unrealistic: stemming the violence should first and foremost be the priority, leaving open the option to rebuild a better, and possibly different, version of Syria. Let's use some of the tools that Richard Holbrooke used with the Dayton Accords—let go of the idealism and create the conditions required to force a solution.

The question of how to dismantle these networks for the long term is not and cannot be answered solely by a military response—

regardless of which military is responding. Terrorism is not an existential threat to the United States and requires a multilayer approach that is not linear and should encompass locally derived goals. The US government should envision kinetic operations as only one part of a broader strategy to stabilize a country in conflict, or we will continue to find ourselves in a perpetual war.

The entities responsible for carrying out counterterrorism work in the United States carry out divergent actions with no coherent purpose. This lack of coherent purpose makes it easy to fall into the trap of misreading activities, such as strikes or raids, as ends in and of themselves. They are divorced from a strategy or series of policies that might have a more cumulative impact on terrorist actors or communities, providing them with operating space. From Southeast Asia to the Middle East and North Africa, the US government often has turned to kinetic operations, a tactical function, as a substitute for a strategy. As hinted at earlier, these operations offer a veneer of "doing something" when there is a sense of urgency in the face of a perceived or real risk, even if the efficacy of using kinetic operations is questionable. They can be useful in the short term to prevent or limit control of territory, or if a terrorist organization has settled into a power vacuum, kinetic ops can buy time for stabilization efforts to take root. But if they are not incorporated into a broader strategy, kinetic operations cannot be successful in combating terrorist threats—particularly because kinetic operations are a tactical and episodic response to a strategic and enduring challenge.

One thing we know well about groups formed by the anvil of Zarqawi's vision is that they have a habit of wearing out their welcome. Offer a viable opportunity for everyday people to have a real life, and they will respond to it. The United States has tried and failed to respond to such an opportunity by spreading our version of democracy in the Middle East. In contrast to a replica of what we have, an open society that the Middle East would find sustainable has to be designed by those who believe in the solution.

Most important, we have spent too many lives and too much time, money, and energy focused on creating a military solution to a nonmilitary problem. It's time we focus on nonkinetic options such as diplomacy. Diplomacy can help ensure that kinetic measures are bolstered by removal of the power vacuum terrorist organizations rely upon, ensuring that others can't step in behind them.

Threat perception and the way in which governments measure and assess risk play a pivotal role in counterterrorism operations. For instance, a study of terrorism threat perceptions after 9/11 in the United States and Europe revealed substantial differences in public opinion among countries that had little or no experience in terrorism compared with countries that had experienced one or more acts of terrorism. Countries like the United States with little experience in terrorism typically had a high perception of the threat compared with countries that had experienced more acts of terrorism and which therefore had a lower threat perception prior to September 11, 2001. As a result, threat perceptions in the United States have tended to be too high. Government policies should be based on risk assessments, not on threat perceptions, and policy makers should acknowledge publicly the vulnerabilities that free societies face and the reality that not all risk can be mitigated.

The big challenge for the US government going forward will be to act less like a hegemon imposing solutions and picking winners, and instead to think of ourselves as part of a complex network that can ultimately provide for better futures than the alternatives. If Iraq showed us anything, it was that a severe lack of capability in this regard could not be overcome simply by imposing our military's might. Considering our routine failures in public policy here at home, in an environment that is familiar, I find the likelihood of the

United States demonstrating any sort of consistent skill in influencing conditions abroad very low at this point.

———

I have no doubt there are analysts and targeters at Langley right now focused on defining threats against the United States. They're surely losing sleep and dreading the late-night calls just as much as I did. I know all too well the toll a multinational, cross-continental hunt like theirs can take upon everyone involved. As removed as some of those individuals might seem from everyday life in America, they are just people, like me, dedicated to their job and focused on protecting our country.

———

To all the women and men who are currently working in the national security sector and to those who aspire to, I am cheering you on every day. There is still a lot of work to be done, and our national security apparatus needs women now more than ever.

Acknowledgments

To my coauthor, Davin Coburn, without whom this book wouldn't exist. To my agent, Cait Hoyt at CAA, thank you for your support, dedication, and patience. To the editors and staff at Little, Brown, thank you so, so, so much for your patience and sticking with me, especially Judith Clain and Vanessa Mobley, Sareena Kamath, Betsy Uhrig, Elizabeth Garriga.

Thank you to Mark Zaid and Bradley Moss for helping me dislodge the book out of the government review. Special thanks to Dennis Gleeson, Bill Harlow, John Nixon, Yashar Ali, Joby Warrick, Rodney Faraon, David Priess, and Jeffrey Smith and Charles Blanchard at Arnold & Porter Kaye Scholer for their advice and encouragement. Thank you to Morgan Fairchild, Brett McGurk, Clarissa Ward, Martha Raddatz, John McLaughlin, Clint Watts, Ali Soufan, and Doug Ollivant, for your pre-read and feedback.

To the Warkids for keeping me sane; you are all amazing. I would also like to thank my colleagues at Foreign Policy Research Institute: Ronald Granieri, Barak Mendelsohn, and Michael Noonan; and Elmira Bayrasli at Foreign Policy Interrupted.

Without these people in media that gave me a platform, I wouldn't have been able to get my story out: Greg Barker, John Battsek, Claudia Rizzi, Jake Swantko, Diane Becker, Razan Ghalayini, Gayle Lemmon-Tzemach, Lauren Wolfe, Barbara Gaines, David Letterman, Rachel Burstein, Don Lemon, Janelle Griffin, Maria Spinella, Joy

Reid, Rukmini Callimachi, Mike Madden, Adam Serwer, Kriszta Satori, Michael Rauch, Michael Weiss, Lee Farren, PBS *Frontline,* and HBO Docs. CAA staff who have given me opportunities and support: Tiffany Ward, Michelle Weiner, Hannah Epstein, Amie Yavor, Andy Roth, Christina Cohan, Erik Telford. Also thanks to Karga 7, Claire Kosloff, Julia LoVetere, and Daniela Lockwood.

To my colleagues at the CIA, thank you for continuing to serve your country.

To my AOPi's, thank you for the support for the past thirty years!

My Twitter community and friends: Morgan Fairchild, William Gibson, General Michael Hayden, Sarah Carlson, Cindy Otis, Bob Baer, Lisa Kaplan, Chris Diehl, Dave Gutelius, Cindy Storer, Susan Hasler, Barbara Sude.

Thank you to the staff at the publication review board for your hard work.

To my family and friends, thanks for listening to my frustration while the book was in review for three years. This book is also dedicated to my grandmother and my mom, miss you and wish you were here.

Notes

Introduction

p. 3 **May of 2011:** Peter Baker, Helene Cooper, and Mark Mazzetti, "Bin Laden Is Dead, Obama Says," *New York Times,* May 1, 2011.

p. 3 **Navy SEALs:** Ibid.

p. 3 **Abbottabad, Pakistan:** Ibid.

p. 3 **shot Usama bin Ladin multiple times in his head and chest:** Matthew Cole and Anna R. Schecter, "Who Shot Bin Laden? A Tale of Two Navy Special Operators," NBC News, November 6, 2014.

p. 3 **Agency personnel tracked bin Ladin's trusted courier:** Marc Ambinder, "How the CIA *Really* Caught Bin Laden's Trail," *The Week,* April 29, 2013.

p. 4 **the godfather of terrorism in Iraq:** John F. Burns, "U.S. Strike Hits Insurgent at Safehouse," *New York Times,* June 8, 2006.

p. 4 **no insurgent group caused more bloodshed:** Henry Schuster, "The World's Most Dangerous Terrorist," CNN, January 21, 2005.

p. 4 **literally thousands of deaths:** Burns, "U.S. Strike Hits Insurgent."

p. 4 **in the actions of the Islamic State:** Joby Warrick, "ISIS, with Gains in Iraq, Closes in on Founder Zarqawi's Violent Vision," *Washington Post,* June 14, 2014.

p. 4 **network known as Al Qaida in Iraq:** Burns, "U.S. Strike Hits Insurgent."

p. 5 **main character from Zero Dark Thirty:** Nada Bakos, "How True Is Zero Dark Thirty? A Former Operative Weighs In," *Pacific Standard,* January 16, 2013.

p. 5   **women initially made up the majority of the CIA targeters:** Robert Windrem, "Hunting Osama bin Laden Was Women's Work," NBC News, November 14, 2013.

p. 5   **I can now speak more freely:** John Hollister Hedley, "Secrets, Free Speech, and Fig Leaves, Reviewing the Work of CIA Authors," *Studies in Intelligence* (Spring 1998): 75–83.

p. 6   **ISIS...has risen from the ashes of Zarqawi's organization:** Warrick, "ISIS, with Gains in Iraq."

p. 6   **ISIS's brutal approach:** Ibid.

Chapter 1

p. 7   **New Headquarters Building, in Langley, Virginia:** CIA History Staff, "50 Years in Langley: Recollections of the Construction of CIA's Original Headquarters Building, 1961–2011" (Washington, DC: Center for the Study of Intelligence, 2012), https://www.cia.gov/library/center -for-the-study-of-intelligence/csi-publications/books-and -monographs/50-years-in-langley-recollections-of-cias-ohb/OHB%20 50th%20Anniversary.pdf.

p. 8   **The Office of Special Plans:** Jeffrey T. Richelson, ed., "Special Plans and Double Meanings: Controversies over Deception, Intelligence, and Policy Counterterrorism," National Security Archive Electronic Briefing Book 456, February 20, 2014, http://nsarchive.gwu.edu/NSAEBB/NSAE BB456/.

p. 8   **roughly a dozen personnel:** Ibid.

p. 8   **the fifth floor of the Pentagon:** Richard Sale, "Exclusive: DIA Targets DOD Unit," United Press International, July 30, 2004.

p. 9   **"Feith-based intelligence":** Robert Dreyfuss and Jason Vest, "The Lie Factory," *Mother Jones,* January/February 2004.

p. 9   **"Has somebody thought of this?":** Department of Defense Press Briefing: Defense Secretary Donald Rumsfeld and General Richard B. Myers, Chairman, Joint Chiefs of Staff, October 24, 2002, http:// fas.org/irp/news/2002/10/dod102502.html.

p. 9   **"purposefully aggressive...connections":** *Iraq and al-Qa'ida: Interpreting a Murky Relationship,* June 21, 2002, https://fas.org/irp/congress/ 2005_cr/CIAreport.062102.pdf.

p. 10   **an uncoordinated product:** Select Committee on Intelligence, United States Senate, "Iraq's Links to Terrorism," part XII of "Report on the

U.S. Intelligence Committee's Prewar Intelligence Assessments on Iraq," July 7, 2004, National Security Archive, George Washington University, http://nsarchive.gwu.edu/NSAEBB/NSAEBB129/part12-terrorism.pdf.

p. 10   **visiting Agency headquarters themselves:** Peter Baker, *Days of Fire: Bush and Cheney in the White House* (New York: Doubleday, 2013).

p. 10   **"unprecedented":** Ray McGovern, "Cheney, Forgery, and the CIA," *Counterpunch,* June 27, 2003.

p. 10   **"highly unusual":** Craig Unger, *The Fall of the House of Bush: The Untold Story of How a Band of True Believers Seized the Executive Branch, Started the Iraq War, and Still Imperils America's Future* (New York: Scribner, 2007).

p. 12   **"link between Iraq developing weapons":** "President Bush Outlines Iraqi Threat: Remarks by the President on Iraq," Office of the White House Press Secretary, October 7, 2002, http://georgewbush -whitehouse.archives.gov/news/releases/2002/10/20021007-8.html.

p. 12   **"American civilians...live and work":** Ibid.

p. 12   **"intelligence operative to deliver it":** Ibid.

p. 13   **"planning for chemical and biological attacks":** Ibid.

p. 14   **burn bags:** Roger Girdwood, "Burn Bags," *Studies in Intelligence* (Summer 1989), https://research.archives.gov/id/7283291.

Chapter 3

p. 47   **"Declaration of War":** "Declaration of War by Osama bin Laden, 1996," *PBS NewsHour,* August 23, 1996, http://www.pbs.org/news hour/updates/military/jan-june98/fatwa_1998.html.

p. 47   **"no more important duty":** Ibid.

p. 47   **February of 1998:** "Al Qaeda's Second Fatwa," *PBS NewsHour,* February 23, 1998, http://www.pbs.org/newshour/updates/military-jan-june98/ fatwa_1998/.

pp. 47–48   **"The ruling to kill the Americans":** Ibid.

p. 48   **the bombing of two US embassies:** "FBI Executive Summary: Bombings of the Embassies of the United States of America at Nairobi, Kenya, and Dar Es Salaam, Tanzania," *Frontline,* November 18, 1998, http://www .pbs.org/wgbh/pages/frontline/shows/binladen/bombings/summary .html.

p. 51   **the sixteen-week-long CAP:** "A Major Agency Success Celebrated 100 Times Over: CIA's Career Analyst Program," CIA Featured Story Archive,

October 30, 2008, https://www.cia.gov/news-information/featured
-story-archive/2008-featured-story-archive/a-major-agency-success
.html.

p. 51 **Sherman Kent School for Intelligence Analysis:** "Training
Resources," Offices of CIA, April 25, 2007, https://www.cia.gov/offices
-of-cia/intelligence-analysis/training-resources.html.

p. 51 **"the basic thinking, writing, and briefing skills":** Ibid.

p. 52 **"Fundamentals of Denial and Deception":** Bob Drogin, "School
for New Brand of Spooks," *Los Angeles Times,* July 21, 2000.

p. 52 **special blue name badges:** Ibid.

p. 52 **computers labeled TOP SECRET:** Ibid.

p. 52 **writing style demanded of analysts:** Bill Welch, ed., *The Analyst's
Style Manual* (Erie, PA: Mercyhurst College Institute for Intelligence
Studies Press, 2008), https://www.ncirc.gov/documents%5Cpublic
%5CAnalysts_Style_Manual.pdf.

p. 52 **BLUF:** Ibid.

p. 55 **two years before I attended:** "A Look Back…Sherman Kent:
The Father of Intelligence," CIA Featured Story Archive, May 6,
2010, https://www.cia.gov/news-information/featured-story-archive/
2010-featured-story-archive/sherman-kent-the-father-of-intelligence
.html.

p. 55 **as far back as 1953:** "Studies in Intelligence Celebrates 60th Birthday,"
CIA Featured Story Archive, September 23, 2015, https://www.cia
.gov/news-information/featured-story-archive/2015-featured-story
-archive/studies-in-intelligence-celebrates-60th-birthday.html.

p. 55 **"have a nice day":** Tim Weiner, "Naivete at the CIA: Every Nation's
Just Another U.S.," *New York Times,* June 7, 1998.

p. 56 **was shot down:** "Genocide in Rwanda," United Human Rights Council, http://www.unitedhumanrights.org/genocide/genocide_in_rwanda.

p. 56 **whom they blamed for the attack:** Ibid.

p. 56 **eight hundred thousand…were slaughtered:** Ibid.

p. 57 **"years after the fact":** "Vice President Cheney Addresses New CIA
Analysts," CIA Press Release Archive, November 8, 2002, https://
www.cia.gov/news-information/press-releases-statements/press
-release-archive-2002/pr11082002.html.

p. 59 **Abu Musab al-Zarqawi arrived in Iraq:** "How ISIS Spread in the Middle East and How to Stop It," *The Atlantic,* October 29, 2015, https://www

.theatlantic.com/international/archive/2015/10/how-isis-started-syria
-iraq/412042/.

p. 60   **the al-Masoum neighborhood of Zarqa's "old town":** Mohammad Ahmad, "Al-Zarqawi's Legacy Haunts the al-Khalayleh Clan,"
Terrorism Focus 3, no. 23 (June 13, 2006).

p. 60   **October of 1966:** Mary Anne Weaver, "The Short, Violent Life of
Abu Musab al-Zarqawi," *The Atlantic,* July/August 2006.

p. 60   **Ahmad Fadil al-Nazal al-Khalayleh:** Ibid.

p. 60   **one of ten children:** Ahmad, "Al-Zarqawi's Legacy."

p. 60   **third-largest city:** Weaver, "The Short, Violent Life."

p. 60   **population of some 850,000:** Ibid.

p. 60   **"Chicago of the Middle East":** Loretta Napoleoni, "Profile of a
Killer," *Foreign Policy,* October 20, 2009.

p. 60   **a farmer and herbal medicine salesman:** Ahmad, "Al-Zarqawi's
Legacy."

p. 60   **dropped out of high school at the age of seventeen:** Jeffrey
Gettleman, "Zarqawi's Journey: From Dropout to Prisoner to an
Insurgent Leader in Iraq," *New York Times,* July 13, 2004.

p. 60   **the nearby Palestinian refugee camp:** Weaver, "The Short, Violent Life."

p. 60   **Fadil died the year after Khalayleh dropped out:** Ahmad,
"Al-Zarqawi's Legacy."

p. 60   **a drunk and a thug:** Gary Gambill, "Abu Musab Al-Zarqawi: A
Biographical Sketch," *Terrorism Monitor* 2, no. 24 (December 15, 2004).

p. 60   **in the garbage-strewn Masoum cemetery:** Ahmad, "Al-Zarqawi's Legacy."

p. 60   **two-story concrete-block family home:** Gettleman, "Zarqawi's
Journey."

p. 60   **He raped local women to assert his dominance:** Stanley McChrystal, *My Share of the Task: A Memoir* (New York: Portfolio, 2013).

p. 60   **the green man:** Jeffrey Gettleman, "Abu Musab al-Zarqawi Lived a
Brief, Shadowy Life Replete with Contradictions," *New York Times,*
June 9, 2006.

p. 61   **arrested for drug possession and sexual assault:** McChrystal,
My Share of the Task.

p. 61   **more foreign fighters:** David Kenner, "The Men Who Love the
Islamic State," *Foreign Policy,* February 4, 2015.

p. 61 **the hometown of Mohammed Salameh:** Kim Murphy, "Bomb Suspect's Family Is Confused but Hopeful," *Los Angeles Times,* March 12, 1993.

p. 61 **led Khalayleh to Zarqa's Al Hussein bin Ali mosque:** "Abu Musab al-Zarqawi," *The Independent,* June 8, 2006, https://www.independent.co.uk/news/obituaries/abu-musab-al-zarqawi-481622.html.

p. 62 **burn his tattoos:** Stanley McChrystal with Tantum Collins, David Silverman, and Chris Fussell, *Team of Teams: New Rules of Engagement for a Complex World* (New York: Portfolio, 2015).

p. 62 **Khalayleh himself headed off to fight:** Napoleoni, "Profile of a Killer."

p. 62 **stopping first in Peshawar, Pakistan:** "Key Events in the Life of al-Zarqawi," *New York Times,* June 8, 2006, https://www.nytimes.com/2006/06/08/world/08timeline-zarqawi.html.

p. 62 **then traveling on to Afghanistan:** Loretta Napoleoni, *Insurgent Iraq: Al Zarqawi and the New Generation* (New York: Seven Stories Press, 2005).

p. 62 **arrived in Herat:** "Key Events in the Life of al-Zarqawi."

p. 62 **a roving reporter...for...Al Bunyan al Marsus:** Weaver, "The Short, Violent Life."

p. 62 **soon become his spiritual leader:** Ibid.

p. 62 **seven years Khalayleh's elder:** Adrian Levy and Catherine Scott-Clark, *Deception: Pakistan, the United States, and the Secret Trade in Nuclear Weapons* (New York: Walker & Company, 2007).

p. 62 **had lived for a time in the Palestinian refugee camp:** Nibras Kazimi, "A Virulent Ideology in Mutation: Zarqawi Upstages Maqdisi," *Current Trends in Islamist Ideology* 2 (September 12, 2005): 59–73.

p. 63 **Zarqawi and a handful of other mujahideen fighters:** Joby Warrick, *Black Flags: The Rise of ISIS* (New York: Anchor Books, 2016).

p. 63 **reprimanding women:** Urs Gehriger, "Abu Musab al-Zarqawi: From Green Man to Guru," SignAndSight.com, September 11, 2005, http://www.signandsight.com/features/449.html.

p. 63 **"It was not easy with him":** Ibid.

p. 63 **form a militant group:** Weaver, "The Short, Violent Life."

p. 64 **stashing weapons in his basement:** Weaver, "The Short, Violent Life."

p. 64 **"He never struck me as intelligent":** Gettleman, "Zarqawi's Journey."

p. 64   **sentenced to fifteen years in prison:** Weaver, "The Short, Violent Life."

p. 64   **bench-pressing buckets of rocks:** Gettleman, "Zarqawi's Journey."

p. 64   **doled out prison chores to other inmates:** Ibid.

p. 64   **caught him reading *Crime and Punishment*:** Gehriger, "Abu Musab al-Zarqawi."

p. 64   **"like a child wrote it":** Gettleman, "Zarqawi's Journey."

p. 64   **covered the ward's TV sets with black cloth:** Ibid.

p. 65   **intermediary between the guards and the inmates:** Ibid.

p. 65   **personally bathed an inmate:** Gehriger, "Abu Musab al-Zarqawi."

p. 65   **"He was tough, difficult to deal with":** Napoleoni, *Insurgent Iraq.*

p. 65   **"others would follow suit":** Ibid.

p. 65   **"al-Gharib"—the stranger:** Lawrence Joffe, "Abu Musab al-Zarqawi," *The Guardian,* June 8, 2006.

p. 65   **King Abdullah II granted a royal pardon:** Gambill, "Abu Musab Al-Zarqawi."

p. 65   **a book by Jordanian journalist Fuad Hussein:** Brian Fishman, "Revising the History of al-Qa'ida's Original Meeting with Abu Musab al-Zarqawi," *CTC Sentinel* 9, no. 10 (October 2016).

p. 66   **"We were therefore very pleased":** Gehriger, "Abu Musab al-Zarqawi."

p. 66   **Zarqawi was sitting in a safe house in Kandahar:** Ibid.

p. 66   **infiltrated Zarqawi's prison network:** Weaver, "The Short, Violent Life."

p. 67   **some in al Qaida, including Adl:** Fishman, "Revising the History."

p. 67   **"poor rhetorical skills":** Gehriger, "Abu Musab al-Zarqawi."

p. 67   **With Adl's encouragement:** Weaver, "The Short, Violent Life."

p. 67   **Bin Laden authorized $5,000 in seed money:** Ibid.

p. 67   **a training base outside Herat:** Ibid.

p. 67   **"coordination and cooperation...common goals":** Gehriger, "Abu Musab al-Zarqawi."

p. 67   **"senior associate and collaborator":** George Tenet, *At the Center of the Storm: My Years at the CIA* (New York: HarperCollins, 2007).

p. 67   **with a dozen or so followers:** Weaver, "The Short, Violent Life."

p. 67   **his new group's name, al-Tawhid wal-Jihad:** Jean-Charles Brisard, *Zarqawi: The New Face of al Qaeda* (New York: Other Press, 2005).

Chapter 4

p. 70 **"eviscerated on an editorial page":** Martin Petersen, "What I Learned in 40 Years of Doing Intelligence Analysis for US Foreign Policymakers," *Studies in Intelligence* 55, no. 1 (March 29, 2011), https://www.cia.gov/library/center-for-the-study-of-intelligence/csi-publications/csi-studies/studies/vol.-55-no.-1/what-i-learned-in-40-years-of-doing-intelligence-analysis-for-us-foreign-policymakers.html.

p. 70 **Ismail Khan and some five thousand of his militiamen:** Ibid.

p. 70 **Zarqawi was in Iran:** Mary Anne Weaver, "The Short, Violent Life of Abu Musab al-Zarqawi," *The Atlantic,* July/August 2006.

p. 71 **he settled in the northern mountain town of Khurmal:** David S. Cloud, "Long in U.S. Sights, a Young Terrorist Builds Grim Résumé," *Wall Street Journal,* February 10, 2004.

p. 71 **he paid two men to gun down an unlikely victim:** Matthew Levitt, "Zarqawi's Jordanian Agenda," *Terrorism Monitor* 2, no. 24 (December 15, 2004).

p. 71 **October 28, 2002:** Neil MacFarquhar, "American Envoy Killed in Jordan," *New York Times,* October 29, 2002.

p. 71 **limestone villa in Abdoun:** Michael Matza, "Diplomat from U.S. Shot Dead in Jordan," *Philadelphia Inquirer,* October 29, 2002.

p. 72 **Around 7:15 a.m. that October day:** MacFarquhar, "American Envoy Killed."

p. 72 **Libyan national Salem bin Suweid:** Reuters, "Jordan Hangs 2 for Killing U.S. Diplomat," March 12, 2006.

p. 72 **shot eight times in the head, chest, and abdomen:** MacFarquhar, "American Envoy Killed."

p. 72 **a getaway rental car driven by Jordanian Yasser Freihat:** Associated Press, "Jordan Executes 2 Militants for Slaying of U.S. Diplomat," March 11, 2006.

p. 72 **handed him the gun:** Jean-Charles Brisard and Damien Martinez, *Zarqawi: The New Face of al-Qaeda* (Cambridge, UK: Polity Press, 2005).

p. 72 **sentenced to death in absentia:** *Los Angeles Times* Wire Reports, "Court Sentences Zarqawi to Death in Absentia," December 19, 2005.

p. 72 **menace who should be taken out of the picture:** Jarrett Murphy, "Birthday Gift to Wanted Terrorist," CBS News, October 31, 2003.

p. 73 **"an associate...of Osama bin Laden":** "Transcript of Powell's U.N. Presentation Part 9: Ties to al Qaeda," CNN, February 6, 2003, http://www.cnn.com/2003/US/02/05/sprj.irq.powell.transcript.09/index.html?iref=mpstoryview.

p. 73 **"many of its leaders are known to be in Baghdad":** "Bush: 'All the World Can Rise to This Moment,'" CNN, February 6, 2003, http://www.cnn.com/2003/US/02/06/sprj.irq.bush.transcript/.

p. 73 **killing some five thousand civilians:** "1988: Thousands Die in Halabja Gas Attack," BBC, http://news.bbc.co.uk/onthisday/hi/dates/stories/march/16/newsid_4304000/4304853.stm.

p. 74 **consolidated their power:** Stanford University, "Mapping Militant Organizations: Ansar al-Islam," http://web.stanford.edu/group/mappingmilitants/cgi-bin/groups/view/13.

p. 74 **he aligned his forces with theirs:** Ibid.

p. 74 **"but well considered":** Urs Gehriger, "Abu Musab al-Zarqawi: From Green Man to Guru," SignAndSight.com, September 11, 2005, http://www.signandsight.com/features/449.html.

p. 74 **son of a wealthy factory owner:** Karl Vick, "A Bomb-Builder, 'Out of the Shadows,'" *Washington Post,* February 20, 2006.

p. 75 **Saqa had affiliated himself with Zarqawi:** Mustafa Hamid and Leah Farrall, *The Arabs at War in Afghanistan* (New York: Oxford University Press, 2016).

p. 75 **an experienced facilitator:** Ibid.

p. 75 **Saqa and Zarqawi were sentenced...fifteen years in prison:** Associated Press, "Alleged al-Qaeda Aide Said to Fake Death," January 1, 2006.

p. 75 **Algeria, Morocco, Pakistan, Libya, and two dozen other countries:** George Tenet, *At the Center of the Storm: My Years at the CIA* (New York: HarperCollins, 2007).

p. 75 **such as cyanide gas and aerosolized ricin:** Rolf Mowatt-Larssen, "Al Qaeda's Pursuit of Weapons of Mass Destruction," *Foreign Policy,* January 25, 2010.

p. 75 **CIA knew exactly where Zarqawi was:** Mike Tucker and Charles Faddis, *Operation Hotel California: The Clandestine War Inside Iraq*

(Guilford, CT: Lyons Press, 2009); *Wall Street Journal,* October 25, 2004.

p. 75 **A small team of Agency operatives:** Tucker and Faddis, *Operation Hotel California.*

p. 75 **they found Zarqawi's new home:** Ibid.

p. 76 **testing of those contact toxins:** Ibid.

p. 76 **tinker with blocks of cyanide salt:** Ibid.; Jim Miklaszewski, "Avoiding Attacking Suspected Terrorist Mastermind," NBC News, March 2, 2004.

p. 76 **tried the same with ricin:** Ibid.

p. 76 **animals had become unwitting subjects:** Tucker and Faddis, *Operation Hotel California.*

p. 76 **torturing of a donkey and other animals:** Ibid.

p. 76 **"chemical and biological weapons":** "Interview with Douglas Feith. Jonathan Holmes interviews Douglas Feith, the Under Secretary of Defense for Policy," ABC 4Corners, February 21, 2003.

p. 77 **"chemical and biological weapons techniques":** Condoleezza Rice, interview with Bob Schieffer, CBS News, and Tom Friedman, *New York Times,* on *Face the Nation,* March 9, 2003, http://www.cbsnews.com/news/ftn-3-9-03/.

p. 77 **"producing these toxins":** Greg Miller, "Ongoing Iraqi Camp Questioned," *Los Angeles Times,* February 7, 2003.

p. 77 **"in the National Security Council":** Miklaszewski, "Avoiding Attacking Suspected Terrorist."

p. 77 **"a prime suspect in that regard":** Rudi Williams, "Cheney Says U.S. in Final Stages of Diplomacy with Iraq," American Forces Press Service, March 16, 2003.

p. 77 **"greeted as liberators":** *Meet the Press,* September 14, 2003, http://www.nbcnews.com/id/3080244/ns/meet_the_press/t/transcript-sept/#.VlCXr8qPyaw.

Chapter 5

p. 90 **150,000 US troops in Iraq at the time:** Associated Press, "U.S. Troops at Lowest Level in Iraq Since 2003 Invasion," February 16, 2010.

p. 90 **my new home:** Charles Duelfer, *Hide and Seek: The Search for Truth in Iraq* (New York: PublicAffairs, 2009).

p. 90   **7.5 million passengers a year:** Ibid.

p. 91   **six square miles of airport grounds:** Ibid.

p. 92   **"Any war that Saddam survived was a victory":** Rebecca Santana, "U.S. Troops in Iraq Leaving Saddam Palaces," Associated Press, June 12, 2011.

p. 95   **chose the publicly released photo:** Terry McDermott and Josh Meyer, *The Hunt for KSM: Inside the Pursuit and Takedown of the Real 9/11 Mastermind, Khalid Sheikh Mohammed* (New York: Little, Brown, 2012).

p. 95   **"get out of the way":** Nancy DeWolf Smith, "Osama's Real Hunters," *Wall Street Journal,* April 25, 2013.

p. 95   **"rather than recruiting spies":** Nora Slatkin, "Executive Director Speech: Women in CIA," May 15, 1996, https://www.cia.gov/news -information/speeches-testimony/1996/exdir_speech_051596.html.

p. 95   **1986 class-action lawsuit:** John M. Broder, "CIA Will Settle Women Agents' Bias Lawsuit," *Los Angeles Times,* March 30, 1995.

p. 96   **"pervasive culture of sexual discrimination":** Ibid.

p. 96   **$940,000 in back pay and granting twenty-five retroactive promotions:** Ibid.

p. 96   **"a fantasy of a different sort":** Slatkin, "Executive Director Speech."

p. 96   **"male participants are more likely to take risks":** James Byrnes, David Miller, and William Schafer, "Gender Differences in Risk Taking: A Meta-Analysis," *Psychological Bulletin* 125, no. 3 (May 1999): 377.

p. 96   **"may indeed lead to higher risk aversion":** Helga Fehr-Duda, Manuele de Gennaro, and Renate Schubert, "Gender, Financial Risk, and Probability Weights," *Theory and Decision* 60, no. 2 (May 2006).

p. 97   **"Armed and Dangerous":** United States Department of State Bureau of Intelligence and Research, "The Wandering Mujahidin: Armed and Dangerous," August 21–22, 1993, http://blogs.law.harvard .edu/mesh/files/2008/03/wandering_mujahidin.pdf.

p. 97   **"they are training new fighters":** Ibid.

p. 98   **"That's not real analysis":** Barbara Sude, interview conducted by Peter L. Bergen in *Manhunt: The Search for Bin Laden,* HBO, 2013.

p. 98   **"We are at war":** "Report Cites Warnings Before 9/11," CNN, September 19, 2002, http://edition.cnn.com/2002/ALLPOLITICS/09/18/intelligence.hearings/.

p. 98 **"I want no resources or people spared in this effort":** Douglas Jehl, " '98 Terror Memo Disregarded, Report Says," *New York Times,* April 15, 2004.

p. 98 **"despite the DCI's declaration of war":** "Full Transcript from Testimony on Attacks," *New York Times,* September 18, 2002, http://www.nytimes.com/2002/09/18/politics/19INTEL-TEXT.html.

p. 98 **"did not discharge their responsibilities...manner":** Katherine Shrader, "CIA Missed Chances to Tackle al-Qaida," Associated Press, August 22, 2007.

p. 99 **"we settled on the one issue":** Associated Press, "Wolfowitz Comments Revive Doubts over Iraq's WMD," May 30, 2003.

p. 99 **Seventy-Fifth Exploitation Task Force:** Anthony H. Cordesman, "Intelligence, Iraq, and Weapons of Mass Destruction," Center for Strategic and International Studies, January 26, 2004.

p. 99 **six hundred or so people:** Ibid.

p. 99 **nineteen top suspected WMD sites:** Ibid.

p. 100 **"but we're past that":** Barton Gellman, "Frustrated, U.S. Arms Team to Leave Iraq," *Washington Post,* May 11, 2003.

p. 100 **a new fifteen-hundred-person task force:** Cordesman, "Intelligence, Iraq, and Weapons of Mass Destruction."

p. 102 **"without identifying with or acting upon them":** Stephen Batchelor, *Buddhism Without Beliefs: A Contemporary Guide to Awakening* (New York: Riverhead Books, 1997).

p. 103 **Camp Cropper:** Human Rights Watch, "The Road to Abu Ghraib," June 2004, https://www.hrw.org/reports/2004/usa0604/index.htm.

p. 103 **as many as twenty-six thousand inmates:** Martin Chulov, "Largest of America's Two Prisons in Iraq to Shut," *The Guardian,* September 16, 2009.

p. 103 **included Huda Salih Mahdi Ammash:** John F. Burns, "24 Ex-Hussein Officials Freed from U.S. Custody," *New York Times,* December 20, 2005.

p. 103 **was also in a cell in Cropper:** Ibid.

p. 103 **Tariq Aziz...was there as well:** Tim Arango, "Transfer of Prison in Iraq Marks Another Milestone," *New York Times,* July 14, 2010.

p. 104 **was apprehended and sent to Cropper:** Martin Chulov, " 'Chemical Ali' to Be Hanged Within Days," *The Guardian,* January 17, 2010.

p. 104 **"One day, they [will] start facing bitter facts":** Emily DePrang, "'Baghdad Bob' and His Ridiculous, True Predictions," *The Atlantic,* March 21, 2013.

p. 105 **then distributed among various internment facilities around the country:** Abigail Hauslohner, "Prison Life Inside Baghdad's Camp Cropper," *Time,* June 12, 2008.

p. 105 **built to house around two hundred people:** Scott Higham, Josh White, and Christian Davenport, "A Prison on the Brink," *Washington Post,* May 9, 2004.

p. 105 **somewhere between five hundred and one thousand:** Ibid.

p. 106 **more than three hundred days:** "Marine General: Freed Iraqis Not Rejoining Insurgency," CNN, October 10, 2007.

Chapter 6

p. 109 **bored of talking about the Iraqi Intelligence Service:** "Iraq's Intelligence Services: Regime Strategic Intent — Annex B," April 23, 2007, https://www.cia.gov/library/reports/general-reports-1/iraq_wmd_2004/chap1_annxB.html; "Report of the Select Committee on Intelligence, Postwar Findings on Iraq's WMD Program and Links to Terrorism and How They Compare with Prewar Assessments," United States Select Senate Committee on Intelligence; S Report 109-331, September 2006, https://www.intelligence.senate.gov/sites/default/files/publications/109331.pdf; "Support to Operation Iraqi Freedom," April 25, 2007, https://www.cia.gov/library/reports/archived-reports-1/Ann_Rpt_2003/iraq.html.

p. 110 **Sayf al-Adl:** Ari R. Weisfuse, "The Last Hope for the al-Qa'ida Old Guard? A Profile of Saif al-'Adl," *CTC Sentinel* 9, no. 3 (March 2016).

p. 110 **his main al Qaida contact in Iran:** Robert Windrem, "Newly Released Bin Laden Document Describes Iran, Al Qaeda Link," NBC News, November 1, 2017, https://www.nbcnews.com/news/world/newly-released-bin-laden-document-describes-iran-al-qaeda-link-n816681; Weisfuse, "The Last Hope for the al-Qa'ida Old Guard?"

p. 110 **other foreign fighters would join his ranks:** Aki Peritz and Eric Rosenbach, *Find, Fix, Finish: Inside the Counterterrorism Campaigns that Killed bin Laden and Devastated Al Qaeda* (New York: Public Affairs, 2012).

p. 110 **"but not introduce it into politics":** Efraim Karsh and Inari Rautsi, *Saddam Hussein: A Political Biography* (New York: Grove Press, 1991).

p. 110 **killed more than a million people:** Ian Black, "Iran and Iraq Remember War That Cost More Than a Million Lives," *The Guardian*, September 23, 2010.

p. 111 **Hussein opened an Islamic university:** Michael Slackman, "Hussein Putting His Mark on Islamic Faith," *Los Angeles Times*, November 4, 2001.

p. 111 **He introduced compulsory religious education:** Paul Lewis, "Iraq Bans Public Use of Alcohol," *New York Times*, August 21, 1994.

p. 111 **He shuttered nightclubs with seedy reputations:** Ibid.

p. 111 **import ten million copies of the Koran:** Ibid.

p. 111 **"If we could ban it, we would. We can't":** Slackman, "Hussein Putting His Mark."

p. 111 **he banned alcohol from restaurants:** Lewis, "Iraq Bans Public Use."

p. 111 **Hussein added the words** *Allahu akbar*...**to the Iraqi flag:** Ibid.

p. 111 **Named the Mother of All Battles:** Philip Smucker, "Iraq Builds 'Mother of All Battles' Mosque in Praise of Saddam," *The Telegraph*, July 29, 2001.

p. 111 **pints of Hussein's blood:** Martin Chulov, "Qur'an Etched in Saddam Hussein's Blood Poses Dilemma for Iraq Leaders," *The Guardian*, December 19, 2010.

p. 117 **a slow but steady increase in violence:** Michael J. Boyle, *Violence After War: Explaining Instability in Post-Conflict States* (Baltimore: Johns Hopkins University Press, 2014).

p. 117 **killed a smattering of foot soldiers:** "U.S. Missiles Hit Islamist Strongholds in Northern Iraq," Fox News, March 22, 2003.

p. 121 **described some methods as outright torture:** Siobhan Gorman, Devlin Barrett, Felicia Schwartz, and Dion Nissenbaum, "Senate Report Calls CIA Interrogation Tactics Ineffective," *Wall Street Journal*, December 9, 2014.

p. 122 **Evil Hagrid:** Charles Duelfer, *Hide and Seek: The Search for Truth in Iraq* (New York: PublicAffairs, 2009).

p. 122 **twenty-four different directorates:** "Iraq's Intelligence Services," in *Comprehensive Report of the Special Advisor to the Director of Central Intelligence on Iraq's Weapons of Mass Destruction* 1, annex B (Washington,

DC: Central Intelligence Agency, 2004), https://www.cia.gov/library/
reports/general-reports-1/iraq_wmd_2004/chap1_annxB.html.

p. 122 **each designated with an M:** Ibid.

p. 122 **Another nine smaller regional offices:** Ibid.

Chapter 7

p. 128 **killed each day:** iCasualties.org, "Iraq Coalition Casualties: Fatalities by Year and Month," http://icasualties.org/App/NewsArchive.

p. 128 **Phase 0:** Joint Chiefs of Staff, "Joint Operation Planning," Joint Publication 5-0, Defense Technical Information Center, August 11, 2011,
http://www.dtic.mil/doctrine/new_pubs/jp5_0.pdf.

p. 128 **Phase I:** Ibid.

p. 128 **Phase II:** Ibid.

p. 128 **Phase III:** Ibid.

p. 129 **CPA Order Number 1:** L. Paul Bremer III, "Coalition Provisional
Authority Order Number 1: De-Ba'athification of Iraqi Society,"
National Security Archive, George Washington University, May 16,
2003, http://nsarchive.gwu.edu/NSAEBB/NSAEBB418/docs/9a%20
-%20Coalition%20Provisional%20Authority%20Order%20No%20
1%20-%205-16-03.pdf.

p. 129 **"future employment in the public sector":** Ibid.

p. 129 **Doug Feith was the architect of this plan:** James P. Pfiffner, "US
Blunders in Iraq: De-Baathification and Disbanding the Army," *Intelligence and National Security* 25, no. 1 (February 2010): 76–85.

p. 129 **roughly eighty-five thousand government workers:** Ibid.

p. 130 **"no...Principals meeting to debate the move":** George Tenet,
At the Center of the Storm: My Years at the CIA (New York: HarperCollins, 2007).

p. 130 **"true believers" in Hussein's regime:** L. Paul Bremer III, *My
Year in Iraq: The Struggle to Build a Future of Hope* (New York: Simon
and Schuster, 2007).

p. 130 **CPA Order Number 2:** L. Paul Bremer III, "Coalition Provisional
Authority Order Number 2: Dissolution of Entities," National Security Archive, George Washington University, May 23, 2003, http://
nsarchive.gwu.edu/NSAEBB/NSAEBB418/docs/9b%20-%20Coali
tion%20Provisional%20Authority%20Order%20No%202%20-%20
8-23-03.pdf.

p. 130 **385,000 former Iraqi soldiers:** Thomas E. Ricks, *Fiasco: The American Military Adventure in Iraq* (New York: Penguin Press, 2006).

p. 130 **285,000 workers from the Ministry of Interior:** Ibid.

p. 130 **50,000 guards from Hussein's presidential security units:** Ibid.

p. 131 **"away from work and looking for employment":** Human Rights Watch, "Climate of Fear: Sexual Violence and Abduction of Women and Girls in Baghdad," July 2003, https://www.hrw.org/reports/2003/iraq0703/index.htm.

p. 133 **focused on searching out figures:** Barton Gellman, "Covert Unit Hunted for Iraqi Arms," *Washington Post,* June 13, 2003.

p. 134 **"So it's hard":** "Rumsfeld Denies U.S. Acting Unilaterally on Iraq," Defense Department transcript of interview on CNBC's *Capital Report,* March 6, 2003.

p. 134 **first established in 1980:** Dana Priest and William Arkin, *Top Secret America: The Rise of the New American Security State* (New York: Little, Brown, 2011).

p. 135 **OODA loop:** David K. Williams, "What a Fighter Pilot Knows About Business: The OODA Loop," *Forbes,* February 19, 2013.

p. 135 **a former air force pilot:** Ibid.

p. 135 **during the Korean War:** Ibid.

p. 135 **observe-orient-decide-act planning process:** Paul Tremblay Jr., "Shaping and Adapting: Unlocking the Power of Colonel John Boyd's OODA Loop," master's thesis, United States Marine Corps Command and Staff College, Marine Corps University, April 22, 2015.

p. 136 **shaping the environment rather than adapting to it:** Ibid.

p. 137 **hardwired to the bombs:** Noah Shachtman, "The Secret History of Iraq's Invisible War," *Wired,* June 14, 2011.

p. 137 **fight at the roadside:** Rick Atkinson, " 'The Single Most Effective Weapon Against Our Deployed Forces,' " *Washington Post,* September 30, 2007.

p. 137 **a half mile away:** Manuel Valdes, "Even at Home, Soldier 'Still Looking for IEDs,' " *Seattle Times,* October 28, 2006.

p. 137 **garage door openers:** STRATFOR Global Intelligence, "The Pros and Cons of IED Electronic Countermeasures," December 24, 2004, https://www.stratfor.com/analysis/pros-and-cons-ied-electronic-countermeasures.

p. 137 **wireless doorbells:** Adam Higginbotham, "U.S. Military Learns to Fight Deadliest Weapons," *Wired,* July 28, 2010.

p. 137 **remote-controlled toy car controllers:** STRATFOR, "The Pros and Cons."

p. 137 **kill thousands of Americans:** William R. Levesque, "IEDs Continue to Kill and Maim U.S. Troops Despite Multibillion Dollar Effort," *Tampa Bay Times,* September 27, 2012.

p. 137 **billions of US dollars:** Alex Rogers, "The MRAP: Brilliant Buy, or Billions Wasted?" *Time,* October 2, 2012.

p. 137 **before the devices are even built:** Atkinson, " 'The Single Most Effective Weapon.' "

p. 140 **Hussein's former interrogation chamber:** Ibid.

p. 140 **it was purgatory:** Michael Bronner, "Hussam Mohammed Amin: Former Iraqi Weapons Monitor Describes U.S. Abuse for First Time," *Huffington Post,* November 4, 2009.

p. 141 **"enabled the British government":** Ian Cobain, "Camp Nama: British Personnel Reveal Horrors of Secret US Base in Baghdad," *The Guardian,* April 1, 2013.

p. 142 **"Fear Up Harsh," "Fear Up Mild," and "Pride and Ego Up":** Josh White, "Documents Tell of Brutal Improvisation by GIs," *Washington Post,* August 3, 2005.

p. 142 **the Soviet Union and other Cold War enemies of the United States:** Tony Lagouranis and Allen Mikaelian, *Fear Up Harsh: An Army Interrogator's Dark Journey Through Iraq* (New York: New American Library, 2007).

p. 142 **dietary manipulation:** Carla Anne Robbins, Greg Jaffe, and David S. Cloud, "Interrogation Rules Were Issued Before Iraq Abuses," *Wall Street Journal,* May 13, 2004.

p. 142 **the use of muzzled dogs:** Ibid.

p. 142 **sleep adjustment, and sensory deprivation:** Ibid.

p. 143 **"some kind of special metal stick":** Bronner, "Hussam Mohammed Amin."

p. 143 **gashes in his face that required stitches:** Ibid.

p. 143 **including those sent by the...Red Cross:** Ibid.

p. 143 **"and distribute relief supplies":** American Red Cross, "Summary of the Geneva Conventions of 1949 and Their Additional Protocols," January 2013, https://www.redcross.org/content/dam/redcross/atg/PDF_s/International_Services/International_Humanitarian_Law/IHL_Summary GenevaConv.pdf

p. 146   **trove of Iraqi government documents had been uncovered:** Con Coughlin, "Terrorist Behind September 11 Strike Was Trained by Saddam," *Sunday Telegraph,* December 14, 2003.

p. 146   **"the former head of the Iraqi Intelligence Service":** Ibid.

p. 146   **The paper was dated July 1, 2001:** Ibid.

p. 146   **Atta "displayed extraordinary effort":** Ibid.

p. 146   **"the targets that we have agreed to destroy":** Ibid.

p. 147   **compiled detailed records of airline travel:** Michael Isikoff, "Terror Watch: Dubious Link Between Atta and Saddam," *Newsweek,* December 16, 2003.

p. 147   **ATM withdrawals:** Ibid.

p. 147   **cell-phone usage:** Ibid.

p. 147   **hotel stays:** Ibid.

p. 147   **"conducted extensive travel":** Ibid.

p. 148   **the FBI recorded Atta flying from Fort Lauderdale to Boston:** Ibid.

p. 148   **landed in Las Vegas that afternoon at 2:41 p.m.:** Ibid.

p. 148   **he rented a Chevrolet Malibu from an Alamo rental-car office:** Ibid.

p. 148   **an Internet café called the Cyber Zone:** Ibid.

p. 148   **EconoLodge motel on Las Vegas Boulevard:** Ibid.

p. 148   **he boarded a flight from Boston to Zurich:** Ibid.

p. 148   **He returned to the United States on July 19, 2001:** Ibid.

p. 148   **some 120 men and women strong:** "Global Forensic Services, LLC," ExpertPages.com, http://expertpages.com/details.php/4092_4207_319_121.htm.

p. 148   **More than 8,500 samples of ink:** Gerald M. LaPorte, Marlo D. Arredondo, Tyra S. McConnell, Joseph C. Stephens, Antonio A. Cantu, and Douglas K. Shaffer, "An Evaluation of Matching Unknown Writing Inks with the United States International Ink Library," *Journal of Forensic Sciences* 51, no. 3 (May 2006): 689–92.

p. 148   **since the 1920s:** Ibid.

p. 149   **Whatman filter paper:** James M. Egan, Kristin A. Hagan, and Jason D. Brewer, "Forensic Analysis of Black Ballpoint Pen Inks Using Capillary Electrophoresis," *Forensic Science Communications* 7, no. 3 (July 2005).

p. 149   **the largest ink library in the world:** LaPorte et al., "An Evaluation of Matching Unknown Writing Inks."

p. 150   **"remain unidentified":** John Conyers, *Reining in the Imperial Presidency: Lessons and Recommendations Relating to the Presidency of George W. Bush* (New York: Skyhorse Publishing, 2009).

p. 150   **"is absurd":** "White House Responds to Suskind Charges," NBC News, August 5, 2008.

Chapter 8

p. 152   **HCS-5...was also based at the airport:** Jennifer Franco, "HCS-5 Earns Navy Unit Commendation," US Navy press release, March 30, 2006.

p. 153   **"introduction...or consumption":** "General Order Number 1B (GO-1B)," United States Central Command, http://www.loc.gov/rr/frd/Military_Law/pdf/OLH_2015_Ch22.pdf.

p. 159   **hundreds of individual "bomblets" packed inside a rocket:** Paul Wiseman, "Cluster Bombs Kill in Iraq, Even After Shooting Ends," *USA Today,* December 16, 2003.

p. 159   **The 1.5 million or so bomblets:** Michael M. Phillips and Greg Jaffe, "Pentagon Rethinks Use of Cluster Bombs," *Wall Street Journal,* August 25, 2003.

p. 159   **5 to 15 percent of the bomblets...fail to detonate:** Ibid.

p. 162   **Office of Transnational Issues:** "'Think Ahead'—Directorate of Intelligence," August 28, 2008, https://www.cia.gov/news-information/featured-story-archive/2008-featured-story-archive/think-ahead-directorate-of-intelligence.html; "Careers & Internships: Economic Analyst," August 6, 2018, https://www.cia.gov/careers/opportunities/analytical/economic-analyst.html.

p. 163   **76 percent of Americans in Iraq:** Shannon D. Putnam, John W. Sanders, Robert W. Frenck, Marshall Monteville, Mark S. Riddle, David M. Rockabrand, Trueman W. Sharp, Carla Frankart, and David R. Tribble, "Self-Reported Description of Diarrhea Among Military Populations in Operations Iraqi Freedom and Enduring Freedom," *Journal of Travel Medicine* 13, no. 2 (March 2006): 92–99.

p. 163   **more than one million workdays were lost:** Kathleen Miller, "Million Days Lost to Diarrhea Spur Military's Cure Search," *Bloomberg Business,* December 4, 2012.

p. 163   **on the case to find a quick cure:** Ibid.

p. 164 **in the comfort of his sister-in-law's home:** Agence France-Presse, "Troops Came with Tanks: Neighbours: Tariq Aziz's Arrest," *Dawn*, April 26, 2003.

p. 164 **in the middle of the night:** Ibid.

p. 164 **in the backs of luxury cars:** Ibid.

p. 165 **Cropper:** "Regime Strategic Intent," April 22, 2007, https://www.cia .gov/library/reports/general-reports-1/iraq_wmd_2004/chap1 .html#sect4.

p. 165 **something of a showman:** Dominic Evans, "Tariq Aziz Was Saddam's Voice Through War and Crises," Reuters, June 5, 2015.

p. 165 **Hussein rarely left Iraq:** Jack Healy, "Top Aide to Saddam Hussein Is Sentenced to Death," *New York Times,* October 26, 2010.

p. 165 **even traveled to the Vatican:** "Tariq Aziz, Ex-Saddam Hussein Aide, Dies After Heart Attack," BBC News, June 5, 2015.

p. 165 **He had said Saddam did:** "Report of the Select Committee on Intelligence, Postwar Findings on Iraq's WMD Program and Links to Terrorism and How They Compare with Prewar Assessments," United States Select Senate Committee on Intelligence; S Report 109-331, September 2006, https://www.intelligence.senate.gov/sites/ default/files/publications/109331.pdf.

p. 167 **"Mikhail Yuhanna":** Timothy R. Smith, "Tariq Aziz Dies; Saddam Hussein's Top Minister, Longtime Spokesman for Iraq," *Washington Post,* June 5, 2015.

p. 167 **Born outside Mosul in 1936:** Ibid.

p. 167 **earned his journalism degree:** "Iraq War 10 Years Later: Where Are They Now? Tariq Aziz," NBC News, March 19, 2013.

p. 167 **then joined the upstart Arab Socialist Baath Party:** "An Interview with Tariq Aziz," *Frontline,* January 25, 2000, http://www.pbs .org/wgbh/pages/frontline/shows/saddam/interviews/aziz.html.

p. 167 **changed his name to Tariq Aziz:** Smith, "Tariq Aziz Dies."

Chapter 9

p. 172 **caravans of fortified Chevy Suburbans:** Rajiv Chandrasekaran, "On Iraq, U.S. Turns to Onetime Dissenters," *Washington Post,* January 14, 2007.

p. 173 **a statue of Abbas Ibn Firnas:** Oras Al-Kubaisi, "Abbas Ibn Firnas Statue—Baghdad," Getty Images, http://www.gettyimages.com/detail/

photo/abbas-ibn-firnas-statue-baghdad-high-res-stock
-photography/518707585.

p. 173 **known to many troops as the Winged Man:** John F. Burns, "On Way to Baghdad Airport, Death Stalks Main Road," *New York Times,* May 29, 2005.

p. 173 **onto Baghdad Airport Road:** Ibid.

p. 173 **"Route Irish":** Ibid.

p. 173 **suburbs such as Amariya, Hamra, and Qaddisiya:** Ibid.

p. 173 **Sunni strongholds under Hussein's regime:** Ibid.

p. 174 **the first major attack occurred on the road:** Sarah Childress, "Iraq: How Did We Get Here?" *Frontline,* July 29, 2014, http://www.pbs.org/wgbh/frontline/article/iraq-how-did-we-get-here/.

p. 174 **Death Street:** Burns, "On Way to Baghdad Airport."

p. 174 **IED Alley:** Ibid.

p. 174 **Highway to Hell:** John Geddes, *Highway to Hell: Dispatches from a Mercenary in Iraq* (New York: Broadway Books, 2008).

p. 176 **"Our knowledge of Iraq's ties to terrorism is evolving":** Select Committee on Intelligence, United States Senate, "Iraq's Links to Terrorism," part XII of "Report on the U.S. Intelligence Committee's Prewar Intelligence Assessments on Iraq," July 7, 2004, National Security Archive, George Washington University, http://nsarchive.gwu.edu/NSAEBB/NSAEBB129/part12-terrorism.pdf.

p. 176 **"derived from sources...reliability":** Ibid.

p. 178 **On February 19:** James Risen, "Iraq Said to Have Tried to Reach Last-Minute Deal to Avert War," *New York Times,* November 6, 2003.

p. 178 **United States would be given "first priority" to Iraqi oil:** Ibid.

p. 178 **"full support" for the US negotiation:** Ibid.

p. 178 **assist the Bush administration in its counterterrorism efforts:** Ibid.

p. 178 **help promote America's strategic interests:** Ibid.

p. 178 **allow "direct U.S. involvement on the ground in disarming Iraq":** Ibid.

p. 178 **the offer was deemed incredible:** Julian Borger, Brian Whitaker, and Vikram Dodd, "Saddam's Desperate Offers to Stave Off War," *The Guardian,* November 6, 2003.

p. 179 **family visits once every two weeks:** Abigail Hauslohner, "Prison Life Inside Baghdad's Camp Cropper," *Time,* http://content.time.com/time/photogallery/0,29307,1856440,00.html.

p. 179   **five minutes of physical contact for hugs:** Ibid.

p. 181   **born in Mosul, Iraq, in 1961:** "Pentagon: Top al Qaeda Leader Taken to Guantanamo," CNN, April 27, 2007, http://www.cnn.com/2007/ US/04/27/al.qaeda.gitmo/index.html?eref=yahoo.

p. 181   **risen to the rank of major in Hussein's Iraqi Army:** Bill Roggio, "Senior Al Qaeda Operative Abd al-Hadi al-Iraqi Captured," *Long War Journal,* April 27, 2007, http://www.longwarjournal.org/archives/ 2007/04/senior_al_qaeda_oper.php.

p. 181   **international operations chief:** Ibid.

p. 181   **bin Ladin's ten-man personal shura council:** Seth G. Jones, *Hunting in the Shadows: The Pursuit of Al Qa'ida Since 9/11* (New York: W. W. Norton & Company, 2012).

p. 181   **the show of intellectual force was clearly important for bin Ladin:** Sami Yousafzai, "Terror Broker," *Newsweek,* April 10, 2005.

pp. 181–182   **rebel groups in Jordan...and elsewhere:** Stanford University, "Mapping Militant Organizations: The Islamic State," May 15, 2015, http://web.stanford.edu/group/mappingmilitants/cgi-bin/ groups/view/1.

p. 182   **had fled across the country's western border into Iran:** Douglas Jehl, "Iran Said to Hold Qaeda's No. 3, but to Resist Giving Him Up," *New York Times,* August 2, 2003.

p. 182   **placed under "house arrest":** Craig Whitlock and Munir Ladaa, "Al-Qaeda's New Leadership: Saif al-Adel," *Washington Post,* 2006, http://www.washingtonpost.com/wp-srv/world/specials/terror/adel .html.

p. 182   **"pose a grave and growing danger":** "President Delivers State of the Union Address," White House archives, January 29, 2002, http://georgewbush-whitehouse.archives.gov/news/releases/2002/ 01/20020129-11.html.

p. 182   **"threaten the peace of the world":** Ibid.

p. 182   **"It is both our responsibility...fight":** Ibid.

p. 183   **three explosions:** Douglas Jehl and Eric Schmitt, "U.S. Suggests a Qaeda Cell in Iran Directed Saudi Bombings," *New York Times,* May 21, 2003.

p. 183   **At around 11:15 p.m.:** "One Bombed Compound Owned by Pro-Western Saudi," CNN, May 13, 2003, http://www.cnn.com/2003/ WORLD/meast/05/13/Saudi.jadawel/.

p. 183 **three housing compounds in... Riyadh:** Ibid.

p. 183 **killing three dozen people:** Jehl and Schmitt, "U.S. Suggests a Qaeda Cell."

p. 183 **Iran tightened the reins... borders:** US Department of State, Office of the Coordinator for Counterterrorism, "Overview of State-Sponsored Terrorism: Patterns of Global Terrorism," April 29, 2004, http://www.state.gov/j/ct/rls/crt/2003/31644.htm.

p. 183 **vanishing inside Iran until fairly recently:** Yassin Musharbash, "Saif al-Adel Back in Waziristan: A Top Terrorist Returns to Al-Qaida Fold," *Spiegel Online,* October 25, 2010.

p. 183 **made it safely to meet with Zarqawi:** Yousafzai, "Terror Broker."

p. 183 **"Why is the sheik sending someone else?":** Ibid.

p. 184 **al-Iraqi seems to have found a connection with Zarqawi:** Ibid.

p. 184 **al-Iraqi defended the brash Jordanian to bin Ladin:** Ibid.

Chapter 10

p. 187 **publicly feuded with the UN:** Maggie Farley and Maura Reynolds, "Bush, Schroeder End Feud; Germany Offers Aid in Iraq," *Los Angeles Times,* September 25, 2003.

p. 187 **a fifty-five-year-old... named Sergio Vieira de Mello:** Samantha Power, *Chasing the Flame: Sergio Vieira de Mello and the Fight to Save the World* (New York: Penguin Press, 2008).

p. 187 **thirty-four years as a UN diplomat in war-torn countries:** Samantha Power, "The Envoy," *The New Yorker,* January 7, 2008.

p. 187 **Named the UN's high commissioner for human rights in 2002:** Ibid.

p. 187 **it could never be allowed to become a "country club":** Ibid.

p. 187 **"I gave U.N. peacekeepers shoot-to-kill authority":** Ibid.

p. 187 **it was a key strategic gambit:** Ibid.

p. 187 **"in search for international legitimacy":** Bill Spindle, "Vieira de Mello Took On Big Job with Iraq Position," *Wall Street Journal,* September 2, 2003.

p. 188 **"join in and help create these new institutions":** Ibid.

p. 188 **the UN had set up its offices at the Canal Hotel:** Power, "The Envoy."

p. 188 **"he will also have to distance himself from the Coalition":** Ibid.

p. 188   **the envoy's third-floor office:** Gil Loescher, "Sole Survivor," *Notre Dame Magazine,* Spring 2004.

p. 188   **At the end of the service road was a busy catering school:** Ibid.

p. 189   **there were 117 attacks against coalition forces:** "Report of the Independent Panel on the Safety and Security of the UN Personnel in Iraq," United Nations, October 20, 2003, http://www.un.org/News/ dh/iraq/safety-security-un-personnel-iraq.pdf.

p. 189   **That number rose to 307 in June:** Ibid.

p. 189   **and 451 in July:** Ibid.

p. 189   **killing seventeen people...and wounding more than sixty:** Reuters, "Jordanian Sentenced to Death over 2003 Iraq Bombing," November 5, 2007, http://www.reuters.com/article/uk-security-jordan-sentence -idUKL0571040720071106.

p. 189   **the number of attacks...crept toward 320:** "Report of the Independent Panel."

p. 189   **sending ten thousand troops...rebuilding efforts:** Howard LaFranchi, "Turks Pitch In: New Troops to Iraq," *Christian Science Monitor,* October 8, 2003.

p. 189   **a car bomb detonated outside the Turkish embassy in Baghdad:** Alex Berenson and Ian Fisher, "Bomb at Turkish Embassy in Baghdad Kills Bystander," *New York Times,* October 15, 2003.

p. 189   **fifty-seven people were killed and seven hundred wounded:** Benjamin Harvey, "7 Get Life in '03 Istanbul Bombings," Associated Press, February 16, 2007.

p. 190   **"it is only a matter of time":** Power, "The Envoy."

p. 190   **an orange truck with a brown cab:** "Report of the Independent Panel."

p. 190   **witnesses reported seeing the truck speed up:** Ibid.

p. 190   **spraying the hotel's windows with gravel:** Ibid.

p. 190   **"one million flashbulbs going off all at once":** Power, "The Envoy."

p. 190   **Twenty-three people were killed in the blast:** UN News Centre, "UN Envoy for Iraq Sergio Vieira de Mello Laid to Rest in Geneva," August 28, 2003, https://news.un.org/en/story/2003/08/77882-un-envoy -iraq-sergio-vieira-de-mello-laid-rest-geneva.

p. 190   **Vieira de Mello lay tangled in the rubble:** Power, "The Envoy."

p. 190   **By 7:30 p.m....consciousness:** Ibid.

p. 190   **by 8:00 p.m., he was dead:** Ibid.

p. 190 **the UN pulled the majority of its remaining staffers out of Iraq:** "Regret at UN's Iraq Retreat," BBC News, September 26, 2003, http://news.bbc.co.uk/2/hi/middle_east/3140184.stm.

p. 192 **the most exclusive newspapers in the world:** Rhodri Jeffreys-Jones and Christopher Andrew, *Eternal Vigilance? 50 Years of the CIA* (London: Frank Cass and Company, 1997).

p. 192 **ten-to-fifteen-page collections of articles written by CIA analysts:** Robert Windrem, "What Is a PDB?" NBC News, April 12, 2004.

p. 192 **hand-delivered six days a week:** Ibid.

p. 192 **PDBs...generally have to be read in the company of the delivering Agency officer:** Ibid.

p. 193 **a bomb...was detonated in central Baghdad:** "Terror Strikes Blamed on al-Zarqawi in Iraq," NBC News, May 4, 2005, http://www.nbcnews.com/id/5437742/ns/world_news-hunt_for_al_qaida/t/terror-strikes-blamed-al-zarqawi-iraq/#.VnBl1cqPyaw.

p. 194 **Zarqawi's associates attacked a police station...in Sadr City:** Ibid.

p. 194 **five suicide bombers blew up vehicles:** Ibid.

p. 194 **an attack at the Italian carabinieri training center in Nassiriyah:** Ibid.

p. 194 **Seventeen killed at a police station in Khalidiyah:** Ibid.

p. 194 **three Iraqis killed and twenty-nine wounded:** Ibid.

p. 194 **outside the coalition headquarters in Baghdad:** Ibid.

p. 194 **an attack on a police station in Mosul:** Ibid.

p. 194 **roughly $140 a month:** Ann Scott Tyson, "Increased Security in Fallujah Slows Efforts to Rebuild," *Washington Post,* April 19, 2005.

p. 194 **a bomb in the bed of a red Toyota pickup:** "Terror Strikes Blamed on al-Zarqawi."

p. 195 **Fifty-six people were killed:** Ibid.

p. 195 **blew himself up at an Iraqi Army recruiting station:** Ibid.

p. 195 **forced to divert nearly $2 billion in reconstruction funds:** Howard LaFranchi, "Iraq's Hottest Front Line: The Police," *Christian Science Monitor,* September 17, 2004.

p. 196 **"I live in West Chester, Pennsylvania, near Philadelphia":** Jesse Singal, Christine Lim, and M. J. Stephey, "Seven Years in Iraq: An Iraq War Timeline," *Time,* March 19, 2010.

p. 196 **a twenty-six-year-old telecommunications engineer:** Ibid.

p. 196 **twice gone to Iraq in search of work:** Brian Whitaker and Luke Harding, "American Beheaded in Revenge for Torture," *The Guardian,* May 12, 2004.

p. 196 **a few weeks prior to the video being posted:** Ibid.

p. 196 **"and they refused":** "Militants Behead American Hostage in Iraq," Fox News, May 11, 2004, http://www.foxnews.com/story/2004/05/11/ militants-behead-american-hostage-in-iraq.html.

p. 196 **"coffin after coffin slaughtered in this way":** Ibid.

p. 197 **mental health professionals to counsel analysts:** Shane Harris, "The Shrinks Who Only See CIA Officers," *Daily Beast,* April 4, 2015.

p. 198 **Iraq to al Qaida:** "Zarqawi Letter: February 2004 Coalition Provisional Authority English Translation of Terrorist Musab al Zarqawi Letter Obtained by United States Government in Iraq," https://2001 -2009.state.gov/p/nea/rls/31694.htm; "Letter May Detail Iraqi Insurgency's Concerns," CNN, February 10, 2004, http://www.cnn.com/ 2004/WORLD/meast/02/10/sprj.nirq.zarqawi/.

p. 198 **the PDB I wrote about the correspondence:** Dexter Filkins, "U.S. Says Files Seek Qaeda Aid in Iraq Conflict," February 9, 2004, https://www.nytimes.com/2004/02/09/world/the-struggle-for-iraq -intelligence-us-says-files-seek-qaeda-aid-in-iraq-conflict.html.

p. 201 **swimming without getting wet:** Fulton T. Armstrong, "Ways to Make Analysis Relevant but Not Prescriptive," *Studies in Intelligence* 46, no. 3 (2002), https://www.cia.gov/library/center-for-the-study-of -intelligence/csi-publications/csi-studies/studies/vol46no3/article05 .html.

Chapter 11

p. 204 **The drone program employed by both Presidents Bush:** Dave Boyer, "Bush Policies Still Alive in Obama White House," *Washington Times,* April 24, 2013.

p. 204 **that today is part of its Special Activities Division:** Gary C. Schroen, *First In: An Insider's Account of How the CIA Spearheaded the War on Terror in Afghanistan* (New York: Presidio Press, 2005).

p. 204 **SAD personnel were inserted into Tibet in 1950:** Jonathan Mirsky, "Tibet: The CIA's Cancelled War," *New York Review of Books,* April 9, 2013.

p. 204 **they ran the Agency's covert Air America program:** Associated Press, "CIA Creates Paramilitary Unit to Fight Terrorists," June 4, 2002, http://www.foxnews.com/story/2002/06/04/cia-creates-paramilitary-unit-to-fight-terrorists.html.

p. 204 **the CIA had...plotted the assassinations:** Simon Tisdall, "CIA Reveals Decades of Plots, Kidnaps and Wiretaps," *The Guardian*, June 23, 2007.

p. 204 **the very first ones into Afghanistan following the 9/11 attacks:** "FLASHBACK: Sept. 26, 2001 — CIA Is 'First In' After September 11th Attacks," CIA Featured Story Archive, September 26, 2013, https://www.cia.gov/news-information/featured-story-archive/2013-featured-story-archive/flashback-sept-26-2001.html.

p. 214 **Another attack near a military base in Taji:** Council on Foreign Relations, "Iraq Timeline 2004," December 31, 2004, https://www.cfr.org/timeline/iraq-war.

p. 214 **Then simultaneous assaults in five cities...left one hundred dead:** Christopher Allbritton and Maki Becker, "Slaughter, Chaos in Iraq: 100 Are Killed in Six-City Blitz," *Daily News* (New York), June 25, 2004.

p. 215 **wore yellow headbands:** Ibid.

p. 215 **the mechanic found himself based near Karbala, Iraq:** Jo Dee Black, "Military Moms Help Family See Son Hurt in Iraq," *Great Falls Tribune*, May 24, 2004.

p. 216 **Maintenance Platoon...Armored Division:** Rudi Williams, "Regis Philbin Inspired by Wounded Service Members' Spirit," American Forces Press Service, June 23, 2004.

p. 216 **Forward Operating Base Saint Michael:** Tim Dyhouse, "Always Know It's Going to Get Better," *VFW Magazine*, February 2012.

p. 216 **whose duties included driving...tow truck:** Ibid.

p. 216 **"a matter of when and where you would get it":** Ibid.

p. 216 **"but that wasn't happening":** Ibid.

p. 217 **the 875 US troops who'd already been killed there:** Associated Press, "Insurgents Kill 3 U.S. Troops in Northern Iraq," July 12, 2004.

p. 217 **the 5,300 wounded men and women:** "Insurgent Attacks Kill 8 in Iraq," CNN, July 1, 2004, http://www.cnn.com/2004/WORLD/meast/07/01/iraq.main/.

p. 218   **Ghul was a facilitator:** Select Committee on Intelligence, United States Senate, "Committee Study of the Central Intelligence Agency's Detention and Interrogation Program," December 9, 2014, https://www.congress.gov/113/crpt/srpt288/CRPT-113srpt288.pdf.

p. 218   **a courier tasked with crisscrossing the Middle East:** "Treasury Targets Three Senior Al-Qa'ida Leaders," US Department of the Treasury, Press Center, September 7, 2011.

p. 218   **Ghul would later tell us:** Select Committee on Intelligence, "Committee Study."

p. 218   **missiles for manpower:** Ibid.

p. 218   **perhaps even chemical ones...Ghul said:** Ibid.

p. 218   **In exchange, Zarqawi needed al Qaida personnel:** Ibid.

p. 218   **Al-Iraqi agreed to at least hear him out:** Ibid.

p. 218   **sending Ghul to meet with Zarqawi...in January of 2004:** Ibid.

p. 218   **spread word throughout the border villages:** Ibid.

pp. 218–219   **a tall man in a light jacket and trousers:** Ibid.

p. 219   **they recovered two CDs...flash drive:** Stanley McChrystal, *My Share of the Task: A Memoir* (New York: Portfolio, 2013).

p. 219   **During the forty-eight hours after Ghul's capture:** Ibid.

p. 219   **names of fighters al Qaida was considering sending to Iraq:** Ibid.

p. 219   **four separate e-mail addresses Ghul had for Zarqawi:** Ibid.

p. 219   **the ideological differences...Ghul discuss:** Ibid.

p. 219   **That was hardly the end:** Ibid.

p. 220   **photographed him:** Ibid.

p. 220   **subjected him to a cavity search:** Ibid.

p. 220   **wrapped in a diaper, then a jumpsuit, and blindfolded:** Ibid.

p. 220   **Headphones would have been placed over his ears:** Ibid.

p. 220   **a loose hood would have been draped over his head:** Ibid.

p. 220   **His hands and feet would have been shackled:** Ibid.

p. 220   **loaded onto a small plane:** Ibid.

p. 220   **"placed in [a] standing position against the wall":** Select Committee on Intelligence, "Committee Study."

p. 220   **His hands were suspended...two hours at a time:** Ibid.

p. 220   **"enhanced measures...what he expects to happen":** Ibid.

p. 220   **fifty-nine straight hours of sleep deprivation:** Ibid.

p. 220   **he began hallucinating:** Ibid.

p. 220   **placed in a hanging stress position:** Ibid.

p. 220 **"and mild paralysis of arms, legs and feet":** Ibid.

p. 220 **"notable physiological fatigue":** Ibid.

p. 220 **"when he decides to be truthful":** Ibid.

p. 221 **"new and unique insight...operations":** Ibid.

p. 221 **confirming the nom de guerre of bin Ladin's personal courier:** Ibid.

p. 221 **"announced their allegiance to the Sheikh al-Mujahideen of our time":** Jeffrey Pool, trans., "Zarqawi's Pledge of Allegiance to al-Qaeda: From Mu'asker Al-Battar, Issue 21," *Terrorism Monitor* 2, no. 24 (December 15, 2004), http://www.jamestown.org/single/?tx_ttnews [tt_news]=27305#.VnHgTPFqeaw.

p. 221 **The letter:** "Al-Zarqawi Group Claims Allegiance to bin Laden," CNN, October 17, 2004, http://www.cnn.com/2004/WORLD/meast/10/17/al.zarqawi.statement/.

p. 221 **the past eight months:** Pool, "Zarqawi's Pledge of Allegiance."

p. 222 **"until Islam enters the home of every city-dweller and nomad":** Ibid.

p. 222 **known as Tanzim Qai'dat al-Jihad fi Bilad al-Rafidayn:** Ibid.

Chapter 12

p. 223 **the CIA's seven-man Jawbreaker mission:** "FLASHBACK: Sept. 26, 2001 — CIA Is 'First In' After September 11th Attacks," CIA Featured Story Archive, September 26, 2013, https://www.cia.gov/news -information/featured-story-archive/2013-featured-story -archive/flashback-sept-26-2001.html.

p. 223 **coordinate with Northern Alliance commanders and US Special Operations Forces units:** Ibid.

p. 224 **Office of Russian and European Analysis:** "Offices of CIA: Office of Russian and European Analysis," CIA, January 23, 2013, https:// www.cia.gov/news-information/featured-story-archive/2008 -featured-story-archive/think-ahead-directorate-of-intelligence .html.

p. 224 **Office of Asian Pacific, Latin American, and African Analysis:** "Offices of CIA: Office of Asian Pacific, Latin American, and African Analysis," CIA, January 23, 2013, https://www.cia.gov/news-information/ featured-story-archive/2008-featured-story-archive/think-ahead -directorate-of-intelligence.html.

p. 224 **Office of Near Eastern and South Asian Analysis:** "Offices of CIA: Office of Near Eastern and South Asian Analysis," CIA, January 23, 2013, https://www.cia.gov/news-information/featured-story-archive/2008 -featured-story-archive/think-ahead-directorate-of-intelligence.html.

p. 226 **our team member embedded with SOF:** Stanley McChrystal, *My Share of the Task: A Memoir* (New York: Portfolio, 2013).

pp. 226–227 **that's where cooperation ended:** Ibid.

p. 227 **McChrystal arrived in Iraq:** Ibid.

p. 227 **General Michael Flynn was brought on board:** Ibid.

p. 227 **"our fight against Zarqawi...intelligence":** Ibid.

p. 227 **It is not a secret now:** Matthew Rosenberg, "Michael Flynn Is Harsh Judge of C.I.A.'s Role," *New York Times,* December 12, 2016.

p. 228 **ten times that:** McChrystal, *My Share of the Task.*

p. 228 **his teams needed to be more agile:** Ibid.

p. 229 **and has instead used its own network...classified material:** Bruce Berkowitz, "Failing to Keep Up with the Information Revolution," *Studies in Intelligence* 47, no. 1 (June 27, 2008), https://www.cia .gov/library/center-for-the-study-of-intelligence/csi-publications/csi -studies/studies/vol47no1/article07.html.

p. 229 **illegally pulled 250,000 State Department cables...off the network:** Paul Lewis, "Bradley Manning Given 35-Year Prison Term for Passing Files to WikiLeaks," *The Guardian,* August 21, 2013.

p. 231 **raiding the right homes only around 50 percent of the time:** Dana Priest and William Arkin, *Top Secret America: The Rise of the New American Security State* (New York: Little, Brown, 2011).

p. 231 **"left to clean up the mess":** Ibid.

p. 233 **"former regime elements":** David C. Gompert, Hans Binnendijk, and Bonny Lin, "The Iraq War: Bush's Biggest Blunder," *Newsweek,* December 25, 2014.

p. 233 **"a conviction that's deep in my soul":** Sean Loughlin, "Bush Stands Firm on Iraq, War on Terror," CNN, April 14, 2004, http://www.cnn .com/2004/ALLPOLITICS/04/13/bush.conference/.

p. 233 **some twenty-five attacks in Iraq per day:** Anthony H. Cordesman, "Iraq: Security Trends," Center for Strategic and International Studies, November 19, 2009, http://csis.org/files/publication/091118 _IraqSecTrends.pdf.

p. 233 **late that year...sixty per day:** Ibid.

p. 233 **More than 160 US soldiers...following the official handover of power:** iCasualties.org, "Iraq Coalition Casualties: Fatalities by Year and Month," http://icasualties.org/App/Fatalities.

p. 233 **US military fatalities in Iraq had passed one thousand:** Monica Davey, "For 1,000 Troops, There Is No Going Home," *New York Times,* September 9, 2004.

p. 234 **nearly 5.5 million Sunnis:** Michael Eisenstadt and Jeffrey White, "Assessing Iraq's Sunni Arab Insurgency," Washington Institute for Near East Policy, December 2005.

p. 234 **more than a million of traditional military age:** Ibid.

p. 234 **"the prince of Al Qaida in Iraq":** "Purported bin Laden Tape Endorses al-Zarqawi," CNN, December 27, 2004, http://www.cnn.com/2004/WORLD/meast/12/27/binladen.tape/.

p. 234 **"obey him in his good deeds":** Ibid.

p. 234 **Fallujah, a city of three hundred thousand:** Alex Rodriguez, "'Window...Is Closing' for Fallujah," *Chicago Tribune,* November 6, 2004.

p. 234 **hundreds of non-Iraqi Arabs moving into the city during that year:** Ibid.

p. 234 **loads of cash and a militant vision of Islam:** Hannah Allam, "In Fallujah, a Backlash Against Foreign Fighters: With Their City Under Siege, Iraqis Are Feeling Betrayed," Knight Ridder Newspapers, November 14, 2004.

p. 234 **In April, Zarqawi's men had helped repel a coalition advance:** Ibid.

p. 235 **Zarqawi's men were beginning to wear out their welcome:** Ibid.

p. 235 **longtime residents bristled at the extreme interpretation of religion:** Ibid.

p. 235 **those accused of spying...were murdered on the spot:** Ibid.

p. 235 **Iraqi police arrested Umar Baziyani, a former head of Ansar al Islam:** Robert Alt, "The Supreme Court Has Rewritten a Well-Established Statute," *National Review,* June 29, 2004.

p. 235 **Baziyani had the sort of organizational chart we needed:** Ibid.

p. 235 **Al Qaida in Iraq was in fact headquartered in Fallujah:** Ibid.

p. 236 **his top deputy, a Syrian named Mahi Shami:** Ibid.

p. 236 **including his bodyguard and driver:** Ibid.

p. 236 **Zarqawi had married the daughter of one longtime Palestin-ian associate:** Urs Gehriger and Marwan Shehadeh, "Abu Musab al-Zarqawi: In the Network of the Phantom," *Die Weltwoche,* October 13, 2005.

p. 236 **Zarqawi's key deputies also married one another's daughters:** Ibid.

p. 236 **nine regional operations throughout Iraq:** Jonathan Schanzer, "Inside the Zarqawi Network," *Weekly Standard,* August 16, 2004, https://www.weeklystandard.com/jonathan-schanzer/inside-the-zarqawi-network.

p. 236 **There were seven of those commanders:** Ibid.

p. 236 **Fallujah, Mosul...and Diyala Provinces:** Ibid.

p. 236 **as well as in al-Qaim:** Ibid.

p. 236 **Zarqawi had some fourteen hundred fighters at his disposal:** Ibid.

p. 236 **the attacks Zarqawi claimed credit for:** Jean-Charles Brisard and Damien Martinez, *Zarqawi: The New Face of al-Qaeda* (Cambridge, UK: Polity Press, 2005).

p. 237 **twelve thousand US troops stormed Fallujah:** Dan Lamothe, "Remembering the Iraq War's Bloodiest Battle, 10 Years Later," *Washington Post,* November 4, 2014.

p. 237 **the bloodiest stretch of urban warfare since Vietnam:** Liz Sly, "Al-Qaeda Force Captures Fallujah amid Rise in Violence in Iraq," *Washington Post,* January 3, 2014.

p. 237 **two thousand insurgent and foreign fighters were dead...cap-tured:** Timothy S. McWilliams with Nicholas J. Schlosser, *U.S. Marines in Battle: Fallujah, November–December 2004* (Quantico, VA: History Division, United States Marine Corps, 2014).

p. 237 **More than eighty US troops had been killed:** Ibid.

p. 237 **some 70 percent of the buildings...destroyed:** Dahr Jamail, "Seven Years After Sieges, Fallujah Struggles," Al Jazeera, January 4, 2012, http://www.aljazeera.com/indepth/features/2012/01/20121210 2823143370.html.

p. 237 **including at least one hundred mosques:** Ibid.

p. 237 **he might have dressed as a woman:** Peter R. Mansoor, *Surge: My Journey with General David Petraeus and the Remaking of the Iraq War* (New Haven, CT: Yale University Press, 2013).

p. 237 **strolled through a decimated Al Qaida in Iraq...command center:** Jackie Spinner, "Insurgent Base Discovered in Fallujah," *Washington Post,* November 19, 2004.

p. 237 **A black-and-white banner in Arabic:** Ibid.

p. 238 **Along with computers:** Associated Press, "U.S. Claims Finding Headquarters of al-Zarqawi Group," November 18, 2004, http://usa today30.usatoday.com/news/world/2004-11-18-iraq_x.htm.

p. 238 **notebooks full of fighters' names:** Liz Sly and James Janega, "Suspected al-Zarqawi Base Is Found in Fallujah," *Chicago Tribune,* November 19, 2004.

p. 238 **ammunition:** Ibid.

p. 238 **medicine that had been stolen from USAID deliveries:** Ibid.

p. 238 **letters written by Zarqawi to his lieutenants:** Ibid.

p. 238 **"there is something there for you":** Ibid.

p. 238 **rudimentary drawings of US fighter jets:** Spinner, "Insurgent Base Discovered."

p. 238 **a Ford Explorer...converted into a bomb:** Ibid.

p. 238 **The SUV was registered in Texas:** Ibid.

p. 238 **Inside a metal-sided warehouse:** Daniel P. Bolger, *Why We Lost: A General's Inside Account of the Iraq and Afghanistan Wars* (New York: Houghton Mifflin Harcourt, 2014).

p. 238 **insurgent caches of...artillery rounds:** Ibid.

p. 238 **a crawl space barricaded with a safe:** Bing West, *No True Glory: A Frontline Account of the Battle for Fallujah* (New York: Bantam, 2005).

p. 238 **who'd been abducted...with a pair of French journalists:** Ibid.

p. 238 **what appeared to be a ramshackle movie studio:** Ibid.

p. 238 **a glass with ice in it:** Ibid.

p. 238 **two video cameras...instructions on how to get footage:** Ibid.

p. 238 **the black-and-green flag of Ansar al-Islam:** Ibid.

p. 238 **caked in dried blood:** Ibid.

p. 239 **a pair of simultaneous car bombings:** Associated Press, "Timeline: Major Attacks Claimed by Zarqawi and His Followers," June 8, 2006.

p. 239 **a funeral procession in Karbala:** Ibid.

p. 239 **Najaf's main bus terminal:** Ibid.

p. 239 **Sixty people, mostly Iraqi civilians, were killed:** Ibid.

p. 239 **Abu Omar al-Kurdi:** "Iraq Interim Government Announces Capture of 'Top Zarqawi Ally,'" BBC, January 24, 2005.

p. 239   **veteran of various jihadist camps across Afghanistan:** Ibid.

p. 239   **He was Zarqawi's headline bomb maker:** Ibid.

p. 239   **used in both the UN and Najaf bombings:** Ibid.

p. 240   **hanged by the Iraqi government:** Stephen Farrell, "Iraq Hangs Insurgent Who Killed Shiite Leader in Bombing of Shrine in 2003," *New York Times,* July 7, 2007.

p. 240   **"this lie that is called democracy":** "Purported al-Zarqawi Tape: Democracy a Lie," CNN, January 23, 2005.

p. 240   **"considered enemies of God":** Ibid.

p. 240   **"we are relieved from any responsibility":** William Branigin, "Three Top Zarqawi Lieutenants Arrested," *Washington Post,* January 28, 2005.

p. 240   **More than a dozen small-scale attacks:** Anthony Shadid, "Iraqis Defy Threats as Millions Vote," *Washington Post,* January 31, 2005.

p. 240   **thirty thousand polling stations across Iraq:** "Milestone Elections Begin in Iraq," CNN, January 30, 2005.

p. 240   **14.2 million registered Iraqi voters:** Ibid.

p. 240   **the senseless ongoing violence:** Ibid.

p. 240   **On February 20, midafternoon Langley time:** McChrystal, *My Share of the Task.*

p. 240   **gave a tip to an Arab-American soldier:** Ibid.

p. 241   **task force was busy establishing an ambush:** Ibid.

p. 241   **made preparations to leave the scene altogether:** Michael Smith, *Killer Elite: The Inside Story of America's Most Secret Special Operations Team* (New York: St. Martin's Press, 2008).

p. 242   **Zarqawi grabbed his rifle:** Peter Beaumont, "Upsurge in Iraq Bloodshed as US Seizes Key Militants," *The Guardian,* May 7, 2005.

p. 242   **an ammunition clip:** Ibid.

p. 242   **and a fistful of the cash:** Ibid.

p. 242   **"What sub-tribe is here?":** Ibid.

p. 243   **outside a health clinic in...Hillah:** Associated Press, "Timeline: Major Attacks."

pp. 243–244   **More than 125 people were killed:** Ibid.

Chapter 13

pp. 249–250   **without awareness that they could be tracked:** U.S. House of Representatives, Permanent Select Committee on Intelligence, "FISA Section 702 Debate: Important Facts about FISA Section 702," January 2018.

p. 250 **a gunrunner named Abu Abbas:** Andy Geller, "Zarqawi Top Aide Bagged—Hit Plot Foiled," *New York Post,* May 9, 2005.

p. 250 **responsible for stealing...rockets:** Ibid.

p. 250 **provided the raw materials Abu Omar al-Kurdi used:** Ibid.

p. 250 **Abu Talha, AQI's emir of that city:** "U.S. Military: Al Qaeda Leader in Mosul Captured," CNN, June 18, 2005, http://www.cnn .com/2005/WORLD/meast/06/16/iraq.main/.

p. 250 **had split with Ansar al-Islam:** Richard A. Oppel Jr., "U.S. and Iraqi Troops Capture a Top Militant Leader in Mosul," *New York Times,* June 17, 2005.

p. 251 **as often as once a month:** Ibid.

p. 251 **a logical successor for the top spot:** Bill Roggio, "US Forces Capture Key Zarqawi Commander," *Long War Journal,* June 16, 2005, http:// www.longwarjournal.org/archives/2005/06/the_demise_of_a.php.

p. 251 **Talha oversaw a few hundred fighters:** Oppel, "U.S. and Iraqi Troops."

p. 251 **approximately fifty car bombings:** Ibid.

p. 251 **Talha was a former Republican Guard:** Ibid.

p. 251 **Talha began wearing a suicide vest:** "Coalition, Iraqi Raid Nabs Mosul's Top al Qaeda Operative," Department of Defense, DOD News, June 16, 2005.

p. 251 **He languished in a cell:** Agence France-Presse, "Top Zarqawi Aide Captured in Iraq's Mosul: US," June 16, 2005.

p. 251 **Qaduli was released from an Iraqi prison in 2012:** "Department of Defense Press Briefing by Secretary Carter and General Dunford in the Pentagon Briefing Room," Department of Defense press release, March 2016.

p. 252 **Zarqawi's men abducted three dozen Iraqi soldiers:** Mohammad Barakat, "At Least 17 Bodies Found in Iraqi Desert Town Near Syrian Border," Associated Press, June 10, 2005.

p. 252 **crimes "against Sunnis and their loyalty to crusaders":** Ibid.

p. 252 **the killing of...Dhari Ali al-Fayadh:** Associated Press, "Slaying of Top Shiite May Stoke Ethnic Tension," NBC News, June 28, 2005, http://www.nbcnews.com/id/8202434/ns/world_news-mideast_n _africa/t/slaying-top-shiite-may-stoke-ethnic-tension/#.Vpa20 PFqeaw.

p. 252 **Fayadh's son and two bodyguards were also killed:** Ibid.

p. 252 **a 6,300-word letter:** David Ensor, "Al Qaeda Letter Called 'Chilling,'" CNN, October 12, 2005.

p. 252 **written by Ayman al-Zawahiri:** Ibid.

p. 253 **bullet-pointed the organization's larger plans:** Ibid.

p. 253 **offered a stinging rebuke to Zarqawi:** Ibid.

p. 253 **reflects upon Zarqawi's attacks on the Shia population:** "Letter from al-Zawahiri to al-Zarqawi," Office of the Director of National Intelligence, October 11, 2005, http://fas.org/irp/news/2005/10/dni 101105.html.

p. 253 **the grisly beheading videos:** Ibid.

p. 253 **"media battle":** Ibid.

p. 253 **"hearts and minds":** Ibid.

p. 253 **"on the mausoleum of Imam Ali Bin Abi Talib":** Ibid.

p. 253 **"Has any Islamic state in history ever tried that?":** Ibid.

p. 253 **"the supporter of the resistance in Iraq":** Ibid.

p. 253 **focus first on expelling the Americans from Iraq:** Ibid.

p. 253 **whatever amount of Sunni territory...controlled:** Ibid.

p. 254 **gradually extend the reach of that new Islamic "state":** Ibid.

p. 254 **bring terror to Israel:** Ibid.

p. 254 **Sulayman Khalid Darwish:** "Syrian National Designated by U.S. as Terrorist Financier," Bureau of International Information Programs, US Department of State, January 25, 2005, https://wfile.ait.org.tw/ wf-archive/2005/050125/epf209.htm.

p. 254 **Darwish had trained...at Zarqawi's camp:** Ibid.

p. 254 **Sayf al-Adl, Zarqawi's original champion within al Qaida:** Stanley McChrystal, *My Share of the Task: A Memoir* (New York: Portfolio, 2013).

p. 254 **The former dentist:** Robert Spencer, "Top Zarqawi Aide Killed in US Attack," Jihad Watch, June 26, 2005, http://www.jihadwatch .org/2005/06/top-zarqawi-aide-killed-in-us-attack.

p. 254 **perfecting document fraud:** Sami Moubayed, "Abu al-Ghadia to Build on al-Zarqawi's Legacy in Iraq," *Terrorism Focus* 3 no. 26 (July 9, 2006).

p. 254 **a steady supply of fake passports:** Ibid.

p. 254 **terrorist forces AQI recruited and trained:** Greg Bruno, "Profile: Al-Qaeda in Iraq (a.k.a. al-Qaeda in Mesopotamia)," Council on Foreign Relations, November 19, 2007.

p. 254   **the US Department of the Treasury froze his assets:** "Syrian National Designated by U.S."

p. 254   **add Darwish to the consolidated list of terrorists:** Ibid.

p. 255   **"fracturing the financial backbone...Al Qaida":** Ibid.

p. 255   **At 8:00 p.m. on February 21, 2006:** Louise Roug, "The Day Civil War Erupted in Iraq," *Los Angeles Times,* February 13, 2007.

p. 255   **four men:** Ibid.

p. 255   **dressed in the signature camouflage...of the Iraqi police:** Peter R. Mansoor, *Surge: My Journey with General David Petraeus and the Remaking of the Iraq War* (New Haven, CT: Yale University Press, 2013).

p. 255   **the al-Askari mosque in the ancient Iraqi town of Samarra:** Roug, "The Day Civil War Erupted."

p. 256   **an Iraqi police unit kept surveillance over the mosque:** Ibid.

p. 256   **carried an array of weaponry:** Ibid.

p. 256   **an Iraqi Army battalion was based...down the road:** Ibid.

p. 256   **US troops were stationed...military operations center:** Ibid.

p. 256   **a nine-foot-high wall:** Ibid.

p. 256   **It was supposed to have been locked at 5:00 p.m.:** Ibid.

p. 256   **nine security guards hired by Sunni authorities:** Ibid.

pp. 256–257   **the four members of AQI overpowered the nine guards:** Ibid.

p. 257   **broke through a locked door:** Ibid.

p. 257   **just before 7:00 a.m.:** Ibid.

p. 257   **Six seconds later, a second explosion:** Ibid.

p. 257   **"our 9/11":** Peggy Faw Gish, *Walking Through Fire: Iraqis' Struggle for Justice and Reconciliation* (Eugene, OR: Cascade Books, 2013).

p. 257   **armed Shias flooded into Baghdad on flatbed trucks:** Robert F. Worth, "Blast at Shiite Shrine Sets off Sectarian Fury in Iraq," *New York Times,* February 23, 2006.

p. 257   **self-proclaimed Mahdi Army:** Ibid.

p. 257   **gruesome torture, often involving power drills:** Jeffrey Gettleman, "Bound, Blindfolded and Dead: The Face of Revenge in Baghdad," *New York Times,* March 26, 2006.

p. 258   **and promptly executed them:** Ellen Knickmeyer and K. I. Ibrahim, "Bombing Shatters Mosque in Iraq," *Washington Post,* February 23, 2006.

p. 258   **more than 150 Sunni mosques...bullets:** Patrick Cockburn, "Ten Imams Murdered in Iraq as Sectarian Killings Intensify," *The Independent,* February 23, 2006.

p. 258 **ten imams being killed:** Ibid.

p. 258 **roughly one thousand Iraqis were dead:** Associated Press, "Eight Workers Shot Dead at Baghdad Shop," March 29, 2006, http://usato day30.usatoday.com/news/world/iraq/2006-03-29-firm-employees _x.htm.

p. 258 **2.7 million people would be displaced inside Iraq:** Elizabeth Ferris, "Remembering Iraq's Displaced," Brookings Institution, March 18, 2013.

p. 258 **two million more would flee for refuge:** Ibid.

p. 260 **Operation Larchwood 4:** McChrystal, *My Share of the Task.*

p. 260 **Abu Sayyif:** Ibid.

p. 260 **media specialist in the nearby Abu Ghraib regional cell:** Ibid.

p. 262 **a doughy English speaker...in his midthirties:** Ibid.

Chapter 14

p. 264 **He was a pediatrician by trade:** Stanley McChrystal, *My Share of the Task: A Memoir* (New York: Portfolio, 2013).

p. 265 **one of the other detainees, identified as Mubassir:** Ibid.

p. 265 **an infamous video of Zarqawi wearing a black bandana:** "Defiant al-Zarqawi Shows Face on Video," CNN, April 25, 2006, http://www.cnn.com/2006/WORLD/meast/04/25/zarqawi/.

p. 265 **standing in a landscape barren and beige:** Nelson Hernandez, "Now Playing in Iraq: Zarqawi Outtakes," *Washington Post,* May 5, 2006.

p. 265 **a massive M249 squad automatic weapon:** Ibid.

p. 266 **It released outtakes from the filming:** Ibid.

p. 266 **"we're going to establish an Islamic caliphate":** Richard A. Oppel Jr. and David S. Cloud, "U.S. Uses Iraq Insurgent's Own Video to Mock Him," *New York Times,* May 5, 2006.

p. 266 **"Go help the sheikh":** Ibid.

p. 267 **"It's just a matter of time before we take him out":** "U.S. Airs Video of Zarqawi Bloopers," *Washington Times,* May 5, 2006.

p. 268 **"and shot him twice in the head":** Associated Press, "Deadly Attacks Include Mosque," *Tampa Bay Times,* May 24, 2006.

p. 268 **Rahman's existence wasn't news to our team back at the Agency:** Brian Fishman, "The Man Who Could Have Stopped the Islamic State," *Foreign Policy,* November 23, 2016.

p. 268 **Zarqawi's newest spiritual adviser:** McChrystal, *My Share of the Task.*

p. 268 **Mubassir broke:** Ibid.

p. 269 **Only when Rahman got into a small blue vehicle:** Ibid.

p. 271 **nine Iraqis were killed and forty-four wounded:** Richard A. Oppel Jr., "In Image War, U.S. Shows Video of Bumbling Zarqawi," *New York Times,* May 4, 2006.

p. 271 **was moving at a frenetic pace, assaulting house after house:** "Killing Abu Musab al-Zarqawi and His Legacy: A Discussion with General Stanley A. McChrystal," Brookings Institution, January 28, 2013.

p. 272 **"I could almost smell those pancakes":** Eli Lake, "Secret Weapons," *Newsweek,* September 17, 2012.

p. 273 **a 1953 report:** Panel on Career Service for Women, "Career Employment of Women in the Central Intelligence Agency," November 1953, http://www.foia.cia.gov/typisttrailblazer/pdfs/1953-11-01a.pdf.

p. 273 **"at your operational inconvenience":** Ibid.

p. 273 **"and they are out of the running":** Tasneem Raja, "The Secret History of CIA Women," *Mother Jones,* November 4, 2013.

p. 274 **Those task forces are overseen by the FBI:** "Support to the War on Terrorism and Homeland Security," CIA 2002 annual report, updated January 3, 2012, https://www.cia.gov/library/reports/archived-reports-1/Ann_Rpt_2002/swtandhs.html.

p. 275 **"calling for national unity":** Joel Roberts, "Zarqawi Calls for Civil War in Iraq," CBS News, June 3, 2006.

p. 275 **Midmorning Baghdad time on June 7:** McChrystal, *My Share of the Task,* chap. 13, "Hibhib."

p. 275 **Rahman...was spotted climbing into a silver sedan:** Ibid.

p. 275 **He headed off into Baghdad:** Ibid.

pp. 275–276 **the sedan wound its way through various neighborhoods:** Ibid.

p. 276 **then turned back to its starting point:** Ibid.

p. 276 **the sedan bolted east across Baghdad:** Ibid.

p. 276 **merged onto a six-lane highway running...Diyala Province:** Ibid.

p. 276 **Rahman's car slowed...highway's shoulder:** Ibid.

p. 276 **a stubby blue Kia Bongo pulled up beside him:** Ibid.

p. 276 **Rahman climbed into the passenger side:** Ibid.

p. 276 **finally reaching Baquba:** Ibid.

p. 276 **the truck pulled up outside...a restaurant:** Ibid.

p. 276 **Rahman exited the vehicle and entered the building:** Ibid.

p. 276 **a white pickup with a red stripe on the side:** Ibid.

p. 276 **Rahman emerged from the building...pickup:** Ibid.

p. 276 **no fewer than nine surveillance aircraft were orbiting the area:** Ibid.

p. 277 **now merging onto Route 5 and heading west:** Ibid.

p. 277 **entered the small town of Hibhib:** Ibid.

p. 277 **the pickup turned right again into the driveway:** Ibid.

p. 277 **walked down the driveway to meet them:** Ibid.

p. 277 **"So I'm saying absolutely—whack it":** Ibid.

p. 277 **a man emerging from the shadows outside the home:** Ibid.

p. 278 **they were armed in case of contingencies:** Ibid.

p. 278 **immediately engage the safe house:** Ibid.

p. 278 **one of those planes...midair refueling:** Ibid.

p. 278 **was ordered...leave his wingman:** Ibid.

p. 278 **At 6:11 p.m.:** Ibid.

p. 278 **and then *pulled up* without releasing a bomb:** Ibid.

p. 279 **he locked onto the target...weapon:** Ibid.

p. 279 **just after 6:12 p.m.:** Ibid.

p. 279 **the F-16 was ordered to double back:** Ibid.

p. 279 **GPS-enabled GBU-38:** Ibid.

p. 279 **"to ensure the target set was serviced appropriately":** Craig Gordon, "Death of a Terrorist Leader / How Aide's Betrayal Doomed al-Zarqawi," *Newsday,* June 9, 2006.

p. 279 **Iraqi police stationed nearby arrived on the scene:** McChrystal, *My Share of the Task.*

p. 279 **who arrived...6:40 p.m.:** Ibid.

p. 279 **Police officers were struggling to hoist a stretcher:** Ibid.

p. 279 **closed in on the ambulance:** Ibid.

pp. 279–280 **The Jordanian had actually survived the bombing:** Ibid.

p. 280 **burst the blood vessels in his lungs and ears:** Joshua Partlow and Michael Abramowitz, "Officials Detail Zarqawi's Last Hour," *Washington Post,* June 13, 2006.

p. 280 **broken right leg and massive internal injuries:** Ibid.

p. 280 **team members found the remains...girl:** Ibid.

p. 280 **those of Rahman and another man:** Ibid.

p. 280 **At 7:04 p.m.:** McChrystal, *My Share of the Task.*

p. 280 **"turn the tide of this struggle":** "Statement by the President on Death of Abu Musab al-Zarqawi," White House archives, June 8, 2006, http://georgewbush-whitehouse.archives.gov/news/releases/2006/06/20060608.html.

p. 281 **laid Zarqawi's body...next to Rahman's:** McChrystal, *My Share of The Task.*

p. 281 **the "godfather" of sectarian violence in Iraq:** "Terrorist Leader Zarqawi's Death Called 'Severe Blow' to al-Qaida," Bureau of International Information Programs, US Department of State, June 8, 2006.

p. 281 **"this is an honor for our nation":** John F. Burns, "After Long Hunt, U.S. Bombs Al Qaeda Leader in Iraq," *New York Times,* June 9, 2006.

p. 282 **"the word of God will be supreme":** Associated Press, "Al-Qaida in Iraq's al-Zarqawi 'Terminated,' " June 8, 2006.

p. 282 **"His death will re-ignite yet another wave of revenge":** "Beheaded Man's Father: Revenge Breeds Revenge," CNN, June 8, 2006, http://www.cnn.com/2006/WORLD/meast/06/08/berg.interview/.

p. 282 **roughly thirty-five thousand civilians were murdered in Iraq:** Project Ploughshares, "Armed Conflicts Report: Iraq (2003—First Combat Deaths)," http://www.justice.gov/sites/default/files/eoir/legacy/2014/02/25/Iraq.pdf.

p. 283 **the bloodiest twelve-month stretch...for them:** Gordon Lubold, "2006 Was Deadliest Year for U.S. Troops in Iraq," *Army Times,* January 5, 2007.

p. 283 **"Whenever there is a new al-Zarqawi, we will kill him":** Associated Press, "Al-Qaida in Iraq's al-Zarqawi."

p. 284 **He received the Distinguished Flying Cross:** Greg Jaffe, "Combat Generation: Drone Operators Climb on Winds of Change in the Air Force," *Washington Post,* February 28, 2010.

p. 284 **Two members...received the Bronze Star Medal from McChrystal:** McChrystal, *My Share of the Task,* chap. 13, "Hibhib."

Epilogue

p. 286 **The findings...were at times ghastly:** Select Committee on Intelligence, United States Senate, "Committee Study of the Central

Intelligence Agency's Detention and Interrogation Program," December 9, 2014, https://www.congress.gov/113/crpt/srpt288/CRPT-113 srpt288.pdf.

p. 286 **extensive waterboarding:** Greg Miller, Adam Goldman, and Julie Tate, "Senate Report on CIA Program Details Brutality, Dishonesty," *Washington Post,* December 9, 2014.

p. 286 **mock executions:** Jeremy Diamond, "Top Takeaways from the CIA Torture Report," CNN, December 9, 2014.

p. 286 **"rectal feeding":** Alan Yuhas, "Controversial 'Rectal Feeding' Technique Used to Control Detainees' Behavior," *The Guardian,* December 9, 2014.

p. 286 **no clear actionable intelligence gained from torture:** Brian Bennett, "Senate Report Says CIA Torture Methods Yielded No Useful Intelligence," *Los Angeles Times,* December 9, 2014.

p. 286 **East Coast media were already in high dudgeon:** Miller et al., "Senate Report on CIA Program."

p. 286 **read the New York Times:** Mark Mazzetti, "Panel Faults C.I.A. Over Brutality and Deceit in Terrorism Interrogations," *New York Times,* December 9, 2014.

p. 287 **"how forthcoming he was":** Select Committee on Intelligence, "Committee Study."

p. 287 **a panel discussion at the Council on Foreign Relations:** "CFR and HBO Screening of the New HBO Documentary Manhunt," Council on Foreign Relations, April 16, 2013, http://www.cfr.org/terrorist -leaders/cfr-hbo-screening-new-hbo-documentary-manhunt/ p35447.

p. 287 **a story I'd read on Rudaw:** Wladimir van Wilgenburg, "Kurds of Iraq Played Major Role in Finding bin Laden," Rudaw, September 5, 2011, http://www.rudaw.net/english/kurds/3665.html.

p. 288 **divulged more useful information at a black site:** Eyder Peralta, "'Torture Report': Did Harsh Interrogations Help Find Osama Bin Laden?" National Public Radio, December 9, 2014.

p. 291 **nearly one in five Iraq veterans suffers from PTSD:** Terri Tanielian and Lisa H. Jaycox, eds., "Invisible Wounds of War: Psychological and Cognitive Injuries, Their Consequences, and Services to Assist Recovery," RAND Corporation, April 17, 2008.

p. 291 **have been diagnosed with PTSD:** Jamie Reno, "Nearly 30% of Vets Treated by V.A. Have PTSD," *Daily Beast,* October 21, 2012.

p. 291 **only 35 percent:** Kristina Wong, "Study: Most Troops Don't Seek Military Help with PTSD," *Washington Times,* May 8, 2012.

p. 292 **Abu Ayyub al-Masri:** Eben Kaplan, "Abu Hamza al-Muhajir, Zarqawi's Mysterious Successor (aka Abu Ayub al-Masri)," Council on Foreign Relations, June 13, 2006, http://www.cfr.org/iraq/abu-hamza-al-muhajir-zarqawis-mysterious-successor-aka-abu-ayub-al-masri/p10894.

p. 292 **an Egyptian cohort of Zarqawi's:** Ibid.

p. 292 **trained in al Qaida terrorist camps in Afghanistan:** Ibid.

p. 292 **a bit of bomb-making experience:** Dexter Filkins, "U.S. Identifies Successor to Zarqawi," *New York Times,* June 15, 2006.

p. 292 **ability to shuttle foreign fighters:** Ibid.

p. 293 **a familiarity with the various extremist groups:** Ibid.

p. 293 **masterminding the July 7, 2005, attacks:** Kevin Sullivan, "5 British Men Guilty in Foiled Bombing Plot," *Washington Post,* May 1, 2007.

p. 294 **He's still there today:** Select Committee on Intelligence, United States Senate, "Committee Study of the Central Intelligence Agency's Detention and Interrogation Program," December 9, 2014, https://www.congress.gov/113/crpt/srpt288/CRPT-113srpt288.pdf.

p. 294 **Masri changed AQI's name:** Stanford University, "Mapping Militant Organizations: The Islamic State," https://web.stanford.edu/group/mappingmilitants/cgi-bin/groups/view/1.

p. 294 **He appointed Abu Omar al-Baghdadi:** Khalid al-Ansary, "Iraqis Say Qaeda Deaths Will Not Improve Their Lives," Reuters, April 20, 2010.

p. 295 **killed them both:** Ibid.

p. 295 **"likely living in [the] Peshawar area":** Select Committee on Intelligence, "Committee Study."

p. 295 **"security apparatus would be minimal":** Ibid.

p. 295 **"with a family somewhere in Pakistan":** Ibid.

p. 295 **"always with Abu Ahmed":** Ibid.

p. 295 **A phone number for the Pakistani courier:** Ibid.

p. 295 **had been collected by the CIA two years earlier:** Ibid.

p. 295 **An e-mail address:** Ibid.

p. 295 **six months after that:** Ibid.

p. 295 **in the address books...operatives:** Ibid.

p. 295 **deeply uncertain about his importance:** "Did Enhanced Interrogation Help the CIA Find Osama Bin Laden?" CBS News, December 10, 2014, http://www.cbsnews.com/news/did-enhanced-interrogation-help-the-cia-find-osama-bin-laden/.

p. 296 **"his true role...in the hunt for bin Laden":** Ibid.

p. 296 **"closest assistant":** Select Committee on Intelligence, "Committee Study."

p. 296 **"likely handled all of [bin Ladin's] needs":** Ibid.

p. 296 **Ghul described...letters from bin Ladin:** CIA review team, "Comments on the Senate Select Committee on Intelligence's Study of the Central Intelligence Agency's Former Detention and Interrogation Program," June 27, 2013.

p. 296 **insisted that the courier had "retired" from al Qaida:** Select Committee on Intelligence, "Committee Study."

p. 296 **"our belief that Abu Ahmad...courier or facilitator":** Ibid.

p. 296 **"the long analytic targeting trek that led to Bin Ladin":** Ibid.

p. 297 **"no success in eliciting...bin Ladin's location":** Ibid.

p. 297 **walls as high as fifteen feet:** Issam Ahmed, "Osama bin Laden's Compound: 4 Oddities," *Christian Science Monitor,* May 3, 2011.

p. 297 **no Internet connection or phone line:** Bob Woodward, "Death of Osama bin Laden: Phone Call Pointed U.S. to Compound—and to 'the Pacer,'" *Washington Post,* May 6, 2011.

p. 297 **cell-phone calls were taken well away from the property:** Ibid.

p. 297 **burning their trash in the yard:** Gloria Borger, "Attack on Osama bin Laden Was Years in the Making," CNN, May 4, 2011.

p. 297 **a mysterious third family...top floors:** Mark Bowden, "The Death of Osama bin Laden: How the US Finally Got Its Man," *The Guardian,* October 12, 2012.

p. 297 **Agency analysts referred to him simply as "the pacer":** Woodward, "Death of Osama bin Laden."

p. 297 **"I'm with the same ones as before":** Bowden, "The Death of Osama bin Laden."

p. 298 **"the notion that we have any greater certainty than that":** Ibid.

p. 298   **Shortly after midnight Abbottabad time:** Macon Phillips, "Osama Bin Laden Dead," White House blog, May 2, 2011, https://www .whitehouse.gov/blog/2011/05/02/osama-bin-laden-dead.

p. 298   **President Bush authorized...additional forces to Iraq:** Tom Bowman, "As the Iraq War Ends, Reassessing the U.S. Surge," *All Things Considered,* December 16, 2011.

p. 298   **"It was won. The victory was there":** Ian Schwartz, "Fireworks: McCain vs. Carney on Iraq: 'It's Not a Matter of Disagreement; It's a Matter of Facts,'" RealClearPolitics, September 10, 2014, http://www .realclearpolitics.com/video/2014/09/10/fireworks_mccain_vs_carney _on_iraq_its_not_a_matter_of_disagreement_its_a_matter_of _facts.html.

p. 298   **arrested some five thousand people during the summer of 2007:** Walter Pincus, "'Surge' Has Led to More Detainees," *Washington Post,* August 15, 2007.

p. 298   **brought the total number of detainees...twenty-three thousand:** Ibid.

p. 299   **finishing a doctoral degree in Quranic studies:** William McCants, "The Believer: How an Introvert with a Passion for Religion and Soccer Became Abu Bakr al-Baghdadi, Leader of the Islamic State," Brookings Institution, September 1, 2015.

p. 299   **held by US forces at Camp Bucca:** Ibid.

p. 299   **"we had created a pressure cooker for extremism":** Terrence McCoy, "How the Islamic State Evolved in an American Prison," *Washington Post,* November 4, 2014.

p. 299   **"what the conditions were at the facility during that time":** Jenna McLaughlin, "Was Iraq's Top Terrorist Radicalized at a US-Run Prison?" *Mother Jones,* July 11, 2014.

p. 299   **"the Academy":** McCants, "The Believer."

p. 299   **"they were ticking time bombs":** Ali Hashem, "The Many Names of Abu Bakr al-Baghdadi," *Al-Monitor,* March 23, 2015.

p. 300   **"so he leaves a burning flame":** McCants, "The Believer."

p. 300   **Baghdadi reportedly connected...joined al Qaida:** Ibid.

p. 300   **from Damascus Baghdadi helped oversee...propaganda mill:** Ibid.

p. 300   **he was selected by the group's senior consultative cousel:** Ibid.

p. 300   **fellow radicalized inmates...Camp Bucca:** Ibid.

p. 300   **rename his network...ISIS:** Ibid.

p. 301   **"as they feel imminent danger":** "Zarqawi Letter," US Department of State press release, http://2001-2009.state.gov/p/nea/rls/31694.htm.

p. 301   **summoned civilian Shias to take up arms:** Farnaz Fassihi, Ali A. Nabhan, and Tamer El-Ghobashy, "Thousands Heed Call to Arms in Iraq," *Wall Street Journal,* June 13, 2014.

p. 301   **"their readiness to join a holy war":** Ibid.

p. 302   **"not the group responsible for their actions":** Liz Sly, "Al-Qaeda Disavows Any Ties with Radical Islamist ISIS Group in Syria, Iraq," *Washington Post,* February 3, 2014.

p. 302   **school-age children gun down its prisoners:** Lizzie Dearden, "ISIS Uses Young Boys to Hunt Down and Kill Prisoners in Ruined Syrian Castle for Gory Propaganda Video," *Independent,* December 5, 2015.

p. 302   **publishes annual reports for its financial backers:** Allison Hoffman, "1,083 Assassinations and Other Performance Metrics: ISIS's Year in Review," *Bloomberg Businessweek,* June 18, 2014.

p. 304   **a high perception of the threat:** Christoph O. Meyer, "International Terrorism as a Force of Homogenization? A Constructivist Approach to Understanding Cross-National Threat Perceptions and Responses," *Cambridge Review of International Affairs* 22, no. 4 (2009): 647–66.

About the Author

Nada Bakos is a former Central Intelligence Agency analyst and targeting officer. She was a key member of the team charged with analyzing the relationship between Iraq, al Qaida, and the 9/11 attacks. During the war in Iraq, Bakos served as the chief targeting officer tracking one of the world's most wanted terrorists, Abu Musab al-Zarqawi. In 2006, Zarqawi was killed in a targeted strike conducted by US military forces. She is a senior fellow in the Program on National Security at the Foreign Policy Research Institute and was featured in the Emmy Award–winning HBO documentary *Manhunt*. She has appeared as a guest commentator on PBS's *Frontline*, CNN, ABC, MSNBC, Fox, NBC, and as a guest on *Late Night with David Letterman*. She is also a contributor for publications including the *New York Times, The Atlantic,* and the *Washington Post*. After leaving the CIA, Bakos worked in a key role with Starbucks Corporation Public Affairs and now works as a consultant for a variety of social media and technology organizations.

Also available from Back Bay Books

Assad or We Burn the Country
by Sam Dagher

"Dagher draws on history, interviews, and his own experience as a reporter in Syria to depict an utterly ruthless regime."
—*New York Times Book Review,* Editors' Choice

Top Secret America
by Dana Priest and William M. Arkin

"A breathtaking investigative account of America's vast new secret world... An invaluable book."   —Bob Drogin, *Los Angeles Times*

The Hunt for KSM
by Terry McDermott and Josh Meyer

"Not only eye-opening investigative reporting, but also a concrete indictment of the continued bureaucratic boondoggle that is the War on Terror."   —Eric Liebetrau, *Boston Globe*

BACK BAY BOOKS

LITTLE, BROWN AND COMPANY